Flesh and Fish Blood

FLASHPOINTS

The series solicits books that consider literature beyond strictly national and disciplinary frameworks, distinguished both by their historical grounding and their theoretical and conceptual strength. We seek studies that engage theory without losing touch with history and work historically without falling into uncritical positivism. FlashPoints aims for a broad audience within the humanities and the social sciences concerned with moments of cultural emergence and transformation. In a Benjaminian mode, FlashPoints is interested in how literature contributes to forming new constellations of culture and history and in how such formations function critically and politically in the present. Available online at http://repositories.cdlib.org/ucpress.

Series Editors: Ali Behdad (Comparative Literature and English, UCLA); Judith Butler (Rhetoric and Comparative Literature, UC Berkeley), Founding Editor; Edward Dimendberg (Film & Media Studies, UC Irvine), Coordinator; Catherine Gallagher (English, UC Berkeley), Founding Editor; Jody Greene (Literature, UC Santa Cruz); Susan Gillman (Literature, UC Santa Cruz); Richard Terdiman (Literature, UC Santa Cruz)

1. *On Pain of Speech: Fantasies of the First Order and the Literary Rant*, by Dina Al-Kassim
2. *Moses and Multiculturalism*, by Barbara Johnson, with a foreword by Barbara Rietveld
3. *The Cosmic Time of Empire: Modern Britain and World Literature*, by Adam Barrows
4. *Poetry in Pieces: César Vallejo and Lyric Modernity*, by Michelle Clayton
5. *Disarming Words: Empire and the Seductions of Translation in Egypt*, by Shaden M. Tageldin
6. *Wings for Our Courage: Gender, Erudition, and Republican Thought*, by Stephanie H. Jed
7. *The Cultural Return*, by Susan Hegeman
8. *English Heart, Hindi Heartland: The Political Life of Literature in India*, by Rashmi Sadana
9. *The Cylinder: Kinematics of the Nineteenth Century*, by Helmut Müller-Sievers
10. *Polymorphous Domesticities: Pets, Bodies, and Desire in Four Modern Writers*, by Juliana Schiesari
11. *Flesh and Fish Blood: Postcolonialism, Translation, and the Vernacular*, by S. Shankar

Flesh and Fish Blood

Postcolonialism, Translation, and the Vernacular

S. Shankar

UNIVERSITY OF CALIFORNIA PRESS
Berkeley · Los Angeles · London

THIS BOOK IS MADE POSSIBLE BY A COLLABORATIVE GRANT
FROM THE ANDREW W. MELLON FOUNDATION.

University of California Press, one of the most distinguished university presses in the United States, enriches lives around the world by advancing scholarship in the humanities, social sciences, and natural sciences. Its activities are supported by the UC Press Foundation and by philanthropic contributions from individuals and institutions. For more information, visit www.ucpress.edu.

University of California Press
Berkeley and Los Angeles, California

University of California Press, Ltd.
London, England

© 2012 by The Regents of the University of California

Library of Congress Cataloging-in-Publication Data

Shankar, Subramanian, 1962–
   Flesh and fish blood : postcolonialism, translation, and the vernacular / S. Shankar.
      p. cm. — (Flashpoints ; 11)
   Includes bibliographical references and index.
   ISBN 978-0-520-27252-1 (pbk. : alk. paper)
   1. Indic literature—20th century—History and criticism. 2. Postmodernism (Literature)—India. 3. Indic literature—Translations—History and criticism. 4. Postcolonialism in motion pictures—India. I. Title.
PK5420.S53   2012
891'.1—dc23

                    2011052441

21 20 19 18 17 16 15 14 13 12
10 9 8 7 6 5 4 3 2 1

for my father
K. S. Subramanian
my first and best guide to all things Tamil

யாதும் ஊரே, யாவரும் கேளீர்
[Everywhere is my home, everyone my kin.]

—Kanian Poongundranar (my translation)

Contents

Acknowledgments	xi
Preface	xv
1. Midnight's Orphans, or the Postcolonial and the Vernacular	1
2. Lovers and Renouncers, or Caste and the Vernacular	27
3. Pariahs, or the Human and the Vernacular	65
4. The "Problem" of Translation	103
Conclusion: Postcolonialism and Comparatism	143
Notes	159
Works Cited	167
Index	181

Acknowledgments

Much of the material that makes up this book was presented at various forums over the course of a decade. I am grateful to audiences at the following institutions and meetings for questions and comments: American University, Cairo; Asian Studies Development Program of the East West Center (workshop held at Johnson Community College); Center for the Study of Developing Societies, New Delhi; Central Institute for English and Foreign Languages (now UEFL), Hyderabad, India; Central University of Tamil Nadu (Tiruvarur); Columbia University; Cornell University; Forum on Contemporary Theory (both at the offices of the Forum in Baroda and at annual conventions); International Auto/Biography Association Biennial Conference (2008); International Cultural Studies Program Lecture Series, East-West Center, Honolulu; Madras University; Middlebury College; National Institute of Advanced Studies, Bangalore; Modern Language Association (several annual conventions); University of California, Davis; University of California, Irvine; University of Hawai'i at Manoa; University of Houston; University of Texas, Austin; University of Texas, San Antonio; University of Washington, Seattle; University of Western Ontario; University of Wisconsin, Madison; Annual South Asian Literature Association Conference (2001); Roehampton University, London; Rutgers University; School of Oriental and African Studies, London.

Chapter 1 is a revised version of "Midnight's Orphans, or a Postcolonialism Worth Its Name," first appearing in the journal *Cultural*

Critique (vol. 56, no. 1), published by the University of Minnesota Press (copyright 2004 by the Regents of the University of Minnesota). Sections of chapter 4 were originally published in an earlier version under the title "Postcolonialism and the Problem of Translation" in *New Bearings in English Studies*, edited by R. Azhagarasan, Bruce Bennett, Mohan Ramanan, R. Palanivel, T. Sriraman, and C. Vijayasree. These sections are published here by permission of Orient Blackswan Private Limited, Hyderabad, India. I thank the editors of *Cultural Critique* as well as the anthology for the opportunity to present my preliminary thoughts on vernacular postcolonialism and translation, and the respective presses for permission to reproduce them here in revised form.

Various individuals contributed to my developing arguments by generously reading and responding to them in draft. I especially acknowledge Cynthia Franklin for reading the entire manuscript at a crucial stage and making suggestions with her customary keen insight. The anonymous readings of the manuscript commissioned by Richard Terdiman and Ed Dimendberg, former and present coordinating editors of the FlashPoints series of the University of California Press, were thoughtful, rigorous, and enormously helpful in sharpening the argument and bringing it to its proper potential. I am grateful for the pointed criticisms as well as the enthusiastic support expressed in them. The process of revision was aided in no small measure by the thorough care with which Dick and Ed managed the manuscript through the various stages of review. I am confident *Flesh and Fish Blood* is a better book because of their exacting but committed support. I am grateful too to Mary Francis, Kim Hogeland, Elisabeth Magnus, Caitlin O'Hara, Sandy Drooker, and Tim Roberts for their able assistance through the production process.

More generally, an intellectual community spread out across several continents has played a significant role in helping me think through problems and answers in pursuing this project. In Hawai'i, Cristina Bacchilega, Arindam Chakraborty, Vrinda Dalmiya, Monisha Dasgupta, Keala Francis, Vili Hereniko, Laura Lyons, Paul Lyons, Cheryl Naruse, Jon Osorio, John Zuern, and, again, Cynthia Franklin have been valued readers/interlocutors of my work, or collaborators in the organization of two symposia on translation and humanism that related germanely to the subject of this book, or indeed both. Cynthia Franklin has been an especially important resource in multiple ways over the years and deserves special mention for her fabulous support and generosity with her time. I also want to acknowledge the various participants of the Comparatism and Translation in Literary and Cultural Studies interest group, too many to list individually, and the students in my Translation and Comparatism graduate seminar. I am especially grateful to my students for their enthusiasm and for a stimulating semester of discussions.

Elsewhere, I value the friendship and/or scholarly dialogue provided by Hosam Aboul-Ela, S. Anandhi, Fran Bartkowski, Purnima Bose, Tim Brennan, S. Charusheela, Kanishka Chowdhury, Sheila Contreras, Gaurav Desai, Ayman El-Dessouky, Dermot Dix, Barbara Foley, Keya Ganguly, V. Geetha, Ferial Ghazoul, Bishnupriya Ghosh, Barbara Harlow, Salah Hassan, Andy Hsiao, C. T. Indra, Nalini Iyer, Prafulla Kar, Grace Koh, Chandana Mathur, Louis Mendoza, Satya Mohanty, Supriya Nair, Anjali Nerlekar, Francesca Orsini, M. S. S. Pandian, Lionel Pilkington, R. Radhakrishnan, Venkat Rao, Sundar Sarukkai, Samah Selim, Nirmal Selvamony, Asha Sen, Yumna Siddiqi, Jael Silliman, K. Sivaramakrishnan, Gayatri Chakravorty Spivak, Kate Teltscher, and Bonnie Zare. These individuals have been valuable partners in a continuing conversation about the contours of literary and cultural study in the twenty-first century, in some cases by extending invitations to me to present my work in print or as talks.

This book deals extensively with Tamil literature, film, and culture. My most dependable guides in this regard have been my mother, K. S. Champakam, and especially my father, K. S. Subramanian, to whom I dedicate this book. Conversing with my father about aspects of works discussed here was one of my great pleasures over the years, and a rewarding shared activity by which to remember him in years to come. My son, Ujjayan Siddharth, who has neither read my work in draft nor extended invitations to me to present it, has nevertheless been an important part of what follows—at all the right times and in all the right ways he has brought me to the end of words. The book might have been finished sooner without the limits imposed by his rewarding presence in my life. It would not have been a better book for that.

Preface

As the subtitle indicates, *Flesh and Fish Blood* is concerned with postcolonialism, translation, and the vernacular. The argument of the book represents an encounter with postcolonial studies as currently configured (mainly) in the North American academy as well as an inquiry into postcolonial literature and film from India. My general objective is both to illustrate and to overcome a broad failure with regard to vernacular knowledges in contemporary scholarly engagements with postcolonial societies. By *vernacular knowledges* I mean those oriented away from the transnational, the modern, and the hybrid and toward the local, the traditional, and the culturally autonomous. Because of certain biases that I explore in detail in the book, postcolonial studies has faltered in acknowledging and exploring these vernacular knowledges. Since 9/11, this failure has come to seem ever more costly as it becomes clear that many events in the postcolonial world emanate from vernacular cultural sources about which the United States remains profoundly ignorant. Working with material from and about India, therefore, I set out in this book to open fresh avenues of investigation into postcolonial societies by suggesting that we be attentive to the vernacular.

Accordingly, the first three chapters are largely concerned with an inquiry into the vernacular in relationship to the postcolonial and the colonial. I take up the argument with contemporary approaches to postcolonial *studies* most substantially in the first chapter. In the

Indian context, the vernacular has (or, perhaps, has been made to have) an intimate association with caste. Both chapters 2 and 3, as their titles indicate, are concerned with this topic, though in different ways. Through a reading of R. K. Narayan's novel *The Guide*, chapter 2 pursues the notion of a vernacular postcolonialism introduced in chapter 1 into recent debates about caste (or, more fittingly, the *varna-jati* complex). Chapter 3, which pays special attention to Dalit (formerly "untouchable") literature and literary criticism, follows these debates to a consideration of the status of the human and humanism in anticaste writing. The chapter contributes to a larger critical conversation about humanism in general by offering comparisons between anticaste humanism and the humanism of such scholars as Edward Said and Martha Nussbaum. Along the way, the argument touches on considerations of cosmopolitanism.

My design is to move from the argument about the vernacular in the context of postcolonial studies to a discussion of ensuing theoretical implications. These implications concern translation practice and theory, on the one hand, and comparatism as a methodological option for scholarly scrutiny of postcolonial societies, on the other. And so the book concludes with an examination of translation and comparatism in the context of postcolonialism. Both translation and comparatist modes of inquiry have ebbed and flowed with the vicissitudes of intellectual history. *Flesh and Fish Blood* attempts to assess and reassert—in a judicious manner, for the pitfalls of neither are to be underestimated—the validity of translation and comparatist methods. At their best, translation and comparatism enable rigorous and generous cross-cultural sharing of knowledges, but neither is to be adopted lightly. In the chapters devoted to them, I explore in some detail the felicities and fallibilities of both.

In the pursuit of these themes, the argument ranges over literature and film in Tamil, Hindi, and English. There are critical explorations of both well-known and unfamiliar novels and films. Even as the argument engages Salman Rushdie, R. K. Narayan's novel *The Guide,* and the widely commented-on blockbuster film *Roja* (in Tamil and Hindi), it makes a place for the feminist fiction of Tamil writer Ambai and for the exciting emergent Dalit literature in Tamil. In this manner, I would like to think, the argument of the book endeavors to widen the possibilities for postcolonial studies not only conceptually but archivally. The opportunity to explore Dalit literature and discourses of caste has been a matter of personal satisfaction—as the epigraph to the book, words from the Tamil poet of antiquity Kanian Poongundranar, expresses. These words have often been quoted to articulate anticaste sentiments. I am hopeful that, aside from the issues identified in the subtitle to the book, *Flesh and Fish Blood* will occasion a fuller and more serious engagement with caste and Dalit writing than has been the case so far within postcolonial studies.

Approaching literary study from a complementary direction, I take up the question of world literature in some detail in my chapter on translation, proposing that "literatures of the world" is a more tenable alternative rubric. "Literatures of the world" is at once more modest (less willful) and more adequate to the conditions of possibility underlying the comparative study of literary traditions in the contemporary context. If *world* in the first usage (world literature) primarily conjures up a physical globe contained within an iron grid of longitudes and latitudes, in the second the word is better able to evoke a general social realm of human activity, that is, *world* as evoked for example in the work of Marx and Amartya Sen. The second usage better exemplifies a pluralized and historicized world of human imagination and achievement.

A materialism springing from a particular conception of human endeavor undergirds the second usage. Marx, Raymond Williams notes in *Keywords*, "would include human activity as a primary force" in understanding materialism (1976, 200). And in *The Argumentative Indian* Sen both invokes Buddhism and quotes the words in which the divine Rama is lectured in the Ramayana by "a worldly pundit called Jāvāli on the folly of his religious beliefs: 'O Rama, be wise, there exists no world but this, that is certain! Enjoy that which is present and cast behind thee that which is unpleasant'"; these references, Sen declares, contest Western exaggerations of "the non-material and arcane aspects of Indian traditions" (2006, 159). As the instances of Ambedkar and Periyar readily attest, in what follows I draw on a similar tradition of materialist and worldly Indian thought.

My theoretical orientation in *Flesh and Fish Blood*, then, is consonant with materialism in the above sense—a materialism emerging out of worldliness and human praxis. Where opportunity has presented itself I have explored and underscored the resonances. At the same time, *Flesh and Fish Blood* is not an extended study of materialist method of the kind I undertook in *Textual Traffic*. I have by and large resisted the temptation to launch a more focused, but also distracting, argument about materialism. I think it sufficiently evident from what follows that I find materialist methods—in the plural—congenial; I refer readers who want to know more about how and why to *Textual Traffic*. Here, with the above proposition about materialism in general view, I resolutely keep attention on the topics of immediate concern—postcolonialism, translation, and the vernacular.

CHAPTER I

Midnight's Orphans, or the Postcolonial and the Vernacular

I have no knowledge of either Sanscrit or Arabic.—But I have done what I could to form a correct estimate of their value. I have read translations of the most celebrated Arabic and Sanscrit works. I have conversed both here and at home with men distinguished by their proficiency in the Eastern tongues. I am quite ready to take the Oriental learning at the valuation of the Orientalists themselves. I have never found one among them who could deny that a single shelf of a good European library was worth the whole native literature of India and Arabia.
—Thomas Babington Macaulay, "Minute on Indian Education" (1835)

In 1997, Salman Rushdie celebrated the fiftieth anniversary of India's independence from British rule by coediting *The Vintage Book of Indian Writing, 1947–1997* with Elizabeth West. In the introduction to the anthology, Rushdie claimed that the most interesting literature of post-Independence India was in English.[1] "The prose writing—both fiction and non-fiction—created in this period [the fifty years after Independence] by Indian writers working in English," he wrote, "is proving to be a stronger and more important body of work than most of what has been produced in the eighteen 'recognized' languages of India, the so-called 'vernacular languages,' during the same time; and, indeed, this new, and still burgeoning, 'Indo-Anglian' literature represents perhaps the most valuable contribution India has yet made to the world of books. The true Indian literature of the first postcolonial half-century has been made in the language the British left behind"

(1997c, 50). It is readily apparent from Rushdie's introduction to the anthology that there are, in substance, two evaluatory parts to his argument regarding contemporary Indian literature. One is Rushdie's high estimation of Indian literature in English, expanded on in an interview given around the time of the anthology's publication in which he claimed that because of literature written in English, "India has finally managed to break through into world literature, into the world's language, and to create this great province inside it" (1997b, 36). There can be little quarrel with the general thrust of this part of Rushdie's argument—that the contributions of Indian writers working in English (not the least of which are some of Rushdie's own works) have been of great value. It is the other part—Rushdie's devaluation of literature written in other Indian languages—that has proven controversial and has met with criticism from various quarters.[2]

There is indeed much to be said in defense of the aesthetic value of literature written in Indian languages other than English. However, I am interested less in asserting this value *contra* Rushdie than in tracking what I consider certain other symptomatic *theoretical* and *critical* emphases of Rushdie's argument. For though I begin with Rushdie's provocative comments on contemporary Indian literature (and along the way will offer an assessment of some aspects of this literature), I intend finally to advance an argument about postcolonialism as a theoretical and literary critical project within the North American academy—that is, about what Hosam Aboul-Ela has felicitously christened "institutional postcolonial theory" (2007, 13).[3] Rushdie is not in fact generally regarded as a critic or a theorist. Nevertheless, there is a certain justice in beginning with him. Commenting on Rushdie's "particular prominence," M. Keith Booker notes in the introduction to a recent anthology of critical essays on Rushdie that his work "has been particularly attractive" to postcolonial critics "for whom cultural hybridity is a crucial critical category" (1999, 2–3). Homi Bhabha, whose work I will discuss later in this chapter, is one such critic identified by Booker.

There is a congruence, then, between Rushdie's fiction and certain strands of commentary on postcolonial literature—a congruence that is instructive in a discussion of postcolonial criticism and theory. Critical overviews of postcolonialism have noted the great influence of these strands. Ania Loomba, for example, writes in *Colonialism/ Postcolonialism,* "Postcolonial studies have been preoccupied with issues of hybridity, creolisation, mestizaje, in-betweenness, diasporas and liminality, with the mobility and cross-overs of ideas and identities generated by colonialism" (1998, 173). And Leela Gandhi echoes this description when she writes toward the end of *Postcolonial Theory: A Critical Introduction,* "Postcolonial literary theory, as we have seen, tends to privilege 'appropriation' over 'abrogation' and multicultural 'syncretism' over cultural 'essentialism'" (1998, 153). In this critical context, my turn to Rushdie allows me to demonstrate the widespread nature of the attitudes represented by these emphases and to show that the argument that follows is not relevant only to the domain of criticism and theory narrowly understood as a species of *academic* knowledge.

Of course, I should also note that the tendencies in postcolonial criticism and theory being identified here exist in dialogue and in contestation with other tendencies, especially the materialist criticism of such scholars as Aijaz Ahmad, Timothy Brennan, Barbara Harlow, Neil Lazarus, Satya Mohanty, Benita Parry, Edward Said, E. San Juan, and Gayatri Spivak.[4] Echoes of my argument can be found in their work, and I will have occasion to draw on their enabling and suggestive commentary. At the same time, I am aware there are differences among these critics—and, indeed, between some of their critical perspectives and my argument. In identifying such a broad interpretive stance as materialist criticism, it is useless to look for consensus, even as there is value in recognizing and learning from congruities in critical aims, interpretive methods, and textual archives. I am guided here by Raymond Williams's rejection of a dogmatic specification in advance of materialism's content in *Problems in Materialism and Culture,* where he notes "the necessary social processes through which the materialist enterprise defines and redefines its procedures, its findings and its concepts, and in the course of this moves beyond one after another 'materialism'" (1980, 122). Williams by and large approves this self-correcting advancement, and I believe materialist criticism in the current moment of lull—for so it seems to me—between the theoretical flurry of the seventies, eighties, and nineties and what is to come is best served by a similarly catholic approach. In intervening in postcolonial studies here, then, I aim to strike a balance between a careful endorsement of materialist method on the one hand and a deliberately commodious understanding of materialism on the other.

This chapter begins with readings of three works of contemporary Tamil literature: K. N. Subramanyam's poem "Situation" (an example of the formal and thematic experimentation of the New Poetry movement), Komal Swaminathan's full-length socialist realist (though this

4 | Midnight's Orphans, or the Postcolonial and the Vernacular

characterization is in some ways inadequate) play *Water!*, and Ambai's feminist short story "A Kitchen in a Corner of the House." I have chosen the works to demonstrate adequately both the variety of genres and the diversity of voices within contemporary Tamil literature, deliberately postponing engagement with other developments and movements in Tamil writing, which too are exemplary in this respect, until succeeding chapters. My recourse to these Tamil works is dictated by both my personal biography and the needs of my argument. Literature in Tamil falls among those "vernacular literatures" of India sweepingly dismissed by Rushdie (1997c, xv). Tamil is a modern South Indian language with a tradition of classical literature going back more than two thousand years. Certainly a language marked by a distinguished antiquity, it is also present in a variety of media from film and television to the Web. Nevertheless, as we shall see, because it is seen as a "vernacular language," its very modernity is implicitly questioned in Rushdie's arguments.[5] My main interest in the section that follows is in demonstrating the *thematic* richness of postcolonial Tamil literature in order to suggest, in the final section of the chapter, the limitations of the present configuration of postcolonialism as a theoretical and critical project within the North American academy as well as aligned institutions elsewhere.

IS VERNACULAR LITERATURE TRACTOR ART?

In the introduction to the anthology he coedited, Rushdie asserts, "Parochialism is perhaps the main vice of the vernacular literatures" (1997c, xv). And in the interview, he elaborates further on what he means by this parochialism:

> The besetting sin of the vernacular language is parochialism. It's as if the twentieth century hasn't arrived in many of these languages and the range of subjects and the manner of the treatment of them is depressingly familiar: village life is hard, women are badly treated and often commit suicide, landowners are corrupt, peasants are heroic and sometimes feckless, disillusioned and defeated. The language is a kind of Indian equivalent of what, in the Soviet Union, was called "Tractor Art." When the attempts are made to take notice of some of the developments in the rest of the world, the clumsiness is sometimes embarrassing. (1997b, 36)

For Rushdie, then, the parochial and backward nature of "vernacular literatures"—such as Tamil literature—is easily recognizable in their thematic poverty. But how true is this characterization of vernacular literature? I begin an exploration of this question by turning first to K. N. Subramanyam's 1966 poem "Situation" because this poem would seem to offer the clearest and most direct refutation of Rushdie's claim.[6]

In a preface to a collection of Subramanyam's poems entitled *Puthu Kavithaikal* (*New Poems*), the well-known Tamil poet Gnanakoothan notes, "The words and ideas of previous poets are recognizable in the poems of Ka Na Su from the beginning. But he has used these words and ideas in such a way that they have acquired new meaning" (1989, v).[7] In poetry, as much as in his criticism and fiction, Ka Na Su (as K. N. Subramanyam was known) struggled with the different claims of innovative movements in literature and of tradition. As a poet, he belonged to the New Poetry movement heralded in 1962 by the influential anthology entitled *Puthukurralkal* [*New Voices*], edited by Ci. Cu. Chellappa, in which, in fact, two of his poems were included. As Kamil Zvelebil notes in his essay in *The Smile of Murugan,* New Poetry shows a "radical break with the past and its traditions, though not a negation of the cultural heritage," an "experimentation with language and form of poetry, based on intellection," a familiarity with European and North American modernist poetry, and a "preoccupation" with very contemporary matters (1973, 313–14). Zvelebil concludes his positive assessment of New Poetry by noting the movement's "conscious attempts to evolve a new Tamil idiom, to write, uninhibitedly, about unconventional or even prohibitive themes, to get rid of fashionable foreign influences and to create a truly modern Tamil poetry" (335).[8]

Many of the features identified by Zvelebil in New Poetry are to be found in "Situation" (the translation is by the poet himself):

Introduced to
the Upanishads
by T. S. Eliot;
and to Tagore
by the early
Pound;
and to the Indian Tradition
by Max Mueller
(late of the Bhavan);
and to
Indian dance by
Bowers;
and to
Indian art
by what's-his-name;
and to the Tamil classics

by Danielou
(or was it Pope?);
neither flesh
nor fish blood
nor stone totem-pole;
vociferous
in thoughts
not his own;
eloquent in words
not his own
("The age demanded . . .")

Sanskritic (the Upanishads), national (Tagore), and Tamil traditions make up the cultural heritage of the person described in the poem.[9] But ironically, his only access to these roots is through the work ("fashionable foreign influences"?) of Western cultural authorities like Eliot (Anglo-American), Müller (German), and Danielou (French). Thus the poem thematizes the contemporary cultural predicament of a certain segment of the post*colonial* intelligentsia in Tamil India. Not of the land ("flesh"), not of the sea ("fish blood"), not a worthy (even if inanimate) emblem of his culture ("stone totem-pole"), filled with "words not his own"—the individual described in the poem is, it would seem, the product of what is often referred to in the postcolonial context as cultural imperialism.[10]

The oblique citation of Ezra Pound once again in the final line of the poem suggests the subtlety, erudition, self-reflection, and irony behind this meditation on the contemporary "situation" of the postcolonial intellectual. "The age demanded . . ." is a quotation from Pound's "Hugh Selwyn Mauberley (Contacts and Life)," a long 1920 poem that is, Peter Nicholls notes, "at times a distanced presentation of himself [Pound] and at others a satirical portrait of an ineffectual aesthete" (1995, 190). The phrase makes its appearance in the poem early in the first section, "E. P. Ode pour l'Election de Son Sepulchre," which is a catalog of the various things "demanded" by the age: among other things, "mendacities" rather "than the classics in paraphrase" (Pound 1975, 98–99). Alluding to the just concluded First World War, Pound goes on to note, "There died a myriad, / And of the best, among them, / For an old bitch gone in the teeth, / For a botched civilization" (101). And still later in the poem, the phrase "the age demanded" reappears as the title of a section that continues Pound's ironic and self-deprecating exploration of the relevance of (literary) tradition in the midst of the terrible excesses of modern civilization. This section ends by noting "his final / Exclusion from the world of letters" (110).[11]

"Better mendacities / Than the classics in paraphrase!" and "an old bitch gone in the teeth, / . . . a botched civilization." Clearly these phrases find renewed significance by reference to the postcolonial Tamil intellectual at the center of Ka Na Su's poem. If it is possible to read Pound's poem as an ironic meditation on the modern Anglo-American poet's relationship to tradition and classical literature, a similar preoccupation with regard to the modern Tamil intellectual is at the heart of Ka Na Su's poem. As already noted, Ka Na Su was, like other poets of the New Poetry movement in general, deeply familiar with European modernism, whose central figures often find reference in his work. Of course, in his poem, Ka Na Su resituates this modernist preoccupation within a postcolonial context. Western modernity is not the same as postcolonialism, nor is the predicament of the modernist intellectual the same as that of the postcolonial intellectual. But in "Situation," the example of the modernist intellectual is made to inform in a subtle way the predicament of the postcolonial intellectual. While what the postcolonial age ("botched civilization"?) demands is left somewhat undetermined at the end of Ka Na Su's poem, the contemporary "situation" of a certain kind of postcolonial intellectual finds ironic figuration in the poem.

It seems clear to me that Ka Na Su's "Situation" cannot be characterized, even by unsympathetic eyes, as Tractor Art.[12] Its themes even show a certain affinity with the concerns of that species of postcolonial criticism and theory that has been so important in assigning such a high value to the work of Rushdie. I have already cited a passage in which Keith Booker makes the link between this high valuation of Rushdie's work and postcolonialism by noting that his "cultural hybridity is a crucial critical category" for postcolonial critics like Homi Bhabha. "Situation," too, can easily be described as a hybrid text on a hybrid subject. Written originally in Tamil (in which language its irony is even more pointed), it was translated into English by the poet himself. The cultural hybridity of the poem, then, is not just a matter of citation; such hybridity inheres not just in the manner in which "Situation" incorporates Pound's poem within itself but in its being, if one grants that the author's translation of his own work has a different status from other translations, a bilingual poem. It exists in two languages at the same time. The "hybrid" subject of this bilingual poem is a mimic man. Homi Bhabha has written that in colonial discourse "mimicry represents an *ironic* compromise" between "the synchronic panoptical vision of domination," with its demand for "identity, stasis," and "the diachrony of history," with its demand for "change, difference" (1994, 85–86; italics in original).[13] Thus mimic men and women are called forth by the ambivalence of colonial discourse, but Bhabha goes on to write that "the *menace* of mimicry is its *double* vision which in disclosing the ambivalence of colonial discourse also disrupts its authority" (88; italics in original).

In the economy of a *post*colonial poem such as "Situation," however, the ironic compromise represented by colonial mimicry and the notion that such mimicry is disruptive of the authority of colonial discourse are themselves ironized. The opposite of such irony and mimicry—a certain, if still vexed, notion of cultural autonomy—slips in through the back door: better is the practice of reading the Indian classics in their original languages. In Ka Na Su's hybrid and ironic poem, despite—or, perhaps, through—a deep knowledge of Pound and Euro-American modernism, this desire for cultural autonomy articulates as well as performs an impatience with mimicry. While the poem acknowledges the "multicultural 'syncretism'" and "the mobility and cross-overs of ideas and identities" that lie embedded in notions of colonial mimicry and that have been summarized variously as the most significant emphases of postcolonialism, at least in the North American academy, such desire reaches in other directions—toward notions of cultural autonomy. It is an autonomous access to his own culture that Ka Na Su recommends for the postcolonial intellectual at the center of his poem.

Through irony and mimicry, the poem attempts to snatch such autonomy from the very jaws of irony and out of the hands of inevitable mimicry. In this fashion, the postcolonialism of Ka Na Su's Tamil poem now joins and now diverges from the influential strains of postcolonial theory under discussion here and Indian writing in English that is theoretically and critically abetted by it (such as Rushdie's novels). And both when it joins and when it diverges it slips the noose of Tractor Art.

It may seem at first reading that Komal Swaminathan's full-length play *Water!* cannot slip the noose quite so easily. The play, which I translated into English, is quite different in its main concerns, and indeed in its literary sensibility, from Ka Na Su's poem.[14] *Water!* is Swaminathan's most important play and, arguably, the most important Tamil play of the twentieth century. It was enormously successful when first produced in 1980, partly because it was preceded and succeeded by public furor. *Water!*'s controversial subject matter concerns a drought-stricken village in the far south of India. For five years the rains have failed in the fictional village of Athipatti, and the villagers have repeatedly petitioned the government, to no avail, for relief. Into this situation arrives the vagabond Vellaisamy, who exhorts the villagers to organize themselves and take various actions to better their condition. The villagers try to bring water in a cart; they boycott an election to put pressure on the government; they try to dig a canal to the village. Despite all their efforts, the villagers are defeated by the forces ranged against them. The play ends with the death of Vellaisamy, the dispersal of many of the key villagers, and the village still locked in drought.

Water! was written at the end of a decade of considerable social turmoil within India—ranging from Marxist-Leninist insurrection to Gandhian agitation. In the months immediately preceding the staging of *Water!*, signs of Marxist-Leninist activity had been reported in Tamil-speaking areas of India. Accordingly, censors in Madras attempted to deny permission to Swaminathan's play because of its alleged sympathy for the Marxist-Leninists. By the time the play was first staged, *Water!* had won considerable notoriety as a radical play. A year later it was made into an equally successful film, which encouraged many slum dwellers and villagers to take various actions to procure potable water. The play met with enormous enthusiasm from playgoers and with favorable reviews in the Tamil as well as English-language press. Many reviewers regarded the play as an important milestone in the history of modern Tamil drama.[15] Though drama is, as M. Varadarajan notes, a neglected genre in Tamil literary criticism, it has had an especially intimate relationship to powerful political movements (1970, 269). Many significant political personages have also been important figures in the Tamil theatrical world.[16] It is within this explicitly politicized but critically dismissed dramatic context that Swaminathan's achievement in *Water!* must be placed. The play represents, as indeed Swaminathan's preface to the published version of the play makes clear, a bold and self-conscious engagement with the aesthetic judgments and political conditions of the time.

The Tamil dramatic tradition, and the opportunities and limitations that it represents, constitute one aesthetic context for Swaminathan in *Water!*, but there are others equally important. Swaminathan himself has described his aesthetic sensibility as one informed by "a socialist realism" (in Narayanan n.d.). *Water!* is certainly a Marxist work. In an interview given in 1995, toward the end of his life, Swaminathan noted,

"Marxist literature and thought have provided me a broad-based philosophy of life and I have used it for literary ends" (qtd. in Santhanam 1995, 14). No doubt this "broad-based philosophy" suggests a markedly different aesthetic orientation from the New Poetry sensibility of Ka Na Su's "Situation."

Nevertheless, to present *Water!* as an example of Tractor Art would be to mischaracterize its real thematic and aesthetic complexity. Early in *Water!* the protagonist Vellaisamy reveals that he was born on the day of India's independence: "My father used to say I was born when the flag of the white man came down over Delhi Red Fort and the tricolor went up. The white man was leaving this country. In his memory, my father gave me this name, Vellaisamy. Maybe it's because I was born on the day of independence.... Like independent India, I too live the life of a dog" (Swaminathan 2001, 11). This strange passage full of postcolonial mimicry (Vellaisamy's name can be translated to mean "white master"), ambivalence, and irony reveals Vellaisamy—like Saleem Sinai, the protagonist of Rushdie's novel *Midnight's Children* (1981)—to be a midnight's child. "Initially seen as merely a comic, irreverent and high-spirited novel about a fantastic protagonist whose birth coincided with the independence of India," Meenakshi Mukherjee notes, "*Midnight's Children* was gradually appropriated into a theoretical discourse about nation, history and their narrativity" (1999, 9). And in his foreword to the published version of the play, Swaminathan writes, "The little village named Athipatti is the mirror-image of an India which has now been independent for thirty-two years" (2001, xxxii). Like *Midnight's Children,* then, *Water!* (produced a year before the publication of the novel) is a detailed comment on postcolonial nationhood.

Rushdie's fantastic imaginings, aspirations to a sweeping national allegory, and literary wordplay are aimed at a transnational readership; in contrast, Swaminathan's mode of expression is resolutely attentive to the mundane forms of reality, his primary audience drawn from Tamil India, and his language firmly rooted in the specific dialect proper to the part of Tamil India in which the play is set. Even if both novel and play aspire to comment on the postcolonial condition of India, they do so in very different ways. *Midnight's Children* sets out to be a grand historical novel, while *Water!* is content to explore the same postcolonial history of India through the effects it has had on one drought-stricken village. Perhaps this is the difference between that magic realism with which Rushdie's work is often associated and what

I will call, appropriating for my purposes Rushdie's term of dismissal, a *vernacular* realism—that is, a realism *aspiring* to reproduce the local in all its specificity and drawing substantially, though not exclusively, on vernacular literary and theatrical traditions. Certainly, *vernacular* can carry connotations of being substandard or distinct from literary language. These connotations are evident in Rushdie's uses of the term. However, the term can also connote locality and particularity with regard to geographical region. I draw on the latter connotations in beginning here an elaboration of one of the main arguments of this book.[17]

I have sketched elsewhere Swaminathan's complicated relationship to psychological realism and socialist realism as aesthetic options in *Water!* (Shankar 2001a). *Water!* appears to be a naive play—Tractor Art—if assessed exclusively by the tenets of a psychological realism that emphasizes "rounded" and "interesting" characters and focuses on the motives of human behavior as we have come to understand them from the vast majority of contemporary Western bourgeois literature and drama. There is no real conflict among the "good" characters in the play—no unforgiving anger, no betrayal, no passionate love, no pettiness. Instead, there is a political complexity that is derived at least partly from Swaminathan's commitment to socialist realism. George Bisztray has suggested the following as important characteristics of socialist realism: a programmatic affirmation, a celebration of collectivism, an optimistic outlook, and an emphasis on the educative function (1978, 53–54). *Water!* both expresses and contravenes these tenets of socialist realism. Swaminathan's eschewal of a psychological realism—a realism based on certain notions of individual motivation—corresponds to a socialist realist collectivism. Also present in the play is an emphasis on the educative function. On the other hand, the tragic ending of the play, when Vellaisamy dies and the villagers are defeated in their attempt to bring water, contravenes the programmatic optimism of socialist realism. Assessed in the light of its engagement with socialist realism (both when affirming and when revising), *Water!* appears to be an aesthetically rich play.

Also contributing to this richness is a careful attention to vernacular detail that cannot be explained by reference to socialist realism. The play's language, which offers performative opportunities difficult to capture in a translation, is itself expressive of a vernacularism. With Tamil readers and audiences, the play is famous for its faithful evocation of dialectal variations of spoken Tamil—especially those prevalent among the rural people depicted in the play. Vernacular cultural elements are also to be recognized in some of the characters. In contrast to a communist character such as Kovalu, typifying some of the heroic conventions of socialist realism, are characters like Adaikappan and Kandhaiyan, elderly villagers whose witty dialogue and bantering personalities can be traced back to folk theatrical forms such as *villupaattu* and *therukoothu*. The presence of numerous folk dances and songs in the play also suggests the great influence of these theatrical forms.[18]

In *Water!*, then, socialist realist elements coexist with aspects drawn from Tamil folk culture. I refer to Swaminathan's particular deployment of these latter elements in his play as vernacular realism. The socialist realism, derived from the transnational cultural politics of communism, coexists with the vernacular realism. If—of the three contemporary Tamil texts being discussed here—*Water!* seems in the greatest danger of falling into Rushdie's noose of Tractor Art, it is because of Swaminathan's compounding of a socialist realism with a vernacular realism whose thematic and aesthetic complexity cannot be fully appreciated and cannot even be understood until the text has been returned to its vernacular context. Raymond Williams has suggested that, in a certain productive critical tradition of understanding realism, reality is "seen not as static *appearance* but as the movement of psychological or social or physical forces; realism is then a conscious commitment to understanding and describing these. It then may or may not include realistic description or *representation* of particular features" (1976, 219; italics in original). The varieties of realism alluded to above—magical, psychological, socialist, and, finally, vernacular—should be understood in this light.

The point of my discussion thus far has been to suggest through successive layers of elaboration the inadequacy of characterizing as Tractor Art either an individual text such as *Water!* or a collective body of work such as contemporary Tamil literature. As we have seen, Rushdie mixes what he calls the parochialism of vernacular languages and a caricatured socialist realism in arriving at this questionable formulation. Through its careful and multilayered exploration of the experiences of women, "A Kitchen in the Corner of the House," by Ambai, provides further illustration of the unsuitability of Rushdie's characterizations of literature in languages other than English. While she is most renowned as a writer of short stories, one of Ambai's more interesting works is a volume of feminist literary criticism. *The Face behind the Mask* is an account of the treatment of women in modern Tamil literature and is most valuable for its comprehensive approach to the subject.[19] In the first part of the book, Ambai reviews a wide variety of literary works to examine how they portray women and arrives at a kind of critical taxonomy. The latter portion of the book is a compilation of the information she gathered from a number of important contemporary women writers through questionnaires and interviews. "The need," Ambai notes as she concludes her book, "is to experience the truth of one's self and one's society and find a genuine expression of it"; she goes on to suggest that "such an attempt to write the truth" would permit "the Tamil woman . . . to make common cause with many others who are in different categories of role-playing and not necessarily in the male-dominating-the-female order" (1984, 244).

In many ways, "A Kitchen in the Corner of the House," first published in 1988, exemplifies this supple and sedimented approach to feminism. The story is a study of three generations of Rajasthani women, as perceived by Minakshi (Mina), a Tamil woman married to Kishan, one of the sons of the family. The patriarch of the family is Papaji, the father of Kishan, and the arrangements of the house are firmly in his control. Ambai presents this household as experienced by Mina over a number of visits. Mina, like some of the other younger members of the family, lives elsewhere with her husband. The Tamil Mina is an outsider in this North Indian family, and the story is full of detailed attention to the vernacular specificity of the Rajasthani family and their difference from the Tamil Mina. When on one of her visits she proposes that the dingy kitchen around which the lives of the women of the family revolve be renovated and the view from its window cleared, she faces Papaji's opposition. "Papaji's silent retort" to Mina, Ambai tells us, is "Woman, woman of Mysore [a town in South India, close to the Tamil area]. . . . Dark skinned woman, you who refuse to cover your head, you who talk too much, you who have enticed my son . . ." (1992, 207).

In Papaji's shadow, his wife, Jiji, and stepmother, Bari-Jiji, compete for ascendancy over each other. Formerly, the ascendancy was Bari-Jiji's. But when she loses her husband and falls into the despised condition of widowhood, the positions are reversed. The keys of the household pass from Bari-Jiji to Jiji. Bari-Jiji is reduced to contesting Jiji's domination through subterfuge. Ambai's story ends with an episode in which Jiji falls sick on one of Mina's visits. As Mina watches over her mother-in-law in the "darkened room," a conversation takes place, though we are told "we cannot be certain whether this conversation was actually started by her [Mina], or whether it happened on its own, or whether it only seemed to her to have occurred because she had imagined it so often" (221). Toward the end of this conversation that might not have been a conversation at all, Mina reflects that if all the "clutter" of managing the kitchen in the house "had not filled up the drawers of [Jiji's] mind," she too might have done great things (222). The story ends with Mina's (apparent) exhortation to Jiji to let go, to "sink deeper still," because "when you touch bottom you will reach the universal waters. . . . Your womb and your breasts will fall away from you. . . . And there will be you. Not trapped nor diminished by gender, but freed" (223).

It could be said that "A Kitchen in the Corner of the House," like the "feminist texts" from India reviewed by Rajeswari Sunder Rajan at the end of her book *Real and Imagined Women,* is full of what Sunder Rajan calls "discriminations . . . worth noting" (1993, 143). "Even as we grant that [the feminist texts] operate with a utopian bias," she observes, "we must recognize that they do not create utopian contexts that ignore the tensions of reality . . . ; while they mark what may be described as the brief truces that women seemingly wrest out of history, they do not offer them in the form of a resolution of the conflict between tradition and modernity . . . ; they do reproduce the dialectic of struggle, but not by representing women as unrelentingly external to the social process" (143). Such too are the discriminations of the cautiously utopian vision that concludes Ambai's story. In this sense, "A Kitchen in the Corner of the House" can be added to the feminist texts cited by Sunder Rajan "as significant political advances in the self-representation of women" (143). Furthermore, Ambai, in her desire "to make common cause with many others who are in different categories of role-playing," appends a number of other important themes to her central feminist concern. One of these themes—one I have already tried to indicate through my quotations from the story—is the place of the vernacular within the national community in the context of the historical cleavage of South India from North.

Ambai's story—like Rushdie's novel, Ka Na Su's poem, and Swaminathan's play—offers a wide-ranging comment on the postcolonial condition of India by focusing attention on both the state of women and the limitations of what Benedict Anderson has called the "imagined community" of the nation. In the story, the utopian vision of women's achievement of community *through* a liberation from the constraints of sex and gender is subtly juxtaposed to the sad reality of intranational tensions. Mina's moment of communion with her mother-in-law at the end of the story is contrasted to Papaji's earlier dismissal of her as a "dark skinned woman" from Mysore. In this fashion, the story's conclusion is revealed to be a challenge not only to Papaji's patriarchal power but also to the power of an ethnic prejudice that threatens the utopian vision figured in the "imagined community" of Indian nationhood (an issue of great complexity to which I will have occasion to return in succeeding chapters). Thus Ambai's story reaches beyond the theme of oppression of women and becomes a feminist meditation under postcolonial conditions on the seductions of and obstacles to utopian desire, whether expressed in the notion of nationhood or other types of community.

It might seem that Ambai's vision of a genderless community into which women might escape is a naive notion that feminism has surpassed. But such an objection to Ambai's story would beg the following questions: Whose feminism? What is the address—in the sense of both locus and discursive purpose—of this feminism? It is precisely the universalization of the particular concerns of Western feminism as the concerns of women everywhere that Chandra Talpade Mohanty decried in her widely read essay "Under Western Eyes" (1988). In her critique of Western feminism, Mohanty objected not only to such universalization but also to the construction of the category of a universal Woman oblivious to the particular, material conditions in which particular, material women exist. As she notes in her follow-up essay "'Under Western Eyes' Revisited: Feminist Solidarity through Anticapitalist Struggles" (2002), such a critique does not make impossible the pursuit of other—more legitimate—forms of commonalities among women across the world. Perhaps Ambai's story and her vision of genderless community are deserving of critique—whether such critique is appropriate and what shape this critique might take is not the subject of this chapter—but the critique cannot characterize Ambai's story as backward, that is, insufficiently current, insufficiently developed, without opening itself to the charge of what Mohanty in "Under Western Eyes" calls "ethnocentric universalism" (1988, 199). In other words, Ambai's story cannot become Tractor Art without criticism running the risk of ethnocentric universalism. To make the point in this way is to turn the table on Rushdie's characterization of vernacular literature and suggest the "backwardness" of Rushdie's own charge.

Instead of backwardness, then, in "A Kitchen in the Corner of the House," we find a feminist meditation on utopian possibilities. Varieties of community—of women, of citizens, of ethnic groups—busily lay claim to individual bodies through competing notions of solidarity. Against these notions, Ambai's conclusion brings her reader to the genderless and sexless "universal" community of humanity, a utopian conclusion—nowhere-yet-in-existence conclusion—possible only in the wake of the feminist exploration of the female body in the story. Of the body, Gayatri Spivak writes, "I take the extreme ecological view that the body as such has no possible outline. As body it is a repetition of nature. It is in the rupture with Nature when it is a signifier of immediacy for the staging of the self. . . . It is through the *significance* of my body and others' bodies that cultures become gendered, economopolitic, selved, substantive" (1993, 20; italics in original). Through her many references to menstruation, childbirth, and disease, Ambai draws repeated attention to the ineluctable materiality of the female body *in* nature. It is Ambai's feminism that allows her to delineate the ways in which the women characters (are made to) offer their bodies for the cultured staging of selves (theirs and others). If Ambai wishes—so tentatively, so circumspectly—to have Mina exhort her mother-in-law to disengage from the materiality of womb and breast, it is so that in the utopian freedom of "the universal waters" the ferocious signification of the female self in Papaji's patriarchal culture might be revealed and interrupted. Simultaneously, as we have seen, Papaji posits his and his family's Rajasthani-ness against Mina's Tamil-ness, thus bringing to the surface in the guise of ethnic subnational differences questions of vernacular specificity. The place of gender as well as the vernacular in postcolonial India stands indexed in these ways. Ambai's feminism evokes a utopian universalism in order to explore, among other issues, a specific gendered as well as vernacular postcolonial condition.

"Situation," *Water!*, and "A Kitchen in the Corner of the House" are representative of three very different literary sensibilities within contemporary Tamil literature. These three texts cannot of course be said to describe contemporary Tamil literature exhaustively.[20] My choice of works is not meant to introduce contemporary Tamil literature, a task beyond the scope of this chapter, or indeed this book. It is meant rather to suggest the thematic diversity in contemporary Tamil literature: I have tried to indicate how the appellation Tractor Art is inadequate for any one of these three texts, even *Water!*, which no doubt is the kind of polemical text for which the label is intended. Instead of Tractor Art, we find in the "vernacular literature" represented by these three texts a highly nuanced presentation of a variety of postcolonial themes: the challenge of cultural imperialism, the predicament of the postcolonial intellectual, the postcolonial fates of such transnational cultural movements as modernism and socialist realism, the impasses of postcolonial developmentalism, the place of women within the postcolonial nation, the limits of nationhood, utopian desire, bureaucratic indifference, and so on. My intention has been to expand the horizons of our aesthetic understanding through a series of illustrative readings meant to interrogate the nature of the vernacularity of Tamil literary texts and thus to draw attention to the varied nature of postcolonial experience.

The readings I have offered, I hope, lead us to question the critical attitudes at the foundation of Rushdie's judgment of the vernacular literatures of India, especially as he expresses them in his work as an editor of an anthology. In the preface to another anthology, the monumental *Women Writing in India: 600 B.C. to the Present*, the editors Susie Tharu and K. Lalita present their rationale in selecting the works included in the following manner: "Not all the texts or authors . . . were chosen for the same reasons. We might have included one piece because it was moving, another because the writer was already well known, another precisely because she ought to be better known, or represented a class or other group whose creative activity is rarely taken into consideration in traditional literary histories and the canons they construct. Yet another might be raising an important issue, dramatizing a typical conflict, or representing a formal development" (1991, 1: xxiv).[21] This perspective on the responsibilities of anthologizing offers a profound contrast to Rushdie's views in his introduction: where Tharu and Lalita put forward a highly nuanced grasp of the politics and economics of cultural production, Rushdie seems compelled to fetishize his particular notion of aesthetic value above all else. When read in conjunction with Vinay Dharwadker's observations in the introduction to a special issue of *World Literature Today* titled "Indian Literatures: In the Fifth Decade of Independence," the comments of Tharu and Lalita indicate clearly the limitations and biases of Rushdie's views. Dharwadker notes in his essay, "As a collective nationalistic enterprise that lasted more than a century, the literatures in the Indian languages [he means languages other than English] were able to legitimize themselves easily by claiming to possess the native, authentic, and traditional sources of Indian identity and culture" (1994, 240–41). "In the past ten or twenty years," he goes on to add, "that claim to authenticity has been undermined, not only by the accomplishments of Indian English literature, but also by the inescapable modernity and cosmopolitanism of Indian-language writing itself, and by the emergent diaspora of the Indian languages among immigrant communities around the world" (241).

If the comments of Tharu and Lalita offer a contrast to Rushdie on the principles of anthologizing, Dharwadker's comments suggest a contrasting evaluation of Indian literatures. Rushdie's dismissive reference to vernacular literature as Tractor Art in what is, after all, only an interview would not, perhaps, be worthy of comment were it not, it is now clear, symptomatic of the logic behind the substantial critical and literary intervention represented by his anthology. Since, as Rushdie himself observes, only one writer who does not write in English is included in the anthology (1997c, x), we may then ask, why do Rushdie and his coeditor West not simply call their anthology a collection of postcolonial Indian writing *in English*? Why the desire to eschew what would seem a reasonable circumspection and to exalt Indian writing in English at the expense of the other Indian literatures? In the passage quoted at the beginning of this essay, Rushdie notes, "The *true* Indian literature of the first *postcolonial* half century has been made in the language the British left behind" (1997c, 50; italics added). It would seem that it is in support of this claim to the true India—and also its true postcolonialism—that Rushdie's remarkable comments on Indian literatures are marshaled in his introduction; for it is from these claims to India and its postcolonialism that the canonizing power of Rushdie's anthology flows. And—irony upon irony—in this pursuit Rushdie, spokesperson of the ironic and the hybrid, is forced to retreat to a language of authenticity![22]

POSTCOLONIALISMS: TRANSNATIONAL AND VERNACULAR

The effect of Rushdie's claims of authenticity for Indian writing in English is to make such writing the true literary child of Independence—the true literary inheritor of that postcolonial period inaugurated at the stroke of midnight, August 15, 1947. Ironically, as the epigraph that opens this chapter is meant to illustrate, Rushdie echoes Macaulay's infamous minute on education in advancing his observations. Reciprocally in his argument, and again like Macaulay, the very literatures that claimed to represent India authentically at the height of the nationalist movement are now declared to be inauthentic. In Rushdie's comments they are rendered, we might say, the orphans of midnight. The ghost of Macaulay walks at Rushdie's postcolonial midnight hour. However, as noted at the beginning of this chapter, Rushdie's assessment of the vernacular literatures of India has been contested from a variety of directions. Within India, certainly, the vernacular literatures have sufficiently powerful institutional and popular support. Rushdie's orphaning of the vernacular literatures, I want to argue, can only be symptomatic of a postcolonialism—widely held within the North American academy and its adjuncts elsewhere—understood as a critical and theoretical enterprise privileging the transnational over the vernacular and capable of being contrasted in this respect to another species of postcolonialism.

In this time of the popularity of the postcolonial within the North American academy, much has been written of "the postcolonial condition"—even as many arguments have been made subjecting such a condition to skeptical scrutiny. Anne McClintock, for example, has questioned the accuracy of the term and expressed misgivings about it as "a singular, monolithic term," while insisting that she would not "want to banish the term to some chilly, verbal Gulag; there seems no reason why it should not be used judiciously in appropriate circumstances" (1992, 294). Similarly, Vijay Mishra and Bob Hodge have distinguished between "oppositional" postcolonialism and "complicit" postcolonialism and argued for what they call a "new postcolonialism." "It is precisely if we acknowledge the pervasiveness but not universality of complicit forms of the postcolonial," they conclude, "that we can trace the connections that go back to the settler experience and beyond, and forward to the new postcolonialism" (1991, 289). The essays by McClintock and by Mishra and Hodge, then, have challenged the rapidly institutionalizing definitions of such a term as *postcolonial* even as they have accepted the need for it.

In a similar spirit, I want to suggest that we refine our understanding of "the postcolonial condition" by making a distinction between a *transnational postcolonialism* and a *vernacular postcolonialism*. More often than not, postcolonial theory, especially but not exclusively within the North American academy, has characterized postcolonial societies as hybrid societies. Many of the signature themes of postcolonial criticism and theory have flowed directly out of this characterization of the postcolonial condition. Despite the emphasis on the "hybrid," the ironic effect of this characterization has been, as Ania Loomba points out, to homogenize diverse postcolonial identities and practices under the rubric of a hybridity understood exclusively in the context of a contest between (European) colonizer and ("native") colonized (1998, 178).

The corollary of this emphasis on the hybrid is the erasure of certain other arenas of cultural endeavor, certain other sensibilities or ideologies. Thus influential forms of postcolonial criticism and theory have generally been suspicious of any robust idea of the local or the vernacular, when these terms mark hostility to the hybridizing force of transnational cultural flows. They have also been suspicious of ideas of "tradition" closely linked to the local and the vernacular, finding in appeals to such tradition only a distressing quest for purity and authenticity. It is in this context that we can understand Rushdie's dismissal of the vernacular literatures of India as "parochial." In this context too we might read Homi Bhabha's essay "Minority Maneuvers and Unsettled Negotiations" (1997). This essay uses the term *vernacular* positively, but only by treating it as a rough synonym for *minority* and by separating it from *local, traditional,* and other such terms. Certainly, it is telling that after discussing "vernacular translations," "vernacular cosmopolitans," and the need "to transform social division into progressive minority agency," Bhabha writes of "situations where the driving cataract of history, flowing relentlessly in the direction of the global, does not simply obliterate locality as a kind of obsolete irrelevance but reproduces its own compensatory projections of what tradition, the local, or the authentic *ought to have been*" (458; italics in original).

The main thrust of Bhabha's argument is to establish the value of what he calls the "minority" perspective and an equivalence between it and "vernacular." Reciprocally, however, "minority" becomes the wedge in his argument to separate "vernacular" from "tradition" and "the local," and the latter two, when at all present, are reduced to "compensatory projections" of a globalizing history. And so here too the language of authenticity returns surreptitiously. Bhabha's approach to the contradistinction of the global and the local, the transnational and the traditional, is altogether more careful than Rushdie's dismissal of the vernacular as parochial. Nevertheless, the effect of his argument is to assign a position of inauthenticity to the local and the traditional a priori. The point of departure for analysis is the global, in whose context the local and the traditional, if present, must be understood. The opposite—any idea of the local and the traditional as a point of departure for understanding the global—remains unthinkable. But is not the notion that the driving cataract of history moves relentlessly in the direction of the global a form of metanarrative needing careful elucidation? Such elucidation makes no appearance in Bhabha's essay, and so the discourse of the global validates itself without seeming to do so.

Riveted by the (proto)transnational and transnationalizing force of colonialism and its aftermath, such contemporary theories (commonly summarized as "postcolonial"), despite their complexity in many other respects, have presented a curiously impoverished idea of the appeal of the "traditional" as well as of the "local" and the "vernacular" (as distinct from Bhabha's "minority") on which such an appeal often founds itself. No doubt this is partly because discourses of the traditional in postcolonial societies have themselves often discounted the primacy of the colonial encounter in their arguments and thus have opened themselves to a variety of charges ranging from atavism to romanticized indigenism.

I hope, however, that my discussion of three contemporary works of Tamil literature sheds a different light on the varieties of vernacular culture and discourses of the traditional. I am *not* suggesting that the traditional and the vernacular somehow escape the colonial encounter, that they can be isolated from the category of the colonial. Neither "Situation" nor *Water!* treats the historical effects of colonialism with indifference. I am suggesting, however, that we should be able to argue that the perspectives of the vernacular and related ideas of the local and the traditional (with their orientation toward the autonomous) are no more worthy of automatic dismissal from theoretical discourse than are the perspectives of the transnational and related ideas of the diasporic and the modern (with their orientation toward the hybrid). Sometimes cultural autonomy is the explicit concern of vernacular literature (as in "Situation"). At other times, a subtle critical understanding of degrees of cultural autonomy within a historical "situation" enables a deeper appreciation of the context within which vernacular literature functions. Considered in this light, the notion of the vernacular can certainly be enabling in the journey toward new horizons of aesthetic understanding where postcolonial literature properly construed is concerned. At the same time, it is also possible, indeed necessary, to go beyond a narrowly literary context and propose that an adequate accounting of the postcolonial condition—an issue separate from the question of endorsement or repudiation of particular perspectives—requires a more careful attention to the claims of vernacular as well as transnational postcolonialism than has hitherto been granted within certain influential theories of the postcolonial.

The manner in which I have made the distinction in this chapter between varieties of postcolonialism no doubt founds it in linguistic difference—after all, *vernacular* is chiefly, though not exclusively, as the *Oxford English Dictionary* shows, a linguistic term—and I have no desire to disavow this foundation; but I do want to underscore the point that the distinction is ultimately about varieties of postcolonial *sensibility*, which have a strong relationship to linguistic differences but cannot be reduced to them. It is not as if we must all now rush out to learn the vernacular languages of the postcolonial world. It would be sufficient for the moment if we learned to become more attentive to the diversity of sensibility that actually exists there. Such attentiveness, when suggesting an orientation toward rootedness and cultural autonomy and specific locality, should be distinguished from parochialism (though such parochialism might very well be part of some varieties of vernacular sensibility). The distinction between language and sensibility is also the reason I have preferred to use *vernacular*, despite, as we have seen, its occasional dismissive associations, rather than *bhasha* in my discussions. Bonnie Zare and Nalini Iyer point out that the term *bhasha writing*, used by critics such as G. N. Devy (1992), refers to "texts written in Indian languages other than English" (2009, xii). *Bhasha* means language in many Indian tongues. To use it here would be to willfully emphasize language over sensibility. Additionally, such use would dilute the postcolonial force of my argument—that is, dilute the resonances of my argument for postcolonial locations other than India.

The nuances I am trying to draw attention to here may be elucidated by reference to the careers of Salman Rushdie and R. K. Narayan. The latter, those knowledgeable will agree, is at least as distinguished an Indian writer *in English* as the former. Yet his novels have remained in relative obscurity as far as postcolonial literary criticism as practiced within the North American academy is concerned. There are a variety of reasons for this obscurity, but a crucial one, I would say, is that Narayan is much closer to the pole of a vernacular postcolonial *sensibility*—that is, he shows a greater consciousness of the vernacular in both his subject matter and his philosophical perspectives—than to a transnational one. Accordingly, the transnational postcolonial perspectives under scrutiny in this chapter have been significantly less interested in Narayan—despite his aesthetic and philosophical complexity—than in Rushdie. In the next chapter, I engage in some detail with Narayan's work, especially his most widely read novel, *The Guide*, to illustrate with specific reference to discourses of caste my point regarding Narayan's complexity.

In the meantime, we might note that the corollary too is true. Works of vernacular literature can be located along a spectrum ranging from vernacular postcolonialism at one end to transnational postcolonialism at the other. Thus, among the three Tamil works discussed in this essay, Ka Na Su's "Situation" seems clearly closer to a transnational postcolonial sensibility than Swaminathan's *Water!* This judgment is based not simply on the thematic concerns of these works but also on their formal and aesthetic allegiances. Accordingly, the former lends itself much more readily to analysis using critical tools perfected on the terrain of transnational postcolonialism, though, as we have seen, even here there is a refusal to engage in the facile rejection of the notion of cultural autonomy. Ambai's short story (like *Water!*) is closer to the pole of a vernacular postcolonialism than Ka Na Su's poem in, if nothing else, its foregrounding of intranational—as opposed to transnational—social and political concerns. Even though I have suggested that the notions of transnational and vernacular postcolonialisms should not be reduced to language, as far as literary works are concerned the language used by a writer is of crucial importance in delimiting her audience. While not an inescapable straitjacket, language is a powerful constraining pressure in a variety of ways. Thus we should not be surprised to find that many more works of vernacular literature than literature written in English *tend* to one pole of the spectrum rather than the other.

Critics such as Neil Lazarus and Timothy Brennan have already offered persuasive and sharply delineated critiques of an unqualified privileging of what I am calling transnational postcolonialism. Thus Lazarus pertinently observes, "Even if, in the contemporary world-system the subjects whom Bhabha addresses under the labels of exile, migration, and diaspora, are vastly more numerous than at any time previously, they cannot reasonably be said to be paradigmatic or constitutive of 'postcoloniality' as such" (1999, 136–37). And Brennan's wide-ranging critique of the sensibilities of cosmopolitanism in *At Home in the World* connects at many points with the critique of transnational postcolonialism advanced here. For both Lazarus and Brennan, the vantage point that enables their critiques is the nation-state and what Brennan calls "left nationalisms" (1997, 317). "Nationalism is not dead," Brennan concludes his book. "And it is good that it is not" (317).

So it is. It is good, too, as Brennan himself would no doubt agree, that the vernacular is not dead. Brennan argues elsewhere in his book, "Lost in much of the writing on colonialism and postcolonialism is the mood of languorous attachments to native cultures, still in many ways premarket or anticapitalist, that were (in displacement) sites of nativity. If hybridity can be said to characterize them, then it is a hybridity reclaimed and reinvented as indigenous, defiantly posed against an increasingly insistent metropolitan norm" (10). In Brennan's argument, a certain notion of the indigenous emerges as the counterpoint to the transnational. This recourse to indigeneity is echoed by Arif Dirlik, who notes, "Fundamental to any claim to indigenous identity is an assertion of an inalienable connection between community and land, and, by extension, between society and nature" (2003, 24).

I have preferred the term *vernacular* to do similar work because of my different objectives in this book. *Vernacular* conveys closer association with cultural themes and greater distance from themes of ethnicity and identity. One speaks of "indigenous peoples" but not of "vernacular peoples." To my mind, *vernacular* is able to suggest a sense of local habitation based on genealogy (that *indigenous* indicates much more strongly) without becoming synonymous with it. My desire has been to find a term capable of drawing attention in a historically rich, critically supple, and conceptually broad way to commonly disregarded sensibilities, practices, and modes of being that operate as a counterpoint to the transnational in the postcolonial context. It is the impulse to mark the counterpoint sharply but not so sharply as to be usable only in limited circumstances that has led me to such a term as *vernacular*. The overlap between *indigenous* and *vernacular* indexes how each term expresses a "defiance" (Brennan's apt characterization) of an uncritically transnationalist point of vantage in the postcolonial context. No doubt one term cannot always do the work of the other.

Criticism and theory, then—especially as often practiced within the North American academy, but this point is not necessarily relevant only to such a location—should distinguish between a transnational postcolonialism and a vernacular postcolonialism, without succumbing to the temptation to see the two as polar opposites permitting no gradations in between. This book is not meant to be an argument for the political or otherwise authentication of a vernacular postcolonialism over a transnational postcolonialism (or vice versa). I am aware that my argument proceeds mainly by reference to the Indian context and that the specific nature of the relationship between vernacular and transnational postcolonialisms in India cannot be used to generalize facilely about other parts of the world. I do believe, however, that the set of issues identified in this chapter and succeeding ones is germane to postcolonial criticism and theory in general. To different degrees and in different forms, the need for careful attention to both vernacular and transnational postcolonialisms is relevant to different parts of the postcolonial world. With regard to sub-Saharan Africa, for example, the debates over the appropriate language for literature—whether African literature should properly be written in languages like Yoruba and Swahili or may also be written in English and French—might be said to illustrate a similar tension between vernacular and transnational postcolonialisms.[23] I am aware, too, that I have staged my argument in this chapter on the terrain of literature, raising the possibility of misunderstanding. The textualism of my particular argument here should not be taken to indicate an exclusively textualist understanding of postcolonialism. I have been at pains to regard the literary works discussed as productive clues to certain aspects of the postcolonial situation.

In this chapter, my chief intention has been to outline, through readings of postcolonial literature, some of the pitfalls in current widely held—even near-pervasive—forms of critically assessing and theorizing the postcolonial within the North American academy and to recommend, as far as such criticism and theory are concerned, that we be attentive to both a vernacular and a transnational postcolonialism. We can begin being so only by learning to recognize, analyze, and evaluate a vernacular postcolonial sensibility in ways less reductive and dismissive than are currently the norm. In the pursuit of this goal, perhaps we will need to recover abandoned critical tools and terminology, perhaps to craft new ones. The relationship between Indian writing in English and vernacular literature, the place of the vernacular within the national imaginary, the relationship of the vernacular to caste and to notions of the human (especially in the context of representations of Dalits, the preferred term for those formerly referred to as untouchables), the careful distinctions to be made between vernacular and cosmopolitan sensibilities, the importance as well as challenges of translation as practice and as trope in the postcolonial context, the felicities and fallibilities of comparatism as a methodology capable of drawing into critical light hitherto ignored aspects of the postcolonial—it is at the threshold of these and other issues that we have now arrived. The ensuing chapters will move beyond this threshold, for it is already clear where refusing to take the step across threatens to leave us. We would find ourselves abandoning, orphaning, entire shelves of postcolonial literature, and with, indeed, a far too narrow sense of the postcolonial. The refusal to step across would leave us still in the clutches of Macaulay's ghost.

CHAPTER 2

Lovers and Renouncers, or Caste and the Vernacular

Postcolonial theory is peculiar. In startling ways it is not postcolonial at all. Consider, for example, caste and how little postcolonial theory has to say about it. On the one hand, caste has been the object of intense scholarly scrutiny for centuries. At least from the time of the British entry into India as a colonizing power, it has been steadily made into the very identity of India—its essential nature. Yet in *The Weapon of the Other* Kancha Iliah records his sense that "caste was not a category of socio-historical analysis" in contemporary scholarship (2010, x). Certainly, in the tens of thousands of pages of "postcolonial" commentary on India (that is, from within institutional postcolonialism, or the academic formation known most frequently as "postcolonial studies"), caste is largely absent. Partition, women's issues, sexuality, diaspora, modernity, hybridity, nationalism, religious identity—the list of typical themes when it comes to postcolonial commentary on India is long and diverse, with theorists both devoting attention to issues largely specific to India (Hindu fundamentalism) and connecting India to other postcolonial sites (modernity). In all this commentary, caste has generally been overlooked.

Obviously, some qualification is appropriate. Exceptions exist, mostly recent and perhaps a sign of a growing realization of the need for rectification. One such exception is Partha Chatterjee's *The Nation and Its Fragments*, which includes a chapter on caste. A number of these exceptions—for example, Nicholas Dirks's *Castes of Mind*—are mentioned in the discussion that follows. As the exceptions indicate, the various disciplines contributing to "postcolonial studies" have overlooked caste in multiple ways and to different degrees. Branches of the social sciences and history have taken up caste more seriously than, say, literary criticism. This is hardly surprising, given the questions historians and social scientists ask themselves and the structures of evidence by which they hold themselves accountable. When it comes to India, caste has an unavoidable presence in the "raw materials" of these disciplines. Perhaps this is the reason too that area studies—an older and different model of scholarship than postcolonial studies—has conducted plenty of (sometimes bad) theorizing on caste in India.

To acknowledge caste requires a different frame of reference—a different terminology, a different point of departure—from the one postcolonial studies has generally adopted. Literary postcolonial theory, with its more overt Anglophone preoccupations, registers the bias away from caste more fully than other disciplines. Since Anglophone texts themselves largely disregard caste, the obstacles to contemplating it within postcolonial literary criticism become especially difficult. This is not to say that caste is irrelevant when it comes to Anglophone literature—on the contrary. My recourse to the vernacular is an attempt to name the very difference that will allow us to overcome obstacles to what I regard as necessary postcolonial analysis, including of Anglophone texts. I rely on the notion of a vernacular difference to expose the oversights of "postcolonial theory."

This chapter, then, brings caste more fully into postcolonial theoretical discussions of India—both in its own right and in a way that continues explorations of the difference made by a nuanced idea of the vernacular. As this chapter demonstrates, the relative absence of caste in engagements with India in postcolonial theory is linked to institutional postcolonialism's general lack of interest in the vernacular. Drawing on Vivek Dhareshwar, Dilip Menon observes, "The postcolonial elite in India has used English, both as language as much as 'a semiotic system symbolizing modernity,' to impose . . . secular categories on the social world. This modern subjectivity, framed in English, has allowed caste to be approached only at one remove, as something restricted to the private domain suffused with the vernacular" (2006, 3). Menon's observation is perceptive in linking caste and the vernacular (though some of my own conclusions differ from Menon's because of the broader uses to which I put *vernacular*). Postcolonial studies has largely ignored caste because of the postcolonial elite's preference for

English and Anglophone material. Scholars emerging from within the mode of modern subjectivity identified by Menon have all too often conveniently overlooked the need to translate concerns of caste into the public domain of scholarship.

In this context, theoretical approaches to caste and the vernacular can be mutually clarifying. In the pursuit of both, this chapter enters the terrain opened up by Menon's observation. My argument includes a survey of the notion of caste, necessary given the deficit in knowledge outside specialized circles; a vernacular relocation of that eminent Indian and postcolonial (that is, nationally and transnationally identified, though he was Tamil) writer in English, R. K. Narayan; a perhaps surprising reading of love and renunciation in Narayan's novel *The Guide* (What, one may ask, do lovers and renouncers have to do with caste?); and an exploration of the cinematic adaptation of Narayan's novel into the classic Bollywood film *Guide*, framed by a review of Bollywood film criticism's engagement with the vernacular. Thus, confronting the complication as well as co-implication of caste and the vernacular within the social and political configurations of contemporary India as an independent nation, my argument unravels the one from the other in succeeding sections to arrive finally at a figure lurking in the shadows throughout: the "outcaste." That figure is at the center of the succeeding chapter.

THEORIZING CASTE

Recent studies of caste in India tend to adopt a historicizing thrust—that is, most emphasize caste as a historical category rather than as a quintessentially Indian form of social organization that remains largely unchanged through the centuries. Both drawing on and responding to earlier studies (an older mode of scholarship represented by G. S. Ghurye [1961], M. N. Srinivas [1966], Louis Dumont [1970], and others), more recent studies by Susan Bayly (1999), Nicholas Dirks (2001a), M. S. S. Pandian (2002, 2007), and V. Geetha and S. V. Rajadurai (1998) have sought to underscore the historical changeability of caste rather than its systemic character. The works by Bayly and Dirks are broad surveys, but a similar emphasis on the historicity of caste—its character as a form of social organization responsive not only to religious ideas but also to social, political, and economic forces—can be discerned in more focused works by M. S. S. Pandian and by V. Geetha and S. V. Rajadurai. Pandian's *Brahmin and Non-Brahmin* (2007) explores how Tamil Brahmin identity was produced and contested from a variety of directions in the colonial public sphere of the late nineteenth to mid-twentieth century. In *Toward a Non-Brahmin Millennium* (1998), through meticulous archival work, Geetha and Rajadurai trace the origin and development of Periyar's Self-Respect Movement, which decisively transformed the Tamil public sphere during this same period. Both works are centrally concerned with caste and assume as well as explicate the historicity of caste.[1]

Caste in these studies is not easily defined, for it is precisely their point that the ontology of caste changes in response to historical trends and also varies across geographical spread. Caste is hierarchical—it is a system that distinguishes between lower and upper castes. Caste is based on descent, that is, one is born into a caste and one cannot then choose another. Caste is connected to ritual ideas of purity and pollution, most importantly, concerning "untouchability." Caste subsists on the practice of endogamous marriage—marriage is permitted only within castes. The studies acknowledge these commonly associated "real" characteristics of caste—real in the sense that they capture widely prevalent beliefs and practices—but their main endeavor is to explicate the historical origins and subsequent vagaries of caste. As Bayly (1999) and Dirks (2001a) note in their surveys, a caste can go from being lower to higher over a period of time. Pollution rules too can undergo transformations and can even be contradictory in how they are observed at a particular time and place. Millions who live by and in castes may not acknowledge these mutable characteristics; nevertheless, caste is a demonstrably historical phenomenon.

The works by Bayly and Dirks usefully represent recent scholarship that emphasizes caste's *modernity*. Rather than generalizing about the hoary antiquity of caste, both resolutely focus on caste in its contemporary manifestations. Bayly declares that her aim is "to show that caste as we now recognize it has been engendered, shaped and perpetuated by comparatively recent political and social developments," specifically identifying the post-Mughal eighteenth century as a key transitional moment (1999, 4); and Dirks declares, "Caste (again as we know it today) is a modern phenomenon" (2000a, 5). As their language reveals (both are careful to note their subject is caste "now"), neither Bayly nor Dirks denies the existence of caste in premodern times; however, they emphasize the relatively recent origins of what Bayly calls "caste-centred India" (65). In this fashion, they wrest caste away from the critical perspective of traditionalism and thoroughly engage its historicity.

Rather than a social category through which we access a timeless, traditional India, caste is revealed to be a key element in the fashioning of a modern India. The implications of this shift are immensely consequential for the study not only of caste but also of a colonial and postcolonial modernity in South Asia.

Despite these similarities in their arguments, Bayly and Dirks crucially disagree regarding the role played by colonialism in the constitution of caste systems. Briefly put, Bayly dates the modern origins of the caste system to the eighteenth century, the period of transition from Mughal rule to colonial British rule, whereas Dirks emphasizes the effect of British colonialism. Bayly acknowledges the role played by the British in consolidating and deepening the impact of caste hierarchies and differences through the regulatory and enumerating mechanisms (such as the decennial census) of colonial rule; however, she locates the actual origins of the modern system of caste to a period before colonialism, emphasizes the extent to which Indians were themselves fashioners of the caste system as it exists now, and generally advances the notion that British rule was only one element in a complicated process of re-caste-ing India. In contrast, Dirks asserts, "It was under the British that 'caste' became a single term capable of expressing, organizing, and above all 'systematizing' India's diverse forms of social identity, community, and organization" (2000a, 5). The indictment of colonialism is, thus, far more severe in Dirks than Bayly. His fundamental argument, following Bernard Cohn (1968), is that a textualist interpretation of caste—one that relied on readings of ancient, Sanskrit texts presented by Brahmins who had the most intimate knowledge of these texts—made a dynamic and fluid system more fixed. Through this fixing, the differing but allied projects of the British colonizers (especially) and their upper-caste collaborators were abetted. In other words, Dirks reverses Bayly's order of emphasis. In his account, British colonialism crystallized the caste system as we know it for its own purpose, but the upper-caste collaborators too benefited from this crystallization. Not simply a matter of emphasis, this difference between Bayly and Dirks is greatly consequential for assessing the role of British colonialism.

The word *caste* is Iberian in its origins.[2] Etymologically, it is cognate with *chaste*—a caste is a form of social organization emphasizing chasteness, purity of social identity. Etymology reveals the word's capture of an important aspect—purity—of the system it describes, and yet the word misrepresents in another and more crucial way. In English, the single word *caste* does the work generally done by two words—*varna* and *jati*—in most other Indian languages. As is often the case in this book, translation is at issue here. *Varna* and *jati* are closely related but distinct words. In English, *varna* is caste and *jati* is caste; thus important distinctions are lost in translation. In fact, it is crucial to an understanding of the system of caste and how it works (at least in its present manifestation) to recognize that varna and jati are not the same.

Careful attention to how varna and jati differ underscores the historicity of caste as a system. When it is asserted that Indian society has been divided at least since the time of the Buddha (in whose anticaste discourses evidence for this system is seen) into the fourfold classification of Brahmins (priests or, more accurately, ritualists), Kshatriyas (rulers and soldiers), Vaishyas (merchants), and Shudras (artisans and agriculturalists), varna is being identified.[3] Varna is this fourfold classification, beyond which, as a paradoxical caste of outcastes, are located the "untouchables." Varna is this abstract and theoretical categorization of Indian society—abstract and theoretical because, as anyone with any familiarity with India knows, the system of caste as it functions today (and as it did even in the Buddha's time on the evidence of his discourses) bears little resemblance to this fourfold classification. Brahmins are hardly invariably ritualists any more than Vaishyas are merchants. And, rather than four, in point of fact, there are thousands of castes across India, many of them unique to specific regions or subregions.

Enter jati. Each one of these thousands of castes is a jati, not a varna. Jatis often correlate to varnas (that is, a particular jati belongs to a particular varna), but where varna is a more abstract classification mostly found in texts, jati is an actual socially and culturally delimited community to which an individual belongs. So, in the contradictory everyday life of Indians (mostly Hindus, but often other religious groups too), jati carries more importance than varna. When it comes to marriage, or sharing food, for example, from an orthodox point of view jati identity dictates more than varna identity. It determines an individual's caste practices more than varna. Two jatis belonging to the same varna can mark the boundary of separation between themselves with as much vehemence as two jatis belonging to two different varnas.

Varna, then, is mainly a textual and abstract notion when seen in relation to jati; nevertheless, it has had real historical consequences. As both Bayly (1999, 68-73) and Dirks (2001a, 23) observe, jatis have maneuvered to have themselves defined as belonging to a particular varna in an attempt to "raise" themselves in the caste hierarchy. In its very abstraction, varna serves as a potent, hegemonic idealization of caste as a system and thus becomes a goad to the organization and hierarchization of jati. The increasing correlation of jati and varna—the general assignation of a place within the fourfold varna classification to a jati—possibly results from the impact of British colonialist interpretations of caste. It might be that a relatively fluid and dynamic jati system became increasingly static under British rule, which for its own administrative purposes fixed on the apparent simplicity of the varna system as presented by Brahmin interlocutors. As noted above, this is Dirks's argument. Substitution of the single word *caste* for the words *varna* and *jati*—this act of translation—might even be part of a colonialist quest for simplicity. *Caste* partakes in the tendency of colonial administration to reduce and abbreviate. The cover image to this book, taken from an 1837 manuscript entitled "Seventy-Two Specimens of Castes in India" ("written by T. Vardapillay," according to the inscription, and featuring handwritten captions in Tamil and English), effectively suggests the ferociously abstracting and categorizing impulse of this colonialist logic, even though the manuscript was prepared for American missionaries in South India rather than British administrators. Translation becomes in this logic an instrument of colonial rule. However, the heterogeneity of jati cannot so easily be denied. And so, in an attempt to recognize the *varna/jati* distinction, *jati* is also sometimes glossed in English as "subcaste," only compounding the problem of translation; for calling *jati* a subcaste implies a neatness of division and subdivision as well as articulation of jati with varna that itself denies the heterogeneity of jati.

Preferable to the false precision of the word *caste*, used in conjunction with *subcaste* or not, is the term V. Geetha and S. V. Rajadurai use to describe caste—"the varna-jati complex" (1998, xiii). *Varna-jati complex* better represents the multiple determinants at work within the system we refer to in English as caste. Sometimes, indeed, varna and jati closely correlate, typically at the "highest" and "lowest" ends of the system, as represented by Brahmins and Dalits, for at these ends the hierarchization of the system through ritualized practices is most intently pursued. In other instances, jati and varna are in fact only loosely articulated. The notion of the varna-jati *complex* captures the intricacy of social arrangements at issue here far better than the single word *caste*.

Still, it is not possible to do away entirely with *caste*.[4] The term is especially needed for comparing the varna-jati complex to similar systems of social organization across the world, such as that of the Bunraku in Japan and the Osu in Nigeria. To refer to these Japanese and Nigerian phenomena as varna-jati complexes would be as much an imposition as, I am claiming, referring to the varna-jati complex as caste often is. For reasons of comparison, it helps to have a common term for systems of social organization occurring across the world that seem to share certain features. Originating as an error in translation, *caste* is now this term. *Caste* came into being by emphasizing varna, a concept more abstract and textually delimited than jati. In a sense, this act of translation disregarded the more vernacular aspects of the varna-jati complex, leaving *caste* useful only as a more abstract and general term—that is, mainly as a term that enables the work of comparison. My own references to *caste*, then, either indicate a transnational context or suggest a more abstract, generalized, and formulaic meaning (as, for example, in the phrase "politics of caste").

As terms, *varna-jati complex* and *caste* relate to each other through a complicated set of oppositions. In one sense, each term describes the same social phenomenon from a different vantage point—the former from that of the vernacular and the latter of the transnational. The contrast between the two terms places vernacular resonances and practical heterogeneity (the bewildering variety and contradictoriness of the varna-jati complex) on one side and systemic abstraction and transnational comparison on the other. Though as we see elsewhere in this book this is not the only way the opposition between the vernacular and the transnational can be figured, scrutinizing the translation of the *varna-jati complex* into *caste* underscores how attention to the vernacular enables apprehension of practical heterogeneity. The vernacular, while not synonymous with the practical, provides access to the practical. It names a domain that tends to resist abstraction and systematization.

Within Tamil India, whose recent literary developments are the main concern of this chapter, the politics of the varna-jati complex in translation and untranslated—that is, as we shall see, in English and in Tamil—have had a special salience. The defining political movements in Tamil Nadu during the twentieth century were those professing an anti-Brahmin Dravidianism. Emerging out of "Periyar" E. V. Ramasamy's Self-Respect Movement of the twenties and thirties, these movements effectively conquered political and economic power on behalf of the landed middle jatis by targeting the population of Brahmins in the state, generally put at 3 percent. Periyar was one of the most influential figures of twentieth-century Tamil letters and politics. He was an atheist, a rationalist, and a critic of the varna-jati complex. His understanding of the work needed to challenge the varna-jati complex was thoroughgoing: "Though I have endeavored all along to abolish caste, as far as this country is concerned, this has meant I carry out propaganda for the abolition of God, Religion, the Shastras [scriptures] and Brahmins. For caste will disappear only when these four disappear. Even if one of these were to remain, caste will not be abolished in its entirety" (qtd. in Geetha and Rajadurai 1998, 350). Upholding a view of South India as a Dravidian cultural and political sphere separate from the Aryan North, he espoused anti-Brahminism and Dravidian militancy.[5] He was himself a non-Brahmin. After a brief but checkered career in Gandhi's Indian National Congress, which he came to regard as a Brahminical party, he went on to launch the Self-Respect Movement in the 1920s and to establish in the 1940s the Dravida Kazhagam, the organization that was the progenitor of the two parties that have commandeered political power in Tamil India for most of the past half century.

The Dravidian movements that succeeded Periyar's initiative successfully challenged the Brahmin power he targeted. In some spheres of the Dravidian movements, Brahmins came to be identified not just with caste oppression but also as "Aryans" (that is, in the peculiar racial imagination borrowed from nineteenth-century European imperialism, invaders of a different racial stock) and as devotees of the Aryan language Sanskrit (rather than the Dravidian language Tamil). While the Aryan-ness of Brahmins is certainly a matter of debate (it is doubtful that these racial classifications are historically meaningful), Brahmins, though a small minority, did have, in addition to their enormous caste privilege and all the social and economic benefits that flowed from it, effective control of administrative and professional careers before and immediately after Independence. It was this control that the Dravidian movements targeted with such intensity. By doing so, the Dravidian movements' greatest success quite possibly was in nurturing the economic and social privilege of the jatis immediately below the Brahmins. While some benefits of their legacy reached all the way to the bottom of the varna-jati complex, social and physical violence against Dalits continued to a significant extent, mostly at the hands of jatis immediately above the Dalits. Ravikumar observes, "Since brahmins have been a numerical minority in Hindu society, their violence has mostly been symbolic; whereas the violence unleashed by the castes which are in a numerical majority is physical in nature" (2005, xxiii). While noting Ravikumar's distinction, we need not underestimate the vicious potency of Brahminical symbolic violence. Nevertheless, his observation does underscore that though the Dravidian movements were not themselves necessarily the perpetrators of the physical violence denounced by Ravikumar, they did not solve the issue of anti-Dalit violence.[6]

Caste is complicated—in itself and in how it relates to the politics of Tamil India. I turn now to a reading of R. K. Narayan's novel *The Guide* with this caution in mind. Through recourse to the notion of the vernacular, I show how the paradoxical novel engages with the varna-jati complex and how through this engagement it becomes a different text from the one commonly read in the North American classroom, both when it is dismissed for its exoticism and when it is celebrated for its authentic depiction of a traditional India.[7] To pursue this reading in the next two sections, I begin with a consideration of Narayan in a vernacular context and then proceed to a more focused, and also contrary-seeming, examination of the politics of the varna-jati complex in *The Guide*.

A VERNACULAR WRITER IN ENGLISH

The salience of neither the vernacular nor the varna-jati complex is immediately discernible in Narayan. Narayan is more often regarded as an *Indian* writer in English than as a *Tamil Brahmin* writer in English; as M. S. S. Pandian notes on reading Narayan's autobiography, written in English of course, Narayan "was almost completely silent" about his caste identity (2002, 5). Pandian goes on to observe, "All through the autobiography, caste masquerades as something else and makes its muted modern appearance.... The subtle act of transcoding caste and caste relations into something else—as though to talk about caste as caste would incarcerate one into a pre-modern realm—is a regular feature one finds in most upper caste autobiographies" (6). A similar masked acknowledgment of the varna-jati complex—disavowal and acknowledgment simultaneously—characterizes Narayan's more celebrated fictional writing.

To raise questions regarding the varna-jati complex in Narayan's fiction, we have to detour through that vernacular context marked as necessary by Menon. The Ramayana of Kamban offers convenient entry into this exploration because of its importance in Narayan's work as well as in twentieth-century Tamil letters in general. In contrast to Narayan, in Periyar and the Dravidianist movements hostility to the varna-jati complex was closely articulated with a critique of the Ramayana, the epic story of the incarnation on earth of Vishnu as Rama. The Ramayana came to be read in many sectors of the movements as the story of an Aryan conquest of Dravidian lands. In this interpretation, the varna-jati complex was established among Tamils by Aryan conquest. In other words, the varna-jati complex had no place in the original indigenous culture. As early as the thirties, when Narayan began his career as a novelist, this critique of the varna-jati complex was being vigorously circulated in the vernacular (Tamil) public sphere. Narayan, because of his Brahmin identity, was directly implicated in the historical developments unleashed by the simultaneously anticaste and anti-Brahmin activism of Periyar and the succeeding Dravidianist movements. He responded to these developments in characteristically indirect ways. He wrote repeatedly about the Ramayana, on one occasion even producing a popular retelling of it in English. Buried in these writings is a perspective on the varna-jati complex; but only by reading Narayan in relationship to the fiery debates over the Ramayana in Tamil, that is, by taking him from his Anglophone context and placing him in his vernacular one, can we elucidate the nature and depth of Narayan's transcoded allusions to it.

Since Narayan wrote in English, returning him to his vernacular context cannot mean the same as returning a writer who customarily wrote in Tamil. Although English is also an Indian language, it differs from other Indian languages in crucial ways that have significant literary consequences. English in India is at once a national and an international language. Caught in the insurmountable polemics of language politics, Indian writers in English have generally felt a great pressure to justify their literary enterprise. Accordingly, writers from Raja Rao to Salman Rushdie have advanced a variety of sophisticated as well as more simplistic arguments to dissociate themselves from the taint of alienness.[8] As a literary language, English has been the subject of endless debate, polarized between those who uphold its unique status as a link language in India (its national significance) and those who primarily think of it as an international language (and then perhaps denounce its alien intrusion). Not surprisingly, the peculiar situation of English-language writing in India plays a significant role in the critical discourse on Narayan. Critical approaches aspiring to place his work within a comparative cultural context have usually done so by foregrounding either its transnational links or its status as a national literary phenomenon.[9] Within the varied body of critical opinion, Narayan rarely appears in a vernacular context. He is seen as a *postcolonial* writer or as an *Indian* writer in English. Missing is a study that places him in relationship to his peers from the Tamil literary scene.

To be clear about my argument, two provisos are appropriate. First, K. R. Srinivasa Iyengar's groundbreaking *Indian Writing in English* (1985) does situate writers within a national cultural context that includes developments in a variety of Indian languages. However, the attention to a vernacular context represented by such a broad survey differs from the extended critical and theoretical treatment I have in mind. Moreover, the promising beginning made by Iyengar has largely been ignored by subsequent criticism, certainly by that arrayed under the heading of "postcolonial theory." Second, criticism on Narayan—and on other Indian writers in English such as Salman Rushdie and Shashi Tharoor—is indeed routinely aware of the debt owed by such writers to non-English-language cultural traditions such as the Ramayana and the Mahabharata. However, as they appear in such criticism, the Ramayana and the Mahabharata are vaguely identified as "classical literature" and/or repositories of "national" or "folk" narratives and values. Content to draw on the general fund of stories, cultural associations, and narrative strategies thus identified, the references do not actually cite particular versions of the Ramayana or the Mahabharata or engage with specific vernacular contexts within which the versions appear (see, for example, Narasimhaiah's widely cited essay on Narayan [1987, 137]). Neither Iyengar's survey nor these general references represent adequate theoretical engagement with a vernacular cultural context.

This lack of attention is critically untenable in some fairly obvious ways. Most Indian novelists in English are fluently bilingual. In many cases they read widely in Indian languages other than English, translate from them, or otherwise engage with developments in these allied vernacular cultural spheres. Is nothing to be learnt by placing Narayan in relationship to such Tamil contemporaries as Puthumaipithan and Ka Na Su? Is it entirely meaningless to regard him as a Tamil writer who happened to write in English—that is, as a writer who explored a quintessentially Tamil world in a recognizably Tamil way through the medium of English? I want to suggest that persistent and engaged work on Narayan—the same is probably true of many other Indian novelists who write in English—will reveal the extent to which his work was shaped by a vernacular literary context. The Indian novel in English, while largely consumed by readers outside India, can nevertheless prove to be not just a transnational window *into* India or a national staging *of* India but also, often, a product resulting *from* vernacular debates and intellectual concerns largely invisible to the transnational or even national reader. As I noted in chapter 1, Narayan is generally disregarded in postcolonial criticism when compared to Salman Rushdie because of the devaluation of the vernacular in postcolonial theory. When we return Narayan to his vernacular context I believe we will return some of the complexity to his writing.

With an appreciation of the robustness of the Tamil vernacular cultural sphere, then, I turn to a consideration of R. K. Narayan as a vernacular writer in English. I aim to enrich our understanding of the vernacular, often dismissed by comparison to the sophistication and modernity of the transnational or the national, and to discern how its powerful influence, sometimes difficult to identify, can exist in the most unlikely of places. Narayan's subtle and not-so-subtle ways of drawing on the moral universe of the Ramayana to chart the predicaments of modern India—sufficiently well acknowledged in criticism—aptly allow us to initiate this exercise because of the great significance of debates around the Ramayana within Tamil letters. Narayan himself was quite clear about the importance of the Ramayana to his work: "As a fiction writer, I have enjoyed reading Kamban [who told the story of Rama in the twelfth century in Tamil], felt the stimulation of his poetry and the felicity of his language, admired the profundity of his thought, outlook, characterization, and sense of drama," he writes in the preface to his own retelling (1972, xi). Narayan's recourse to the Ramayana carries many thematic consequences; I focus on drawing out the implications for Narayan's approach to the varna-jati complex.

Narayan's popular retelling of the Kamba Ramayana was published in 1972, a significant date as we shall see. Kamban, Narayan notes at the end of his devout retelling, rejects the darker stories of the Uttara Kanda of Valmiki's Ramayana (the canonical Sanskrit version) and "concludes his tale on the happy note of Rama's return to Ayodhya, followed by a long reign of peace and happiness on this earth. And there I prefer to end my own narration" (171). Nevertheless, as is typical of him, Narayan wears his devotion lightly, allowing in the introduction that "one accepts this work at different levels; as a mere tale with impressive character studies; as a masterpiece of literary composition; or even as a scripture" (ix). References to the Ramayana, sometimes ironic, abound in Narayan's works. Raman, the aspiring rationalist protagonist of *The Painter of Signs* (1976), is one example. Another is the river Sarayu that flows by Malgudi, the fictional town at the heart of most of Narayan's works. The river's name echoes the famed river of Rama's Ayodhya. In *Mr. Sampath* (1956), Ravi imagines Rama walking where Malgudi now stands and creating Sarayu. Through this simple but profoundly important gesture of naming, Narayan enters his entire work—all his Malgudi novels and short stories—into a framework of comparison, now ironic and now earnest, with the fabled utopia of Rama's Ayodhya.

To my mind Narayan's finest work, *The Guide* too is a Malgudi novel in which the Ramayana plays a subtle but significant role. While Raju, the protagonist, involves himself in the affairs of Rosie, Rosie's husband, Marco, is left, we are told by Raju, "to decipher episodes from Ramayan carved on the stone wall in Iswara Temple in North Extension—there were hundreds of minute carvings along the wall. They kept the man fully occupied as he stooped and tried to study each bit. I knew all those panels and could repeat their order blindfolded, but he spared me the labor, he knew all about it" (1958, 56–57). When Raju "steals" Rosie from Marco, the ironic allusion to the Ramayana, the story of Ravana's abduction of Sita from Rama, becomes fully resonant—How well, we might ask, does Raju really know the Ramayana? Later, as she prepares to return to her dancing, Rosie brings up the Ramayana when she asks Raju to find a pandit for her. "I shall . . . want him to read for me episodes of Ramayana and Mahabharata," she says, "because they are a treasure house, and we can pick up so many ideas for new compositions from them" (108). Still later, the Ramayana makes another appearance as Raju, growing into his role of a holy man in Mangala, lectures the children of the villagers. We are told that Raju "spoke to them on godliness, cleanliness, spoke on Ramayana, the characters in epics; he addressed them on all kinds of things. He was hypnotized by his own voice; he felt himself growing in stature as he saw the upturned faces of the children shining in the half-light when he spoke. No one was more impressed with the grandeur of the whole thing than Raju himself" (40).

Readers of *The Guide* have routinely observed that Narayan's novel involves a journey—in Mary Beatina's words, a journey from the "mundane" to the "transcendent" (1993, 2). Raju progresses from being a tourist guide to being first a guide to Rosie and the world of art she represents and then a guide to the transcendent. As the references cited above demonstrate, the Ramayana has its role in marking this journey. It makes its appearance in each of the stages of Raju's transformation. But each of these appearances also serves to reveal that Raju's attitude to the Ramayana is merely instrumental—the epic is something to lead tourists to, a source for dance compositions for Rosie, a tool with which to impress the villagers. In these examples Raju—or for that matter Marco, Rosie, or perhaps even the villagers (some of whom are the most devout characters in the novel)—do not demonstrate a true understanding of the Ramayana. Indeed, as noted above, Raju and Rosie directly contravene the values of the Ramayana in their adulterous relationship. Only when Raju has been led to a certain knowledge of himself is he transformed and thus perhaps accede to the values of the Ramayana, though this point is complicated, as I argue below. Until then, Raju may be superficially knowledgeable about the Ramayana but he is also detached from its values.

Narayan's approach to the Ramayana is part and parcel of his endorsement of Hindu values. Yet even as critics acknowledge this acceptance they tend to depict Narayan's Hindu content as simply "philosophy" or "influence," thus producing a curiously flattened picture of Narayan's achievement as a fiction writer, as if all that Narayan did was to act as a receptor of intellectual currents that lay above and beyond him. Of course, over his long career, Narayan himself contributed to this assessment through his assiduous self-portrayal as an apolitical and nonpolemical writer. Returning Narayan to his vernacular context will go some distance toward rectifying this misperception of his work. Accordingly, I want to proceed now by comparing Narayan's approach to the Ramayana, not to that of other Indian or postcolonial writers in English, but to that of his Tamil literary peers. As a vernacular writer in English, Narayan engaged many of the same issues, including those relating to the varna-jati complex, animating the work of his peers who wrote in Tamil.

The twelfth-century Ramayana of Kamban, whose beauty Narayan so extolled, is one of the earliest and most influential versions of the Rama story and is often regarded as the greatest epic poem in Tamil. Accounts describe Kamban studying Valmiki's Ramayana by night with the help of scholars and composing the verses that make up his version by day. Kamban was not, however, translating Valmiki; he was retelling his story in Tamil. Comparing Valmiki and Kamban, A. K. Ramanujan noted the theological nature of Kamban's work, how Kamban emphasized the divinity of Rama in a manner muted in Valmiki.

"Kampan writing in the twelfth century," he observed, "composed his poem under the influence of Tamil bhakti" (1992, 32). The devotionalism of Bhakti separates Valmiki from Kamban.[10]

No doubt this special devotional status conferred upon the story of Rama by Kamban made it an especially inviting target for Periyar E. V. Ramasamy, who saw in it a narrative of caste supremacy. In 1930, Periyar published a study of the Ramayana in Tamil that achieved extraordinary popularity. Periyar's *Iramayana Pathirankal (Characters in the Ramayana)* was in its tenth printing by 1972, when Narayan published his own retelling. It was translated into English in 1959 as *The Ramayana (A True Reading)*. In this work Periyar critiqued the Ramayana as the product of a war between the Aryan North and the Dravidian South: "The Aryans, when they invaded the ancient land of the Dravidas, maltreated and dishonoured the latter and had written a false and coloured history wholly fallacious. It is this they call Ramayana" (3). To Periyar, Rama was a northern Aryan tyrant who had ruthlessly destroyed the Dravidian hero Ravana in order to conquer and subjugate the South. The Ramayana was to him a Brahminical and caste-ridden story deeply antithetical to the values of the Dravidian Tamils.[11]

Periyar's ideas did not stop at literary criticism as we conventionally understand it. They played a crucial role in his broader political program. Periyar was a terrific propagandist. Dramatic versions of the Ramayana based on Periyar's interpretation were placed on the stage. Sometimes these enactments involved actors beating images of Rama with leather sandals, an act of such impiety and impudence it still boggles the mind. In 1956, nine years after India had achieved independence, Periyar acted on a rather literal understanding of the notion of incendiary interpretation. He was arrested in Chennai (then Madras) as he was attempting to lead his followers in burning pictures of Rama on Marina Beach as a protest against Brahminical and North Indian domination. As a consequence, a veritable political crisis convulsed Tamil India.

Even as Periyar was attacking the Ramayana in this fiery fashion, though, C. Rajagopalachari (Rajaji), a contemporary Tamil political leader comparable to him in stature, was engaged in expanding its influence as a religious text. Until two years before Periyar's picture-burning adventure (1954), Rajaji had been chief minister of Madras Presidency. On his departure from the chief minister's office under difficult circumstances, he undertook to retell the Sanskrit Valmiki Ramayana in weekly installments for the Tamil magazine *Kalki*, later describing this as "the best service I have rendered to my people" (1957, 7). In 1957 this version of the Ramayana was issued in book form in English. Like Periyar's commentary, Rajaji's retelling was popular and influential both in Tamil and in English. In the preface to the English version, Rajaji makes no reference to Periyar or his recent outrageous challenge to canonical notions of the Ramayana. The two men, though intellectual and political antagonists, were friends. Nevertheless, it is difficult not to be reminded of Periyar when we read Rajaji's words justifying the value of the Ramayana. Like his mentor Gandhi, Rajaji was a selective reformer of Hindu tradition rather than a radical antagonist of the kind Periyar was. He concluded his preface on a note of curiously modulated endorsement of the Ramayana: "In presenting this English version to a wider circle of readers spread all over the world, I think I am presenting to them the people of Bharat [India] just as they are, with all their virtues and their faults. Our classics really embody our national character in all its aspects and it is well the world sees us as we really are, apart from what we wish to become" (1957, 8). Given, however, that little commentary exists within the main narrative itself regarding these "faults," we might ask whether Rajaji's new modesty is not an afterthought, a response both to the new external audience for the translation and, more significantly, to the public furor created by Periyar's picture-burning Tamil insider critique of the Ramayana. Between the retelling in Tamil in *Kalki* by Rajaji and the appearance of the English version three years later, I suggest, falls the contrary shadow of Periyar.

These two contrasting examples from modern Tamil intellectual life illustrating the rich use of the Ramayana for social and political contestation and general edification could be multiplied. While in a British Raj prison for "sedition," V. V. S. Aiyar—a nationalist figure and a contemporary of Periyar and Rajaji—wrote an unabashedly celebratory exposition in English of the Ramayana of Kamban. His *Kamba Ramayana: A Study* (1965) lacks even the qualifications hinted at by Rajaji.[12] In literature, too, rereadings of the Ramayana are many. Puthumaipithan, also a contemporary of Periyar and Rajaji and widely regarded as the most influential Tamil prose fiction writer of the twentieth century, wrote a famous short story, entitled "Saba Vimochanam" ("Deliverance from a Curse") (1976), that retells from Ahalya's perspective the episode from the Ramayana in which the sage's adulterous wife is released from a curse by dust from Rama's feet. In Puthumaipithan's short story, Ahalya is transformed into a modern protagonist riven by doubts and ambivalences. In his novella *Asura Ganam* (*Demon Breed* [1985]), Ka Na Su draws on the Ramayana in telling the story of a young man, Raman, who finds himself in a strange liaison with a classmate, Hema, and her mother. He is both attracted to Hema's mother, whom he privately refers to as Soorpanaka (the so-called demoness from the Ramayana), and filled with violent hatred for her. Superficially, *Demon Breed* is a coming-of-age story—at the end of the novella, Raman marries Hema and leaves behind forever a self-indulgent youth. But more interesting is Ka Na Su's reworking of the Rama-Sita-Soorpanaka triangle of the Ramayana. The story is suffused with Raman's peculiar morbidity—whenever he hears the *nadaswaram*, he is reminded not of weddings and celebrations but death. He is antisocial, saved only by his ironic recognition of his own perversity. If Kamban's Rama was loyal, heroic, and virtuous, Ka Na Su's Raman is altogether less edifying. Depending on how one reads it, Ka Na Su's novella is an ironic commentary on Kamban's Ramayana, or a dark meditation on the wrongheadedness of ordinary human beings, or indeed both at the same time.

Periyar, Rajaji, V. V. S. Aiyar, Puthumaipithan, Ka Na Su: I want to suggest that R. K. Narayan's own relationship to the Ramayana is in dialogue with the varied Tamil responses to the Ramayana represented by these contemporaries. If we read Narayan's comments regarding the Ramayana in the context of the wide-ranging contestation over the Ramayana among Tamils, we begin to see how Narayan's project, both in his particular retelling of the Ramayana and in his work more generally, is one of recovery and rehabilitation. "It may sound hyperbolic," he writes in the preface to his version of the Ramayana, "but I am prepared to state that almost every individual among the five hundred millions living in India is aware of the story of the Ramayana in some measure or other. Everyone of whatever age, outlook, education, or station in life knows the essential part of the epic and adores the main figures in it—Rama and Sita" (1972, ix). Clearly, as he could not but know, he was not just hyperbolic but plainly wrong about this. His need to express this opinion, then, suggests his deep investment in the values of the Kamba Ramayana.

Narayan's version of the Ramayana was published, as I have noted above, in 1972. In the early seventies, media attention was focused yet again on Periyar's lifelong confrontation with the values of the Ramayana. The ban on the Hindi version of Periyar's book on the Ramayana was lifted by the Allahabad High Court in 1971. The same year widespread controversy erupted over a procession by Periyar's followers to expose the casteist basis of Puranic and religious texts. When some onlookers threw footwear at the procession, the marchers used the same footwear to beat a portrait they were carrying of Rama beheading the low-jati Sambuka. Writing of these incidents, Pandian notes, "As one would expect, the procession produced a political storm in the state and drew all-India attention" (2007, 194). Can it be possible that Narayan was unaware of these battles over the Ramayana even as he was preparing his version of the story of Rama for publication? Can his celebration of the Ramayana be unrelated to the attacks on it by Periyar and his followers? It seems unlikely when we consider that Narayan's reading and rereading of the Kamba Ramayana matches Periyar's for its lifelong commitment and is connected to his achievement as a writer.

I have noted the references to the Ramayana in *The Guide* marking important points in Raju's progress from the mundane to the transcendent. Now I would like to suggest that as he narrates this journey Narayan rewrites the Ramayana in a secular mode, simultaneously engaging in a masked way the varna-jati complex. *The Guide* opens with Raju, the roguish protagonist, being released from the prison to which he has been sent for forgery. Rather than return to his old life, Raju tries to disappear into a village, significantly named Mangala (or "Auspicious"), where he is not known. There he meets Velan, an ostensibly simple villager who mistakes Raju for a saint. Velan's innocent devotion leads Raju to greater and greater levels of selflessness. Interwoven with the story of Raju's experiences in Mangala is Raju's own account, told to Velan, of his life prior to prison—his career as a tourist guide, his love for the married dancer Rosie, his abandonment of his mother. Raju tells Velan this story in a noble but fruitless attempt to disabuse Velan of his blind devotion. Raju begins by playing the role of a saint in order to enjoy the food and respect Velan makes available to him, but slowly he is led to practice what he preaches. Finally, when the rains fail in Mangala he undertakes a fast aimed at making it rain again. The novel ends, famously, on an ambivalent note—Raju claims to Velan that he can feel it raining far away in the hills, but his assertion is not affirmed by any other aspect of the narrative. Does it in fact rain? From the point of view of the narrative, an answer is irrelevant, for *The Guide* is not a religious novel but rather one about the place of religion in society. Equally irrelevant is whether Raju dies (another ambiguity at novel's conclusion). The climactic point of the novel is not the ambivalent ending but the altogether less equivocal passage in which Raju reflects on the transformation within him: "'If by avoiding food I should help the trees bloom, and the grass grow, why not do it thoroughly?' For the first time in his life he was making an earnest effort; for the first time he was learning the thrill of full application, outside money and love; for the first time he was doing a thing in which he was not personally interested" (1958, 212). It would be possible on the basis of this epiphany that Raju undergoes to read *The Guide* as belonging to that familiar literary genre, the novel of self-discovery. We might then compare *The Guide* to such classic European novels as James Joyce's *Portrait of the Artist as a Young Man*. But my earlier review of Narayan's particular investments in the stories and values of the Ramayana invites additional readings that might resist subsumption of *The Guide* within a European tradition and reveal alternative vernacular inflections.

Such alternatives become apparent when we attend to the secular retelling of the Ramayana in *The Guide*, made clear by comparing Narayan's treatment of Raju with his treatment of Rama as well as Ravana, the ostensible enemy, in his retelling of *The Ramayana*. In Narayan's *Ramayana*, Rama must himself slowly progress to a knowledge of his divinity—to the knowledge that he is an avatar of Vishnu. Accordingly, Rama's missteps, indeed his morally questionable actions, such as the murder of Vali from ambush and the trial by fire of Sita, are explained away as the actions of one who was a mortal man and a divine incarnation at the same time (1972, 97, 163–64). The Ramayana becomes the story of the revelation of the divinity of Rama not only to its readers or auditors but indeed to Rama himself. Thus, toward the end of his retelling, Narayan writes, "The gods . . . had an uneasy feeling that Rama had, perhaps, lost sight of his own identity. Again and again this seemed to happen. Rama displayed the tribulations and the limitations of the human frame and it was necessary from time to time to remind him of his divinity" (163–64). In a further twist, Ravana too is drawn into this narrative of self-discovery. When Ravana dies, Narayan writes, "Now one noticed Ravana's face aglow with a new quality. Rama's arrows had burnt off the layers of dross, the anger, conceit, cruelty, lust, and egotism which had encrusted his real self, and now his personality came through in its pristine form—of one who was devout and capable of tremendous attainments" (159). Ravana, brought back to his true self, then proceeds to heaven.

The Guide explores this Hindu notion of self-discovery within a secular mode. Raju's secular self-transformation matters more than a particular assertion of religious faith. Regardless of whether Narayan himself espouses such a faith, the novel withholds an active endorsement of it. *The Guide* is to my mind philosophical rather than religious—it is an exploration in the guise of a wry narrative about a rogue named Raju of the Hindu faith in the universal nobility of the human being (found also in other Indic traditions). Is this not the lesson taught in Raju's helpless and inevitable accession to the faith Velan reposes in him? To recognize these aspects of *The Guide* is not to deny that Narayan's celebration of the Ramayana is disturbingly uncritical given the uses to which the Ramayana has been put in the pursuit of Hindu fundamentalism. The Ramayana serves as a key text for such organizations as the Rashtriya Swayamsevak Sangh (RSS) and the Bhratiya Janata Party (BJP) in their anti-Muslim diatribes and their attempts to refashion India as a Hindu nation. The controversies surrounding these developments hardly register in Narayan's work; though Narayan's sensibility seems mainly a tolerant secularism, the unabashedly Hindu values on which this sensibility is founded raises difficult questions that cannot be ignored. At the same time, the world of Narayan's fiction cannot be facilely equated with the world of the RSS or the BJP—his rehabilitation of Ravana at the end of his retelling of the Ramayana is but one indication that it cannot.

The Guide, then, reinscribes the values of the Ramayana by upholding it and asserting its centrality in Indian culture, albeit in a putatively secular mode. In its use of the Ramayana, *The Guide* can be seen to be a social and political novel. Where Periyar's approach to the Ramayana was inflammatory and radical in the most thoroughgoing way, Narayan's is devout and preservationist. Compared to Puthumaipithan or Ka Na Su, his recourse to the epic is altogether less transgressive. Puthumaipithan challenges the Ramayana in a manner that is in its own way as radical as Periyar's. Ka Na Su's appropriation too invites a critical rereading of the epic, albeit more obliquely because of the first-person narration he adopts. When placed next to these writers who wrote primarily in Tamil, Narayan turns out to be the more timid writer, further illustrating points I was keen to make in the first chapter—that the vernacular postcolonial cannot be adduced purely from language (that is, a vernacular sensibility cannot be confused with vernacular language) and that the transnational postcolonial (here, postcolonial writing in English) is not necessarily the domain of the transgressive and the bold.

It may seem that these points are rather banal, and so they are. Yet it is necessary to make them, as Salman Rushdie's egregious introduction to his anthology makes clear. Less banal perhaps, and equally important to underscore, is the need to be *theoretically* attentive to vernacular sensibility as it expresses itself in postcolonial contexts. While the origins and provenance of such a sensibility cannot be read facilely, the vernacular in my usage nevertheless marks an important orientation within the postcolonial. Narayan's preservationist project is not fully animated until we situate him in his vernacular context with a robust understanding of what this means—in the mode of critically engaging the vernacular rather than simply delineating "influence" or "allusions." When we do this, Narayan becomes a more interesting writer. Narayan was at bottom a Tamil and a Hindu writer who wrote in English. Finally, this Tamil-ness and Hindu-ness is the key both to Narayan's success and to his relative obscurity outside India. On the one hand, the provincial and predominantly Tamil and Hindu town of Malgudi that he created is rich fodder for an ethnographic curiosity about India. On the other, to many readers across the world he appears intellectually less challenging than he really is because of the fundamental alienness of his writerly vision.

The critical response to Narayan's work over the decades tells us as much about what demands are made of "postcolonial fiction" as it does about him. Earlier I argued that Indian writing in English carries a special burden in making a place for itself as an Indian literature. The medium in which it is written—the English language—has accordingly attracted tremendous attention from both critics and writers. No doubt important literary concerns demand such attention; nevertheless, this particular focus has also kept criticism in thrall to what I have called the axes of the transnational and the national, making it difficult to see the various ways in which the vernacular has conditioned Indian writing in English. Narayan is a postcolonial writer in English, an Indian writer in English, and a vernacular writer in English. Viewed mainly as a postcolonial writer or an Indian writer in English, he is diminished as a literary figure. Narayan's work, including *The Guide*, is deeply engaged in a foundational struggle over values, conducted over the terrain of the Ramayana, roiling the Tamil public sphere. Only by the development of a new and robust understanding of *vernacular* as a critical term does Narayan's engagement become evident. This same attention to the vernacular allows us to scrutinize Narayan's accompanying attention to the varna-jati complex, which perhaps surprisingly is in some ways at odds with his devotional attitude to the Ramayana.

In *The World, the Text, and the Critic,* Edward Said approvingly identifies "criticism whose focus is the text as something other, as something historically and materially more, than a critical occasion. By 'material' in this case I mean the ways, for example, in which the text is a monument, a cultural object sought after, fought over, possessed, rejected, or achieved in time" (1983, 150). Referring to this as "the text's situation in the world," Said calls for a criticism that studies literature "in a more situated, circumstantial, but no less theoretically self-conscious way. There is no point in my further qualifying 'situated' and 'circumstantial,' since it should be obvious that I mean 'worldly' and 'historical': literature is produced in time and in society by human beings, who are themselves agents of, as well as somewhat independent actors within, their actual history" (151–52). Today (yesterday or tomorrow, a rigorous notion of history suggests, the case could be different), restoring *The Guide* to its vernacular context shows us how this text fights over cultural objects even as it is fought over itself; such a restoration reveals for us the text's situatedness, its worldliness, its historicity, in a word, its materiality—albeit a materiality that the text itself works partially to obscure.

LOVERS AND RENOUNCERS

Reading *The Guide* in a materialist spirit is clarifying when it comes to the varna-jati complex. It allows us to recognize both preservationist and transgressive aspects of the novel by noting its engagement of the Ramayana's monumentality (in Said's sense of the term). It allows us to note the way the novel participates in a struggle in *time*, in history, over the values of the Ramayana. Such a materialist reading requires care because the novel engages largely in the kind of masked citation of the varna-jati complex—both disavowal and acknowledgment—identified by Pandian. For the most part, Narayan abjures explicit references, though to the discerning reader the varna-jati complex is everywhere in the general ambience and cultural practices represented. Moving from the preservationist to the transgressive attributes of the novel—as I mean to do now—shows that the contours of the novel's engagement with the varna-jati complex are neither easily identified nor predictable.

Rosie stands as the one exception to the reticence on the part of the text when it comes to the varna-jati complex. With her, tellingly if also complicatedly, the varna-jati complex erupts into the ostensibly casteless world of Malgudi. Early in Raju's romancing of the married Rosie the following exchange takes place between them (as recounted by him to Velan):

> "You see," she began, plucking my sleeve. "Can you guess to what class I belong?"
> I looked her up and down and ventured, "The finest, whatever it may be, and I don't believe in class or caste. You are an honor to your caste, whatever it may be."
> "I belong to a family traditionally dedicated to the temples as dancers; my mother, grandmother, and, before her, her mother. Even as a young girl, I danced in our village temple. You know how our caste is viewed?"
> "It's the noblest caste on earth," I said.
> "We are viewed as public women," she said plainly, and I was thrilled to hear the words. "We are not considered respectable; we are not considered civilized."
> "All that narrow notion may be true of old days, but it's different now. Things have changed. There is no caste or class today." (73)

Here Narayan's language, slipping imprecisely between the terminology of caste and class, shows confusion in even raising the issue of the varna-jati complex; it reflects in this regard a general imprecision in the political discourse of that time about the relationship between class and caste as social categories.[13] At the same time, betraying a telling diffidence, Narayan leaves unstated one of the most horrifying aspects of Rosie's origins in the "caste" of *devadasis,* or temple dancers—that these women ostensibly dedicated to God were often made available to the wealthy men of certain upper jatis as concubines. Rosie's description of herself as a "public woman" is the closest that Narayan's language comes to acknowledging what was often dire sexual exploitation—and indeed Raju's confession that he is "thrilled" at Rosie's description of herself suggests his own appetite for such "public women." Naming the varna-jati complex (caste) is hard enough; engaging with its violences and brutalities appears impossible.

There is a further complication. As both Amrit Srinivasan (1985) and Sassia Kersenboom (1991) observe, devadasis are located in a somewhat anomalous manner within the varna-jati complex. They do not strictly constitute a jati by themselves, for the women dedicated as devadasis in temples, while mostly inheriting their position by birth, were drawn from a variety of different jatis through rituals of consecration. Thus Srinivasan notes "the misuse of the term 'caste' in relation to the devadasis in the colonial literature. According to the devadasis themselves there exists a devadasi 'way of life' or 'professional ethic' (*vrtti, murai*) but not a devadasi *jati*" (1985, 1869). Narayan's language reveals little knowledge of these subtleties—while devadasis endured subjection through the varna-jati complex, they could not accurately be described as in themselves a jati. Still, the purpose of this remark is not to devalue the importance of the varna-jati complex in Narayan's novel but rather to note, to the contrary, how a discourse of caste derived from colonial times will not be denied. Even if in hesitant, imprecise, and masked ways, the novel reproduces such a discourse and engages with the varna-jati complex profoundly, both through the importance assigned in the narrative to Rosie's romance with Raju and through less clearly marked ways.

Certainly, Narayan's reservation in naming the varna-jati complex and its violences, read in the context of his rehabilitation of the Ramayana during a time when his contemporaries were widely critiquing it, signals a naturalization of the privileges and brutalities of the varna-jati complex. Only from the uncritical vantage point of higher-jati identity can the varna-jati complex escape with such nominal treatment. However, while such a reading is not only plausible but necessary to register, I believe it coexists in the text with another, more transgressive, reading. If we look in the right places we find within *The Guide* a critique of the varna-jati complex—in at least two, mutually contradictory, ways.

The first critique involves the very fact of Raju's relationship with Rosie. Raju's romantic involvement with Rosie defies the taboos of the varna-jati complex. Because of it Raju loses his mother, who cannot abide Rosie not only because she is already married but also because she is a dancing girl, a devadasi (that is, prohibited by the moral code of the unnamed but probably Brahmin jati to which Raju belongs). He loses many of his friends over her too. Narayan presents the relationship with ambivalence: he casts Rosie as a seductress and a "snake" woman, even as he presents the constraints of her life with some sympathy, noting through Raju toward the end of the novel that "neither Marco [Rosie's husband] nor I had any place in her life, which had its own sustaining vitality and which she herself had underestimated all along" (198). As for Raju, Narayan shows him to be avaricious and full of material indulgences, as well as genuinely in love with Rosie. His love contravenes both received notions of devadasi concubinage and the exclusionary rules of Raju's jati. Ultimately Raju leaves Rosie behind; but for its duration his relationship with her acquires the structure if not the fact—for they never actually wed—of the inter-jati marriages recommended by Periyar's Self-Respect Movement as a way of confronting the varna-jati complex.

Peiyar encouraged, and in fact publicly staged, inter-jati marriages to overcome the taboos and privileges of the varna-jati complex. He also enthusiastically supported such practices as divorce (pointing out that divorce provided a way out from unhappy and abusive marriages) and extolled romantic love for its capacity to unite two persons in a relationship of equality regardless of social structure.[14] Raju and Rosie's relationship embodies many of these qualities of the Self-Respect Movement. Through this relationship *The Guide* explores the modernist critique of the varna-jati complex offered by the rationalist and atheistic Periyar—a critique that held the commingling of jatis through marriage and personal relationships and the breaking of other taboos as the surest path to the abolition of the varna-jati complex.

The Guide does not, however, ultimately endorse this particular anticaste strand of the narrative, for the novel eventually moves beyond the transgressive love relationship between Raju and Rosie. After his prison stay, Raju does not return to Rosie but rather is led gradually down a different path until he attains the status of a swami or a guru, that is, of a renouncer—beyond family, beyond romance, beyond material comforts, beyond even food, and, significantly for our purposes here, beyond the varna-jati complex. Renunciation is the second and alternative way in which the novel proffers a critique of the varna-jati complex. As Susan Bayly points out in her study, within the Hindu worldview the ascetic renouncer is an alternative ideal to the Brahmin ritualist (16–17). Where the Brahmin ritualist is of the world (and of the varna-jati system that is of the world), the ascetic renouncer is in the world but not of it. In theory at least (for in practice various accommodations did occur), ascetic renouncers operated outside the varna-jati complex. If they were spiritual leaders, as Raju becomes, they typically accepted devotees regardless of jati and explicitly articulated ideas that challenged the varna-jati complex. The Buddha exemplifies this phenomenon. In less extensive ways, so does Gandhi. The example of the ascetic renouncer testifies to the existence of avenues to critique the varna-jati complex from within the modalities of Hindu thought. At the same time, it also suggests the great power of the varna-jati complex, for it is only through such a comprehensive act of renunciation that the varna-jati complex seems capable of being left behind. *The Guide* articulates this renunciatory transcendence of the varna-jati complex (and indeed other aspects of life) in its final pages. Because Raju appears to the villagers initially in the guise of a swami or an ascetic renouncer he is not defined by his jati as he is, albeit putatively, elsewhere in the novel. Nor does Raju relate to the villagers according to their jati identities. In short, Raju as renouncer moves beyond the varna-jati complex in his interaction with the villagers.

Finally, Narayan's allegiances lie with this second mode of critiquing the varna-jati complex. The parodic structure of the novel and its inconclusive ending make it difficult to claim decisively one position rather than another for the novel. Obfuscation is itself an important part of the novel's mode of address and a sign of its inability to come to a clear position on the varna-jati complex. This indecisiveness echoes the novel's attitude to Rosie, the central figure for this aspect of the narrative, viewed sometimes sympathetically and other times with misogyny. Nevertheless, despite this indeterminacy, ultimately the novel sides with the ascetic renouncer mode of critique rather than romantic love in the choice that Narayan has Raju make. To assert this is not to read renunciation as vernacular or traditional and romantic love as cosmopolitan or modern, for neither can facilely be aligned in this manner. It is only possible to argue that, within the structure of Narayan's novel, renunciation is presented sympathetically in contrast to the self-indulgent and modern life Raju previously led in Malgudi with Rosie. That Raju achieves this renunciation in the village of Mangala (or, as noted above, the village of "auspiciousness") and not the town of Malgudi seems to indicate the religious nature of this choice. And so we return—to the extent that return is possible in a novel so full of irony—to the upper-caste bias in Narayan's work. The ascetic renouncer ideal functions within Hinduism in contradictory ways; in Narayan it enables an ambivalent reclamation of a religious mode that is at one and the same time accommodative of values conventionally seen as supportive of the varna-jati complex (the preservationist aspect of Narayan's project) and critical of it and its prejudices (the transgressive element). In this, as in his recovery of the values of the Ramayana, Narayan shows himself struggling with the social and political developments of twentieth-century India, but in ways that betray his own upper-caste inheritance.

Revealed in Narayan's *The Guide* are the tensions and contradictions of secular, liberal, modern but Brahmin ideology. Brought back to its vernacular context, *The Guide* is shown to be marked by jati even as it aspires to go beyond it, to be simultaneously devotional and agnostic, at one and the same time preservationist and transgressive

54 | Lovers and Renouncers, or Caste and the Vernacular

of dominant values. It emerges as a far more willful and historically sedimented text than is usually credited.

BOLLYWOOD ITERATIONS

In 1965, *The Guide*, the English-language novel set in Tamil India, was made into *Guide*, a Hindi-language film set in Rajasthan, illustrating thereby a triple translation—from novel to film, from English to Hindi, from a location in South India to one in North India. As such, the novel and its film adaptation offer fresh opportunities to explore the ways in which languages, cultures, identities, textual economies and discourses can be articulated, rearticulated, and disarticulated within the theoretical empire of the postcolonial. At the same time, because of the variety of postcolonial cultural phenomena brought into focus in this particular instance of filmic transformation, theoretical categories themselves invite articulation, disarticulation, and rearticulation in the course of the exploration.

What is at stake in reading Narayan as a postcolonial writer or an Indian writer as opposed to a Tamil writer? What is the significance, if any, of the Tamil-ness of a novel like *The Guide*? What is the relationship of Hindi to the "imagined community" of India? How does Bollywood, understood strictly as Hindi-language Bombay (or Mumbai) commercial cinema, articulate or disarticulate folk or local, or, of special interest to my argument, vernacular identities and knowledges? What are the relationships and disjunctures between and among those aspects of postcolonial experience invoked by the critical terminology of *vernacular, national,* and *transnational*? What happens when the varna-jati complex is approached from within a national framework rather than a vernacular one? These and similar questions sketch out my terrain of inquiry as I follow Raju's story through its translations. In pursuing these questions, I draw on the distinction I have made and maintained between the transnational and the vernacular. As I have noted, one cannot comprehend the sum of "the postcolonial condition" without acknowledging the existence of both of these dimensions and indeed a spectrum of positions in between, including that of the national.

Many transformations result from adapting Raju's story into a Bollywood film. In another context, I would be especially attentive to the interesting changes in narrative structure and in Rosie's character. Now I concentrate on aspects of the film that reveal its alignment with a particular imagination of the national community and the place of the varna-jati complex and the folk within it. *The Guide* may be read as a novel of the nation—not a national allegory like *Midnight's Children*, but rather a novel that explores aspects of national self-imagination. Narayan accomplishes this obliquely—mainly through reference to Gandhi, to whom he compares Raju during the process of his transformation into a saint (see, for example, 1958, 92–93). Through this reference, the novel's narrative links the philosophical theme of self-discovery to an exploration of a sustaining myth of the nation within Nehruvian ideology—Gandhi as Mahatma. Simultaneously, a politics of contestation and recuperation—always tangential and self-effacing in Narayan—is uncovered not only in the vernacular sphere but also in the space of the national. Through his gently ironic narrative mode, Narayan simultaneously evokes and parodies the myth of Mahatma Gandhi, offering, as we have come to expect, an exploration rather than a conclusion.

In *Guide*, the film, the accommodations with a much more sharply sketched Nehruvian ideology of national "unity in diversity" are greater and immediately evident.[15] Raju in the film speaks many of the different languages of India as a tourist guide; he travels across diverse Indian landscapes when he is released from jail; and the "Piya Tose Naina Laage Re" ("Beloved, My Eyes Have Found You") song-and-dance sequence becomes a deliberately staged spectacle of national unity.[16] Ironically, in the process of this accommodation the main geographical location of the film must be changed from Tamil Nadu to Rajasthan, Raju's identity must be changed from Tamil to Rajasthani, and Rosie's dancing, clearly identified as the Tamil-associated Bharata Natyam in the novel (Narayan 1958, 143), must become a mélange of different Indian dance forms best described as Bollywood dance. Narayan's novel may not cite its vernacular sources overtly, but it nevertheless finds an important part of its sustaining energy within a particular vernacular sphere of contestation and recuperation. It would be tempting to argue that in contrast the film expunges all marks of the vernacular in its articulation of the national; but the nation is of course an abstraction incapable of articulating itself except through various appropriations and expropriations of the vernacular. As I argue at greater length in chapter 4 with regard to the differences between the Tamil and Hindi versions of the Mani Ratnam film *Roja*, a notion of Hindi-centered subjectivity—itself constructed out of vernacular sources, no doubt—typically appropriates for itself the place of the national in Bollywood cinema. Thus, while both film and novel have a complex relationship to the vernacular, the manner in which each relates to it is different.

Guide is not unusual in its dependence on the ideology of nationhood. The intimate relationship between Hindi-language Mumbai-based Indian popular cinema, or Bollywood, and the imagined community of India is both well acknowledged and a subject of sustained critical scrutiny. As the task of producing an adequate theoretical framework for the understanding of Bollywood has gathered momentum, a number of film scholars have moved beyond analyses of individual films to a more general assessment of Indian popular cinema as such. Many of these critical formulations have adopted a nationalist framework in arguing for the cultural and aesthetic value of Bollywood. Understanding cultural value primarily in a political sense, they have borrowed heavily from the treasury of nationalist ideology.

Partly, they have been led to this critical stance by their assessment that dismissals of Bollywood have routinely had similar recourse, albeit for a different purpose, to nationalist ideology. The scholars and filmmakers critical of Bollywood fault it for its imitativeness (especially with regard to Hollywood films) and for a manipulative attitude to its audience; the defense of Bollywood, on the other hand, has surmounted the charge of imitativeness mainly through an assertion of an alternative aesthetic—a distinctively Indian aesthetic—at work in this cinema. Thus both attitudes to Bollywood are governed by what may be called a nationalist or crypto-nationalist critical paradigm. Here my point is not that criticism of Bollywood has been exclusively concerned with its relationship to nationalism but rather that the overarching theoretical framework in many general assessments displays such a concern.

Rosie Thomas, for example, declares that "Indian cinema has, throughout its long history, evolved as a form which has resisted the cultural imperialism of Hollywood," thus revealing its affinity to a nationalist postcolonial cultural politics (1985, 116). Later in her essay, Thomas sets out approvingly what Indian filmmakers themselves regard as the essence of Indianization (121) and notes that "there is of course good evidence that Hindi films have evolved from village traditions of epic narration, and the dramas and the characters, as well as the structure, of the mythological epics are regularly and openly drawn upon" (123). Vijay Mishra (1985) makes a similar point regarding the Mahabharata and the Ramayana but presses the argument much further than Thomas, declaring that the narrative conventions of Bollywood films remain fully committed to those already articulated in the epics. Although Mishra's sweeping assertion seems overstated, the impetus for his argument might be seen to arise out of a desire to consider the films within an Indian context. Both Thomas and Mishra articulate critical positions that appear compatible with versions of the nationalist paradigm.

Sumita Chakravarty provides another version of such an argument. In *National Identity in Indian Popular Cinema: 1947–1987*, she insists that "contemporary concerns find 'creative utterance' in the commercial cinema, despite the widespread impression that the Bombay film is a hopelessly backward-looking, regressive, and random phenomenon" (1993, 16). Her study, she declares, "provides an interpretive framework within which the Hindi film can be apprehended as a distinct aesthetic and cultural system" (10)—indeed, as her discussion demonstrates, as an artifact of an "*Indian* culture" (10, italics in original). Both her theoretical model of "imperso*nation*" and the title of her book make her debt to the nationalist critical paradigm amply clear (6–7, italics in original).[17]

It might be argued that critics such as Thomas and Mishra set out an indigenist and folkloric, rather than nationalist, framework for the assessment of Indian popular cinema. I would aver, however, that these perspectives are subsumed within a nationalist framework. A nationalist hegemonic cultural project, pursuing in this context an Indian distinctiveness, has often found it useful to integrate into itself the cultural sensibility of "the folk," "the indigene," and "the traditional"— in short, "the vernacular," the related term I prefer for its greater critical suppleness. This subsumption of the vernacular within the national in criticism echoes a similar subsumption in the films themselves. All too often in the films, the vernacular is drained of any animating power and presented in what may be called a "museumizing" register.

Such is the case with the aforementioned "Piya Tose Naina Laage Re" song-and-dance sequence in *Guide*, which appears even as Rosie begins her climb to fame. The sequence is a collage of several performances of Rosie in different locations, split by a brief scene that presents Rosie at home with Raju. In these different performances, Rosie is seen wearing costumes vaguely reminiscent of a particular part of India, such as Kerala. The backdrops used in these performances (palm trees or mountains, for example) too suggest the diversity of Indian landscapes. Reinforcing this element of diversity (national unity-in-diversity), Raju, as Rosie's lover and manager, himself appears within the sequence in different garbs ranging from a Western suit to an *achkan* (Nehru's favored dress). Taken as a whole, the sequence suggests a pan-Indian context to its viewers in multiple ways and through various layers—an external pan-Indian film audience is constructed for *Guide* the film through the representation of an enthusiastic internal pan-Indian audience for Rosie the dancer. *Guide* becomes an act of "imperso*nation*" in Sumita Chakravarty's sense.

In the pursuit of this imperso*nation* the "Piya Tose Naina Laage Re" sequence at once recovers and rejects the vernacular. The sequence nominally gestures to the vernacular by presenting a series of vernacular identities in a highly inconsistent—thin, as opposed to ethnographically thick—fashion. Neither the costumes nor the settings are anything more than vague allusions to Malayalee or Tamil or Gujarati or Assamese identities. In the long section within the sequence allegedly referring to Kerala, a Malayalee identity is indicated by the dancers' loose hair and flesh-colored blouses and by a boat moving apparently through a backwater. Even as a vernacular custom of not wearing blouses is acknowledged, the actual practice is deemed inappropriate for a pan-Indian sensibility. What is important is not thick vernacular content but simply the gesture toward the vernacular—reduced to an exhibit, the vernacular becomes an alibi for the nation's self-conception as an imagined community of citizens who both represent diversity and tolerate it.

Thus, in this brilliantly imagined and composed sequence, the vernacular is emptied of all significant content—museumized, shorn of all threatening specificity—so that the self-imagination of the nation ultimately remains untroubled. Appropriated in this way, the national needs the vernacular. It is by now a matter of critical consensus (following Partha Chatterjee [1986, 1993] and Benedict Anderson [1991], for example) that nationalism is the rival of (neo)colonialism in the "Third World," even as it remains a first cousin, indebted to many formulations having their origins in the colonial encounter. Nationalism contests (neo)colonialism. Indeed, in the "Third World," it is the very name for that which contests the (neo)colonial. In this context, nationalism, attracted by the connotation of authenticity emanating from the vernacular, has resourcefully integrated vernacular vocabulary into its own idiom, and Bollywood expresses this expropriation in formal as well as thematic ways, as film critics recognize.

However, film criticism has not sufficiently attended to the distinction I am maintaining between the national and the vernacular. The transactions between the three dimensions of the postcolonial I have identified—the vernacular, the national, and the transnational—are complex, contradictory, overdetermined. Film criticism, as my overview above indicates, makes it possible to understand the cinematic version of *The Guide* mainly as a cultural artifact expressive of the nationalist project, not as one with a troubling mode of representing the vernacular. The differences between the novel and the film that relate to the vernacular become difficult to recognize. Tamil identity is expunged from the film in selective and problematic ways—Raju, for instance, is transformed from a Tamil into a Rajasthani, while the marginal character of Raju's secretary, with the easily recognizable Tamil name of Mani, is retained unchanged. Film criticism, centered on the category of the nation, has noted the ways in which Bollywood films refer to the vernacular, but it has not provided an adequate accounting of the contradictory and, indeed, coercive ways in which the subsumption of the vernacular takes place within the cultural system of Bollywood films. In short, here is yet another instance in which attention to the vernacular represents a new horizon of theoretical possibility for postcolonial criticism today, yet another way such attention casts light on disregarded aspects of postcolonial society. Accordingly, such heedfulness poses vexatious questions about the way "postcolonial theory" is currently configured—about its foundational categories of analysis, its unacknowledged biases, its textual archives.

Of course, caste—or rather the varna-jati complex—too enters into this discussion, though again perhaps in surprising ways. Scrutiny of the varna-jati complex and its accompanying politics as they appear in *Guide*, and of the film's difference on this issue from its literary predecessor, leads us to what may be regarded as unanticipated conclusions. Certainly, in the literary predecessor to *Guide* the varna-jati complex is not the only issue around which vernacular resonances are to be heard. In restoring the novel to its vernacular context, one might just as easily have brought other topics of interest into focus. Nevertheless, attention to vernacular resonances in the novel makes issues regarding the varna-jati complex more audible to us as readers, though we cannot conclude from this that the varna-jati complex always leads us to the vernacular any more than the converse. The example of the film *Guide* is equally instructive in this regard.

References to the varna-jati complex in *Guide* are made more directly than in the novel, with the cinematic Raju loudly inveighing against it at various points. The film's critique of the varna-jati complex is advanced in scenes pitting Raju against two Brahmins living in the village in which he ends up after being released from prison. These Brahmins are entirely absent from Narayan's novel, though they certainly should be seen as emerging from the novel's anticaste subtext. Invented for the film, they help mark an orthodox position on the varna-jati complex against which Raju can take a brave contrary stand. These Brahmin adversaries of Raju are introduced early in the film. When the villagers are speaking admiringly of the new swami who has appeared in their midst, the two Brahmins, played comically by the actors, declare that not just anyone can be accepted as a swami. As keepers of traditional knowledge, the Brahmins take upon themselves the task of testing the newly arrived swami, whom they perceive as a threat to their authority. First, they demand of him his name. Raju responds to this request by asking in a philosophizing tone what they will do with a name, thus echoing the novel's anticaste subtext. Ask not a sadhu or holy man his name or jati (the subtitles dutifully, but not inappropriately in this case, translate the word as "caste"), Raju asserts, but rather his wisdom. Goaded in this fashion, one of the two Brahmins promptly reels off a Sanskrit *shloka* and dares Raju to interpret it. Raju's initial response is silence, which is greeted with derision by the Brahmins. Since he clearly does not know Sanskrit, what hope is there that he will be able to interpret the *shloka*? the Brahmins ask contemptuously.

When Raju finally speaks, his retort is fascinating for what it says about the politics of the varna-jati complex in mid-twentieth-century India. Speaking in English, Raju confronts the two Brahmins with the following words: "Don't laugh like two big fools. You are a couple of crackpots. And for generations you have been fooling the innocent people. It is about time you put a stop to this." Now it is the Brahmins who are rendered speechless. Raju triumphantly echoes the Brahmins' own dismissal of him: Since they clearly do not know English, what hope is there that they will be able to interpret his words? The final victory is his. By taking recourse to English, Raju out-debates the two orthodox Brahmins who try to run him out of the village. Recognizing the threat he poses to their authority (and thus their material well-being), the Brahmins intended to show Raju up as a charlatan. Raju not only defends himself successfully; he manages to expose *them* as charlatans.

Tradition signified by Sanskrit confronts modernity signified by English—traditional Brahmin deceit of generations is destroyed by the modern sound of English. So it would seem. Given Menon's assessment of the role of English in the politics of the varna-jati complex, this interpretation should give us pause. The signification of English as external to the social formations of the varna-jati complex and thus capable of debunking the authority of the Brahmins is both predictable and suspect. Even as the sequence depicts the salvational properties of English, it unwittingly reveals English's own limitations. In these scenes, no character other than Raju understands English. The actual content of what Raju says can be understood only by those members of the film's audience who know English. The particular critique of Brahmin privilege that Raju's words represent is meant, a little reflection suggests, for an Anglophone postcolonial elite that is in no wise external to the varna-jati complex. The rest of postcolonial society will have to content itself with the symbolic power of English as a language and trust in Raju's own knowledge when it comes to the content of his words.

We should recognize that *Guide* identifies and contests the varna-jati complex within a context of nationalist assertion. The varna-jati complex makes its appearance in the film mainly to advance nationalism as an inclusive, tolerant, and modern ideology. Because some merit attaches to this notion of nationalism as the enemy of varna-jati prejudice, such a presentation has its attractions. The varna-jati complex, directly identified in the film, is made the object of a thoroughgoing polemic, quite different from the novel. It would be appropriate to recognize that the sphere of the national does not represent in each and every instance a coercive, that is, intolerant or intolerable, exercise of power. In *The Discovery of India*, Nehru identified caste in particular as a baneful social phenomenon responsible for weakening India. "In the context of society, today," he noted, "the caste system and much that goes with it are wholly incompatible, reactionary, restrictive, and barriers to progress. There can be no equality in status and opportunity within its framework, nor can there be political democracy and much less economic democracy. Between these two conceptions conflict is inherent and only one of them can survive" (1946/1981, 257). It is precisely the film's commitment to a Nehruvian ideology of nation building that enables its critique of the varna-jati complex.

At the same time, though the references to the varna-jati complex in the movie are made directly, in a manner quite different from the novel's "masked citation," these references have little vernacular specificity. What the film presents, rather abstractly, is the varna-based opposition between Brahmins and non-Brahmins; it demonstrates little interest in filling out these references to the varna-jati complex in culturally specific ways—ways specific to Rajasthan. As we have seen, the film instead gestures to the vernacular—and it is only gesture—more through folk dance and music than through the varna-jati complex. It is worth emphasizing here that the vernacular cannot be defined a priori. The *content* of what appears as the vernacular cannot be fixed beforehand. The place of the vernacular is filled differently in different contexts and can be identified and understood only by reference to what exists in relationship to it. The different analyses enabled by the notion of the vernacular when it comes to the novel as opposed to the film demonstrate the critical nuance called for here.

Though they are presented with little vernacular specificity, the two Brahmin characters outwitted by Raju play an important role at the end of the movie. At a crucial moment Raju, finding it difficult to keep up the fast he has undertaken to bring rain, decides to run away. As luck would have it, in his flight from the village he runs straight into the Brahmins. Realizing what he is doing, the Brahmins laugh at Raju and quickly gather the villagers to show them that their beloved swami has absconded. However, when the Brahmins throw open the doors of the temple where he lives to reveal his absence, Raju is seated within in his saffron robe. Raju has relented and, unknown to the Brahmins, returned. The villagers promptly chase away the Brahmins, who do not reappear in the movie.

Having in this fashion finally settled accounts with a varna-jati traditionalism, the movie is freed to pursue religion. The remainder of the movie quickly devolves into religious preaching that is itself traditionalist, albeit differently so from the traditionalism of the Brahmins. As Raju grows weaker from fasting, his fame grows. A great and fervent crowd gathers around him. His mother returns. Eager to receive the blessing of the great swami, she comes without any knowledge of who the swami really is. She is succeeded by Rosie, who, as she walks toward Raju in the hot sun, discards her jewelry. The now plain Rosie is reunited with the dying Raju to the refrain from a love song "O Mere Jeevan Saathi" (O My Life's Partner) that appeared earlier in the movie: "We will never part / Our hands will never be separated." Soon, Ghafoor, the Muslim driver Raju had known as a tourist guide, also arrives to grieve for his dying friend. Raju lets him into the temple against the initial wishes of his followers. Through all these arrivals, Raju's mercenary side (represented by Raju the tourist guide) and his spiritual side (represented by Raju the Swami) battle it out in allegorical scenes representing his state of mind. Finally, the Swami wins and Raju attains ultimate knowledge—that the old Raju, the tourist guide Raju, represents pride and selfishness; that there is nothing in the world but his transcendent self. Raju dies surrounded by his loving family and friends even as it begins to rain.

The differences between this ending and the novel's are many and stark. Where the novel's ending has Raju stand in the river utterly alone but for Velan (Who is guiding whom by this point in the narrative?), the movie has Raju die in the warm if grieving embrace of family and friends. Where the novel refuses to say whether or not Raju dies or it rains, the movie kills him in a great climactic scene of torrential rain. Where the novel concentrates on Raju's realization that he should act without regard for self, the movie uses Raju's death to assert the transcendent autonomy of the self (signified in the final scenes by the face of Raju, played by the great Bollywood star Dev Anand, filling the screen to the refrain "I am beyond everything. Only I exist. Only I, only I, only I"). Where the novel's ending is deliberately ambiguous and agnostic about God and the place of religion in society, the movie's is full of firm statements and ferociously religious. Where the novel is a narrative of personal renunciation, the movie is one of religious martyrdom.

Through the two Brahmin characters, the varna-jati complex is invoked within a religious text such as *Guide* to be quickly contained and then dismissed so that the narrative may now proceed to celebrate religion. While this impulse is not necessarily ignoble, it is worth recalling Periyar's assertion that the varna-jati complex cannot be contested without fighting God, religion, the shastras, and Brahmins, all at the same time. In this regard, when read with appropriate attentiveness, Narayan's explorations, albeit disingenuous at many levels and always reluctant, convey more of the contradictory potency (perhaps *virulence* is a better word) of the varna-jati complex in modern India. Unlike the movie, his novel says little directly about the varna-jati complex; but by hinting at a far more radical notion of renunciation (beyond God, religion, the shastras, Brahmins, and more), it also suggests a deeper and more profound critique of the varna-jati complex. Some of this greater nuance no doubt results from generic difference—strategies of ironic narration are much more easily available to a modernist novel than to a Bollywood film. Irony makes it easier for Narayan to propose a choice between love against the taboos of the varna-jati complex and renunciation, and then to choose renunciation in an open-ended manner inviting multiple interpretations. In contrast, the melodramatic spectacle of *Guide* drives the narrative not to a similar choice but rather to love *and* renunciation—that is, loving martyrdom, a far different matter really from true renunciation.

Despite these differences, there is one significant similarity between novel and movie that is also worth remembering at the conclusion of this chapter. Though I have dug below the surfaces of both novel and movie to uncover their investments in the varna-jati complex, neither text makes anything more than a nominal place for those figures perhaps most illustrative of the iniquities of the varna-jati complex in the eyes of the general public—the "outcastes," the so-called untouchables, at the very bottom. Devadasi Rosie, certainly horribly victimized by the varna-jati complex, does find a place; but neither ironic novel nor melodramatic film represents Dalits. To these "outcastes," absent from both novel and movie, I now turn.

CHAPTER 3

Pariahs, or the Human and the Vernacular

What's in a word? If the word is *pariah*, more than one would think.

Google *pariah* and the hits will show how the word has become a coveted name for, among other things, a movie about lesbians of color, a marching percussion theater group, and a video game.[1] In its most common usage, *pariah* means, the *OED* informs us, "a member of a despised class of any kind; someone or something shunned or avoided; a social outcast."[2] The word's associations of outsider status are so common that some usages are no doubt meant to be subversive through an immoderate underscoring of the word's accepted meaning. This kind of usage means to invest the word with cool oppositionality—the pariah as oppressed outcast certainly, but also as a refuser of bourgeois conventions of respectability.

Delve into *pariah*'s deep history, however, and another, somewhat forgotten, world of meaning—intimately associated with the varna-jati complex—appears. The *OED* indicates that *pariah* entered the English language in India in the eighteenth century (or earlier) from Tamil. *Pariah* is the Romanized rendering of பறையன் (*paraiyan*), which designates a group of "untouchables" in South India (Tamil Nadu and southern Kerala).[3] The Paraiyar—the name, some claim, is derived from a drum (the *parai*) closely associated with them—are the largest and most prominent of the Dalit jatis of South India. Thus, over the course of a couple of centuries, the Tamil name of an oppressed Dalit jati is transformed into a common English word for a socially shunned group or person.

Numerous insights about translation under colonial conditions might be gleaned from this example. Though I postpone a longer discussion until the next chapter, one lesson suggests how over time translation obscures the specific associations of the varna-jati complex but not the sense of social marginalization. Digging out and discarding the vernacular content of the word *paraiyan*, translation renders *pariah* a word signifying exclusion from the community of human beings. Obscuring at one level, translation is revealing at another. Translation makes evident the urgent questions about humanity buried within *paraiyan*. Because of the history of exclusion made visible, the word translated as *pariah* invites reflection on notions of the human.

Pariah originates in India, but the kind of cogitation provoked by the word could and should range more widely. While caste has come to be associated strongly with India, caste systems occur across the world. A Human Rights Watch report notes, "Caste is descent-based and hereditary in nature. It is a characteristic determined by one's birth into a particular caste, irrespective of the faith practiced by the individual. Caste denotes a system of rigid social stratification into ranked groups defined by descent and occupation. Under various caste systems throughout the world, caste divisions also dominate in housing, marriage, and general social interaction—divisions that are reinforced through the practice and threat of social ostracism, economic boycotts, and even physical violence" (2001, 1). Certainly, the attempt to define caste here is somewhat simplistic; nevertheless, the report usefully goes on to list, aside from "the *Dalits* or so-called *untouchables*" of all the countries of South Asia, the following as also examples of outcaste groups: "the *Buraku people* of Japan, the *Osu* of *Nigeria's* Igbo people, and certain groups in *Senegal* and *Mauritania*"(1).[4] Though beyond the scope of this book, a scholarly inquiry might gainfully compare varieties of caste as they appear across the world as well as juxtapose caste and other hierarchical social systems of oppression such as apartheid. Clearly such a comparative scrutiny of caste might offer significant benefits to postcolonial studies.

This chapter, still intent upon the vernacular, remains in India, indeed Tamil India. Enabled by the turn to the vernacular, I explore various notions of the human and humanism through representations of the Dalit in the Tamil literary context. I begin with a few general remarks on Dalit identity and literature and a close reading of the manifesto of the Dalit Panthers. Building on this discussion, I first consider two novels, Perumal Murugan's *Seasons of the Palm* and P. Sivakami's *The Grip of Change*, juxtaposing both to Narayan's novel *The Guide*; and then I explore the celebrated personal account of Christian Dalit life by Bama in conjunction with the testimonio of the Hindu Dalit woman Viramma. Tracking the human throughout, I conclude by drawing out implications for ongoing debates in the North American academy about humanism and cosmopolitanism; I show how a focus on the vernacular reveals weaknesses in the formulation of both.

DALIT IDENTITY AND LITERATURE

No modern critique of the varna-jati complex from a Dalit perspective is more important than that initiated and elaborated by B. R. Ambedkar over the course of several decades during the first half of the twentieth century. A towering figure in the contemporary politics of the varna-jati complex, Ambedkar's political and intellectual legacy is crucial in shedding light both on the complex's general structure and on the particular place of the Dalit within it. Ambedkar was born an "untouchable" Mahar in 1891 in Marathi-speaking western India, in the then Bombay Presidency. Educating himself against great odds (he earned advanced degrees from both the London School of Economics and Columbia University in New York City), Ambedkar rose by the end of his life to serve as chairman of the committee that drafted the constitution of independent India, thus earning for himself the designation "Father of the Constitution." Venerable as this title sounds, Ambedkar's relationship to mainstream Indian politics was decidedly vexed. "After 1933," Valerian Rodrigues notes, "Ambedkar fought a relentless battle against Gandhi" (2002, 23). The reasons for Ambedkar's famously contentious rivalry with M. K. Gandhi were not dissimilar to Periyar's; Ambedkar too found the Indian National Congress Brahminical and upper caste in its cultural and political orientation. His skepticism regarding the kind of hegemonic majoritarian politics represented by Gandhi led directly to his final public act of significance—secession from the mainstream as represented by Gandhi's beloved if reformed Hinduism. A few months before he died in 1956, Ambedkar converted to Buddhism along with half a million of his followers. In Buddhism, Ambedkar found a powerful indigenous—it mattered little that it had almost vanished from India by this time—tradition of critiquing the varna-jati complex. Ambedkar's neo-Buddhist critique, though different from Periyar's rationalistic atheism in significant respects, was every bit as uncompromising.[5]

Among Ambedkar's lasting contributions to Indian politics, a new language of Dalit assertion may be added to neo-Buddhism. In the context of the varna-jati complex, the term *dalit* itself, it is widely held, was popularized by Ambedkar. Originally, the Marathi word did not refer to "untouchables." In her essay "Dalit: New Cultural Context for an Old Marathi Word," Eleanor Zelliot quotes the following definition for the word, drawn from the 1975 reprint of the 1831 edition of Molesworth's Marathi-English dictionary: "Dalit: 1. Ground. 2. Broken or reduced to pieces generally" (1992, 267). *Dalit* becomes a common combative designation for "untouchable" jatis across India only after Ambedkar.[6]

In the 1970s, a radical group, the Dalit Panthers, made its own mark on current usage of the word, especially within intellectual circles. The Dalit Panthers (the parallel with the Black Panthers of the United States was deliberate) was a phenomenon of the Marathi-speaking areas. "A militant organization founded by two writers, Namdeo Dhasal and Raja Dhale in April 1972," the group was, Zelliot notes, "famous for its celebration of 'Black Independence Day' on 15 August of that year, the Silver Jubilee of India's independence, and for its mass physical reaction to violence against Untouchables or Buddhists in the villages" (1992, 267–68). The Dalit Panthers worked toward political as well as cultural assertion. They articulated an Ambedkarite vision of Dalit struggle in an influential manifesto issued in 1973 on the first anniversary of their existence. Though the Dalit Panthers fragmented soon thereafter, their manifesto represents, Barbara Joshi observes, "important themes in the thinking of activists in a variety of Dalit organizations" (1986, 140). It is an indispensable document for an exploration of Dalit identity.

As manifestos commonly do, the Dalit Panthers Manifesto sets out a plan of action. However, in the context of our current discussion, more relevant than its practical exhortations is the manifesto's rather broad definition of Dalits. Moving beyond a purely jati-based definition (the notion that Dalits are properly members of "untouchable" jatis), the manifesto first includes Scheduled Tribes (the name, derived from the schedule of the Indian constitution in which they are listed, for communities commonly regarded as aboriginal) and then grows even more expansive:

Truly speaking, the problem of Dalits, or Scheduled Castes and Tribes, has become a broad problem; the Dalit is no longer merely an Untouchable outside the village walls and the scriptures. He is an Untouchable, and he is a Dalit, but he is also a worker, a landless labourer, a proletarian. And unless we strengthen this growing revolutionary unity of the many with all our efforts, our existence has no future. The Dalit must accordingly accept the sections of masses, the other revolutionary forces as part of his own movement. . . . Then alone shall we possess the right to be called human beings at all. It was for this that Doctor Ambedkar made us realize our humanity even in our state of beast-like exploitation. (Dalit Panthers 142)

Later, the group reiterates this broad definition even more pointedly in the brief section entitled "Who Is a Dalit?": "Members of Scheduled Castes and Tribes, neo-Buddhists, the working people, the landless and poor peasants, women, and all those who are being exploited politically, economically and in the name of religion" (145).

Viewed in whole, the manifesto betrays a contradiction in defining *Dalit*. The seeds of a tension between two types of usage are to be found within *Dalit*. Commenting on the uses of the term in the wake of the manifesto, John Webster notes, "There has thus been a narrow definition, based on the criterion of caste alone, and a broader one to encompass all those considered to be similarly placed or natural allies" (2007, 76). *Dalit* is sometimes used in the manifesto in the conventional way as a marker for "untouchable" jatis, even as elsewhere the spirit is to broaden the definition. Because of the manifesto's influence, this tension has been carried forward into public discourse. Certainly, the more common usage—in newspapers, for example—is still the narrower one, but the broader usage plays an important role in theoretical investigations of Dalit identity, for, as S. M. Michael writes, "It is based on an attempted, though by no means realized, solidarity of the poor and the discriminated classes of the people" (2007, 125).

In one important intervention into these debates entitled *Why I Am Not a Hindu: A Sudra Critique of Hindutva Philosophy, Culture and Political Economy*, Kancha Iliah elaborates the concept of Dalitbahujan. His book illuminates the challenges of resolving the tension between what has been identified above as the narrow and broad meanings of *Dalit* through an argument advanced in a related framework of social critique. As the title of his book indicates, Iliah's objective is to contest hegemonic notions of Hinduism. In this context, he writes that by *Dalitbahujan* he means, "people and castes who form the exploited and suppressed majority" (1996, ix). He explains the need for the term as follows: "The concept 'Bahujan' simply means 'majority.' ... The problem is that it does not point to what the nature of that majority population is" (viii). The addition of *Dalit*, then, provides vital shape to majority identity; the word anchors his forceful attempt to contest the idea of a Hindu majority. Dalitbahujan and Hindus, he argues, are different in every respect—in the gods they worship, the rituals they practice, the food they eat, and so on. Written in the mid-1990s, Iliah's polemic responds to Hindu fundamentalist (the Hindutva of the subtitle) attempts to incorporate the various jatis (including the so-called untouchables) into the community of Hinduism. In a contrary spirit, Iliah brings together the so-called untouchable jatis and those immediately above them—the lowest of the Sudra jatis—under the umbrella of Dalitbahujan. In *The Weapon of the Other*, a later work, he further fleshes out his project by identifying the Dalitbahujan intellectual legacy as follows: "The Dalitbahujan alternative should be worked out on the basis of the theoretical formulations and practices of the Buddha, Phule, Ambedkar and Periyar" (2010, 98). He can advance such a project, however—he acknowledges the problem himself (1996, ix)—only by glossing over the many differences between Sudras and Dalits. Despite his innovations, the same tension between aspiration and actuality that characterizes the Dalit Panthers' *Dalit* might be said to characterize Iliah's *Dalitbahujan*. Thus, in *The Weapon of the Other*, Iliah asserts more wishfully than factually, "Though there are contradictions among different productive castes within the Dalitbahujan bloc, such contradictions are fundamentally amicable since they are constantly mediated by labour processes and can be resolved peacefully" (2010, 98).

If definitions of Dalit identity are not straightforward, then neither are those of Dalit literature. The Dalit Panther Manifesto was closely associated with a significant movement in the production of Dalit literature in Marathi in the seventies. Since then, the movement has spread to other languages.[7] In Tamil, Dalit literature constitutes an exciting new area of creative activity. Anushiya Sivanarayanan rightly notes that "Dalit literature is an entirely new genre within Tamil literature, and Tamil scholars—many of them non-Dalit—find themselves scrambling trying to find a new poetics for this emergent literature" (2004, 56). Some of this Tamil Dalit writing is beginning to appear in English translation, compounding the problem of an adequate poetics through which to explore it. If critics within the indigenous culture have to refashion their analytical tools to access Dalit literature, then the critical task grows even more difficult as this literature circulates more widely through translation. Added to the need for a new poetics is lack of knowledge about the cultural context. How to provide this context without succumbing to the temptation to glibly generalize? How to bring to the fore nuances of contestations over jati privilege that must accompany any poetics of Dalit literature for an audience not attuned to such contestations? As I will argue in the next chapter, it helps to regard this critical task as itself one of translation. For too long we have viewed literary translation as simply a textual process, neglecting to recognize the "culture of translation"—that is, we have neglected to operate with a broad notion of translation that includes (indeed regards as indispensable) the vital critical work of creating an appropriate *culture* of reading with a sophisticated and profound understanding of what translation is and how it functions in societies.

Some of the context for understanding the Dalit text, whether translated or untranslated, is to be found in Sharankumar Limbale's *Toward an Aesthetics of Dalit Literature* (2004). Limbale begins his attempt to generate an adequate critical framework for understanding Dalit literature with the following assertion: "By Dalit literature, I mean writing about Dalits by Dalit writers with a Dalit consciousness. The form of Dalit literature is inherent in its Dalitness, and its purpose is obvious: to inform Dalit society of its slavery, and narrate its pain and suffering to upper caste Hindus" (19). This seems uncomplicated enough, but Limbale later proposes: "Harijans and neo-Buddhists are not the only Dalits, the term describes all the untouchable communities living outside the boundary of the village, as well as Adivasis, landless farm-laborers, workers, the suffering masses, and nomadic and criminal tribes. In explaining the word, it will not do to refer only to the untouchable castes. People who are lagging behind economically will also need to be included" (30). In offering this remarkably expanded definition of *Dalit* (and by implication Dalit literature), Limbale emulates not only the Dalit Panthers' manifesto but also Arjun Dangle, whose seminal collection *The Poisoned Bread*, published in 1992, brought much attention to the notion of Dalit literature. Dangle notes in an essay included in that collection: "Dalit literature is one which acquaints people with the caste system and untouchability in India, its appalling nature and its system of exploitation. In other words, Dalit is not a caste but a realization and is related to the experiences, joys and sorrows, and struggles of those in the lowest stratum of society" (1992a, 264–65). Limbale echoes Dangle in relying in foundational ways upon the Dalit Panthers' manifesto in his attempt to define Dalit literature.

If the Dalit Panthers refuse to focus narrowly on Dalit identity, Limbale in a congruent move finds the definitive features of Dalit literature in a radical humanism that opposes the aesthetic values of *savarna* (higher jati) literature. He does so by contesting and appropriating the savarna formula of godliness "satyam, shivam, sundaram" (truth, auspiciousness, beauty). In the place of savarna interpretations of truth, auspiciousness and beauty, founded on the exaltation of the varna-jati complex and the denigration of Dalits, Limbale offers a Dalit *"satyam, shivam, sundaram"*: "Human beings are first and foremost human—this is satyam. The liberation of human beings is shivam. The humanity of human beings is sundaram" (1992a, 20–22). Finally, it is this materialist humanism—a humanism grounded in this world and in the conduct of human beings toward one another—that permits Limbale to adopt an expansive definition of Dalit-ness.

As with identity, then, so with literature. The tension between a broad and a narrow usage that we have observed with regard to Dalit as an identity seems to reappear in the more literary contentions of Limbale. On the one hand, it might be argued that in him, as in the manifesto, *Dalit* becomes simply one of the many synonyms for *oppressed* and that a much-needed focus on Dalit literature as the literature of a particular jati risks being lost. On the other hand, Limbale's study bears within it the signs of a countering view; it appears to contradict its own abstract and expanded definition of Dalit-ness by working only with examples defined as Dalit in the narrower sense. In this latter aspect, it would seem to affirm *Touchable Tales* (2003), a short collection of responses to the recent boom in Dalit publishing in several languages in India edited by S. Anand, which evidences that not all approaches to Dalit writing nest it within an expansive humanism.

I believe, however, that it is possible to see these contradictions in Limbale, as well as in the manifesto from which he draws, not as confusion but as formidable omens of the struggle to recognize the historicity of the varna-jati complex—its multiple determinants and its multiple modes of exclusion—while maintaining attention on the much-neglected category of Dalit. Limbale's desire, it would seem, is to endorse a humanism while at the same time advocating specific attention to Dalits and Dalit literature (in the narrow sense). Despite the risk of incoherence, his critical stance avoids the reification of Dalit identity and resists reproducing the rigidities of the varna-jati complex in the act of contesting them. Even if in a mode of opposition, the temptation to advance jati identities as ineluctable can be perilous. The more appropriate critical stance would seem to be to acknowledge the specificity of Dalit oppression without freezing Dalit identity. Limbale's formulations, like those of the manifesto, attempt to balance competing needs in approaching Dalit literature. What remains central to his method, as it emerges from his theoretical assertions in combination with his critical practice, are the following features: the centrality of Dalit (in the narrow sense) identity and experience as exemplary; the need to pay special attention to literature written by Dalits; a recognition of the importance of witnessing in Dalit literature; the need to be attentive to ancillary communities such as the Adivasis (the so-called aboriginal communities) and the rural poor; attention to the varna-jati complex and its atrocities; and a commitment to humanism.

These features—adding up to a kind of materialist intervention into Dalit aesthetics—serve as useful guidelines for the inquiry into representations of Dalits in Tamil literature that follows. However, while my exploration keeps in view these general features (thus engaging, one might say, in an act of translation for a broader audience coming fresh to the subject), the specific thrust of my argument is to examine the role of humanism and notions of the human in Dalit literature. In my usage, I will in the interest of clarity restrict myself to the narrow definition of *Dalit*, taking recourse to Iliah's *Dalitbahujan* when I want to indicate a broader coalition of social constituencies; at the same time, my general critical stance will be to acknowledge and explore the implications of the broader humanist definition advanced by the Dalit Panthers, Dangle, and Limbale and echoed by Tamil critic Rajkautaman (2005, 21).

As noted, four texts, originally produced in Tamil, contribute to a representation of Dalits within a Tamil context and are central to my argument. Viewed from the vantage point of Limbale's approach, Perumal Murugan's novel *Koolla Madari* (translated into English by V. Geetha as *Seasons of the Palm* [2004]), P. Sivakami's novel *Pazhaiyana Kazhithalum* (translated by the author herself as *The Grip of Change* [2006]), Bama's *Karukku* (translated by Lakshmi Holmstrom [2000]), and the testimonio *Viramma* (translated from French by Will Hobson in 1997; the French itself is a translation from original oral Tamil narratives), are, despite their differences, still comprehensible in the context of Dalit aesthetics.[8] The last three offer representations by Dalit women, and the first, by a Dalitbahujan rather than a Dalit writer, provides us with striking access to the imagined subjectivity of a Dalit boy.

The critic Rajkautaman has observed that "the purpose of Dalit literature is not pleasurable reading," indicating thereby the importance of witnessing (2005, 26, my translation from the Tamil). In their contrasting styles, the novels, the memoir, and the testimonio demonstrate the range of possibilities within the aesthetics of Dalit representation—the aesthetics of bearing witness against the atrocious system that is the varna-jati complex.

Such are the vernacular works to which we must have recourse to critique the varna-jati complex from the perspective of those who are targets rather than beneficiaries. The varna-jati complex has long been a theme in Tamil literature (as indeed we saw in the previous chapter), but only recently have Dalit and Dalitbahujan writers collectively begun to create an often disturbing if also vivid account of Tamil Dalit communities (in the plural, because there is not in fact a single such community). In this writing, the notion of the vernacular is again at issue. Dalit and Dalitbahujan writing offers yet another way to explore the relationship between the varna-jati complex and the vernacular. Reciprocally, it is the vernacular sphere of Tamil representations and self-representations that enables a critical engagement with Dalit identity and literature. Indeed, were the current argument to restrict itself to Anglophone material, an analysis from a Dalit perspective would be impossible, for very little such writing takes place in English; most of what appears in English does so as translation from Tamil and other languages. As Ravikumar notes, "For dalits, language—English—is still a barrier" (2003, 9). In this context, Tamil Dalit writing appears as a counterpoint to *The Guide* and suggests the ways in which any notion of the postcolonial that excludes the vernacular is inadequate. My discussion of the varna-jati complex here and in the previous chapter, then, could be regarded as symptomatic. My arguments underscore the importance of engaging the vernacular and point toward the kind of critical work that becomes possible once "postcolonial theory" abandons the archival terrain of an exclusionary postcolonialism.

HUMAN(IST) SACRIFICE

A comparative reading of R. K. Narayan's *The Guide*, Perumal Murugan's *Seasons of the Palm,* and P. Sivakami's *The Grip of Change* is illuminating for an inquiry into humanism in the context of what is commonly referred to as "caste politics." All three writers articulate or perhaps more accurately, in the case of Narayan, betray a desire to

Pariahs, or the Human and the Vernacular | 75

transcend the constraints of the varna-jati complex; as we shall see, all three invoke the notion of sacrifice. But what is the content of this sacrifice? And what does the sacrifice enable? The answers to these questions, fruitfully approached through attention to the (absent, in the case of Narayan) representations of the Dalit, bring out differences. Ultimately, these differences are suggestive when these works are considered in the context of humanist approaches to the varna-jati complex.

Whether one views the references to the varna-jati complex in *The Guide* as enabling or problematic, the Dalit as subject finds no place in it, or indeed in its cinematic adaptation. Rosie is not Dalit, though jati differences are manifested in the novel and become both a problem and a seduction for the savarna hero through her: her jati differences become both an intolerable sign of the savarna hero's privilege and an invitation to him to perfect himself as an ethical subject. Figured and also dissimulated as Rosie, the varna-jati complex is an impediment to Raju's spiritual progress, his further exaltation. Though Narayan depicts her with some sympathy, Rosie remains *instrumental* in the novel, which cares more about Raju's advancement than hers. Where Raju's ending is positively saintly, Rosie, still entangled no doubt in the petty and mundane ambitions of the dance world, disappears from the narrative. Her difficulties, while mentioned, remain on an altogether less exalted level. Her life, constrained by the varna-jati complex in a far more fundamental manner than Raju's would seem to be, hardly gets the attention it merits. To make this criticism is not to ask the novel to do something other than what it sets out to, but simply to register its limitations. An analogous argument could be made of *Guide* the movie. Indeed, the movie makes several changes to the depiction of Rosie that result in a further reduction in her agency—for example, by having her attempt suicide the movie makes a victim of her in a way the novel does not. To the extent that novel and film critique the varna-jati complex, they do so from a privileged and gendered point of vantage and certainly not from the perspective of a Dalit subjectivity (wholly absent from both).

Unlike *The Guide*, Perumal Murugan's Dalitbahujan novel *Seasons of the Palm*, though not by a Dalit author, places the Dalit subject at its center. If the novel is best characterized by reference to Iliah's notion of *Dalitbahujan*—that is, if it is advantageously regarded as a Dalitbahujan novel—it is not because Murugan, who is neither Dalit nor savarna, seems to personally exemplify Iliah's argument. Rather than personal identity, narrative is at issue here. *Seasons* might be characterized a Dalitbahujan novel because it explores the intertwined lives of Dalits and the Sudra jatis immediately above Dalits in the varna-jati hierarchy. Regardless of authorial identity, *Seasons* exemplifies Iliah's assertions through narrative. At the core of the novel's narrative are both an assertion of Dalit subjectivity and an exploration of Dalitbahujan experience as constituted across jati divides.

The novel's Dalitbahujan narrative does not work through a simple idealization of cross-jati solidarity. The narrative does not provide a purely optimistic view of the relationship between the destitute Dalit Chakkili children at the heart of the story and their Gounder overlords, located immediately above them in the varna-jati hierarchy. As readers, we encounter many oppressions and jati taboos that divide the two communities. At the same time, we learn about the innumerable ways in which Chakkili and Gounder lives are linked intimately socially, economically, even physically (especially important to recognize in the context of untouchability). If the novel may be described as Dalitbahujan, it is not because it advances an upbeat polemic about a shared identity. Rather, the label is earned by the novel's closely observed account of Dalit psychology in a Dalitbahujan context. Though centered on Dalit characters, the novel's thematic core is the relationship between Dalit Chakkilis and Gounders. The description of the novel as Dalitbahujan certainly seems appropriate when we regard its narration of the intimate lived reality of Chakkilis and Gounders. The horrific ending, to which I turn later, underscores this intimacy, even as it suggests the difficulties in viewing the interrelationships in a purely positive light. At the same time that *Seasons* may best be characterized as a complex Dalitbahujan novel about Dalits rather than a Dalit novel, Limbale's aesthetics too can be usefully brought to bear on it to elucidate its refusal of a naive apotheosization of inter-jati relations. Certainly Limbale's humanism, instigator of the contradictions in his argument as well as the source of his argument's vigor, finds a powerful echo in Murugan's tale of friendship and loss across jati divides.

In different ways, both Iliah and Limbale, then, offer us entries into a reading of *Seasons*. So does V. Geetha's title for the English translation. *Seasons of the Palm* is not a literal translation of the Tamil title—some might say it is not a translation at all. The original Tamil title *Koolla Madari* means "Short Madari" (Madari is a Chakkili jati name specific to the Kongu Nadu region) and is a reference to the chief character of the novel. "Koolla Madari" has a resonance in Tamil absent in a literal translation into English. As if to compensate, Geetha's invention, certainly more lyrical and evocative than a literal translation of the Tamil title into English would have been, zeroes in on the palm tree, one of the central symbols of the novel, even as it draws attention to the novel's structure.[9]

Geetha's title presents an insightful reading of the novel's symbolism and structure. The palm tree, ubiquitous feature of the Kongu Nadu landscape in which the novel is set, finds numerous references in Murugan's narrative. The lives of the chief characters are lived around, under, and sometimes upon it. The trunk of the palm tree, we are told, "is hard and rough and scratches the climber's chest"; it can "scar a climber's chest and cause it to bleed" (2004, 51). At the same time, the palm fruit's "soft, fleshy kernel is fragrant and delicious" (51); and the tree is the source of the intoxicating toddy coveted by all. Thus the palm tree marks both difficulty and delight in a manner parallel to the novel's narrative of Dalit lives. As for the *seasons* in Geetha's title, the word reveals how this ambivalent narrative of difficulty and delight is organized. The novel is divided into three parts—"Dust," "Fine Mud," and "Dry Earth" ("Parched Earth" might be a better translation). The novel begins in the dusty pre-monsoon period, moves through the succeeding revivifying monsoons, and ends in the hot, dry season. The titles of the parts identify the earth—on which the farming and herding communities of Gounders and Chakkilis depend—as it is transformed by the seasons. The three parts also provide structure to the story of the chief character, the Chakkili boy Shortie.

Though written in 2001, *Seasons* is set in the late sixties, that is, before the emergence of a highly vocal Dalit rights movement. The novel opens with quiet but masterful observation of Shortie and his fellow Chakkilli friends Tallfellow, Stumpleg, Belly, Matchbox, and Stonedeaf, all of whom are around the age of puberty. On a typical day, Shortie and his friends gather to graze the goats of their Gounder masters. One by one, Murugan introduces each child and his or her story. Stumpleg is the feared bully. Belly and Stonedeaf are assertive girls. Stonedeaf, the older of the two, is the object of Tallfellow's lustful desire. And so each child—locked in a life of relentless labor for the Gounders, but not therefore without spirit and humanity—is evoked by Murugan's sensitive narrative. Murugan not only provides marvelous portraits of these children but also suggests the complex ways in which their lives are linked to their Gounder overlords. Some children work from morning till evening and then return to their Chakkili homes. Others, like Shortie, live with their Gounder overlords and earn a yearly wage that is paid to their parents. None goes to school. The only future the children can aspire to is serving their overlords.

Jati separates Shortie from another important character—Selvan, the son of Shortie's Gounder master. Aside from his fellow Dalit friends, Shortie's most important relationship is with Selvan. Murugan introduces Selvan, who is a little younger than Shortie, midway into the novel. Much of "Fine Mud," the middle section of the novel, is taken up by the relationship between Shortie and Selvan. Though separated by jati, the two boys spend considerable time together. Between them, the taboos of the varna-jati complex are left mostly unobserved. When not in school, Selvan plays with Shortie and his Chakkili friends, trying to lord it over them because of his higher social status, or else helps Shortie with the goats. Often the two boys sleep with the goats at night, Selvan on a cot and Shortie on the ground, except that all too often Selvan invites Shortie to sleep on the bed with him, contravening jati laws. Other laws too are broken, for Murugan presents the relationship between the two boys with a hint of homoeroticism, a budding intimacy kept secret from Selvan's father.

Murugan's deft portrayal of the relationship between the two boys combines tenderness with an honest depiction of the myriad ways in which social taboos intervene in the friendship. Shortie addresses Selvan as "Master," and Selvan thinks nothing of ordering Shortie about, calling him such choice names as "naked dog" (146). When Selvan loses in a game, he frightens Shortie by threatening to report on him (114–15); and when a goat is lost, it is Shortie alone who must bear the punishment (230–32). Despite these differences, Shortie involves Selvan in most of his activities and feels protective toward the younger boy. We are told, "Shortie feels a gush of love for Selvan" (139). Selvan too shows admiration and affection for Shortie. *Seasons* movingly and plausibly evokes tenderness in the context of overwhelming caste brutality.

Like *Seasons*, P. Sivakami's celebrated Dalit novel *The Grip of Change* (1989) depicts Dalit characters and the relationship between Dalit and non-Dalit jatis. Widely touted as the first novel in Tamil by a Dalit woman, it was translated from English by the author herself. Meena Kandasamy describes *Grip* as "a novel of critical realism" and notes that "it evoked a great deal of discussion because it went beyond condemning caste fanatics by using fiction to describe how we were shackled, and tangled among ourselves" (2006, 193). Unlike *Seasons*,

Grip is more properly described as a Dalit novel. Again, I make this observation not primarily because of the identity of the author. Though *Grip* is concerned with inter-jati relationships between Dalits and those immediately "above" them, it is much less intent on exploring their shared—that is, Dalitbahujan—psychology, culture, and politics. In this context, the several differences as well as similarities between the two novels may be usefully explored to illuminate some of the choices available to writers working within the terrain of Dalit aesthetics. As we shall see, a comparison of the two novels suggests that Limbale's humanism may be approached in multiple ways.

Grip is the story of Kathamuthu, an old-style Dalit (more specifically Paraiyar) leader, confronted with the rape of a Dalit woman by her employer, a man of higher jati. When he finds Thangam at his doorstep begging for help, Kathamuthu skillfully manipulates the administration as well as the varna-jati politics of the locality on her behalf. By doing so, he manages to get Thangam a modicum of justice and also to use this incident of inter-jati violence to win concessions on behalf of the Paraiyar jati. In this respect, *Grip* depicts a politically assertive Dalit subjectivity largely absent from *Seasons*. Yet it does not find Kathamuthu morally beyond reproach. Even as Kathamuthu fights for justice, he acquires Thangam as his third wife and enters into a divisive struggle over property with his brother Kalimuthu when he returns home after years of working in Malaysia. Even within the domain of politics conventionally understood, Kathamuthu's actions are presented with ambivalence. While his campaign brings concessions for the Paraiyar community, it also results in Pariayar huts being burnt and in higher jati landlords refusing to employ Paraiyar workers.

As a study of a local Dalit leader, *Grip* is subtle, though its subtlety is of a different order than *Seasons*. Where the world of *Seasons* partakes of the innocence of childhood, *Grip* depicts the rough-and-tumble world of adult politics. The novel effectively conveys the micropolitics—the politics of village and locality—that govern administrative responses to caste crises. The novel is sympathetic to Kathamuthu at the same time that it vehemently indicts his sexism as well as "big man" mode of operation. Though Kathamuthu is the protagonist of *Grip*, the novel may be read as his spiritual obituary, for at its end, Sivakami tells us, "Kathamuthu was like a defanged snake" (2006, 124). His politics of patronage and deal making is in the process of being superseded by that of younger Dalit men and women, who have a more systemic analysis of their oppression. At the novel's conclusion, Kathamuthu's daughter Gowri is writing a paper with the title "An Organization of Scheduled and Backward Castes," suggesting a broader vision of varna-jati politics than Kathamuthu's narrow focus on his own jati and evocative of Iliah's Dalitbahujan even if only at the political level (126). Meanwhile his son, Sekaran, has allied himself with Chandran, who is a union leader rather than a jati leader on the model of Kathamuthu. Even as Kathamuthu dreams of becoming Member of the Legislative Assembly, young Dalit men and women like Chandran, Sekaran, and Gowri are exploring political models that go beyond narrowly jati-based mobilizations.

Inevitably, the attempt to "go beyond" is not uncomplicated. In response to a question in an interview on whether she wished "to be identified as a dalit writer," Sivakami noted: "Is there a choice? All of us carry the caste tag. But the dalits are oppressed in the name of caste. For the entire nation, caste is a burden. But the dalits alone are made to carry it, as they are the victims of caste. With the tag, I wish to remove the burden of the nation to the best of my abilities" (2003, 25). Her response underscores her faith in the nation at the same time that it recognizes the sacrificial nature of the relationship of Dalits to the Indian nation. It is this ambivalent—at once hostile and resigned—appraisal of jati and jati identity that the conclusion of *Grip* captures. Sivakami's narrative in *Grip* balances a faith in the capacity of nationalism and socialism (labor politics) to move beyond a constraining caste politics with a healthy appreciation of the sacrifices such "isms" demand of Dalits. She notes, for example, of Chandran, "Issues of class and caste were so deeply intermingled that they made him think of those blunt-headed snakes that were like rubber tubes. One could never be sure which end was the head and which end the tail. The problems workers had against the establishment often transformed into caste-related problems. The union's office bearers were chosen on the basis of caste" (2006, 112). While the narrative in *Grip* ultimately sides with a socialistic politics transcending jati, it is by no means sanguine regarding the costs of such a politics.

Seasons too offers a notion of sacrifice, though it arrives at it through a quite different mode of narration. *Grip* begins with a crisis (the rape of Thangam), proceeds to explore its resolution, and then arrives at its ambivalent conclusion. *Seasons* first details the typical lives of Shortie and his friends, not without their joys, and only then introduces the crisis, which demands of Shortie a dire sacrifice. Given the carefully portrayed friendship between Shortie and Selvan, the concluding sections of the novel are harrowing. First, Shortie is beaten and trussed up upside down in a well for having stolen some coconuts. And then, at the very end, Selvan is lost (drowned?) while swimming in this same deep well. Since he is under Shortie's supervision when this happens, the consequences for Shortie are almost beyond contemplation. Though his friends exhort him to run away, Shortie leaps into the well in desperation to look for Selvan. These are the concluding words of the novel:

> He dives into the well. He does not resist the water. He goes down. Quietly. His eyes search the well. He is in white water now, white from the soft earth. And then a few moments later, all is dark. The water is black and cool.
> Now he can see things very clearly. The walls are there, as always, and they seem to invite him. He cannot stop. No, he must go deeper. Further. Further than anyone has ever gone. To the end, where there is only thick darkness. Where he cannot see anymore, where he cannot know how deep it is.
> His legs are free of mud. Of soft earth. They pierce through the water. Taking him down to the deep that knows no end. (Murugan 2004, 319)

Has Selvan drowned? Does Shortie manage to return, with or without Selvan? To pose these questions is to invite a comparison with *The Guide*. Just as we do not know in *The Guide* whether Raju's fasting has brought rain and whether he dies at the end, so in *Seasons* we do not know if Selvan and Shortie have been lost forever. The description of Shortie's jump is evocative, taking the reader beyond a literal account of a frightening descent into a deep well. As in *The Guide*, Murugan's language here withholds meaning just enough to make the act of interpretation speculative. The endings of both *The Guide* and *Seasons* are full of rich ambiguity.

Other comparisons too can be made between the endings of the two novels. Both, of course, involve sacrifice—of Raju in *The Guide* and of Shortie in *Seasons*. However, while they are similar in this respect, crucial differences exist. In *The Guide* sacrifice—Raju embracing possible death for the benefit of the villagers of Mangala—exalts the savarna hero. In *Seasons*, the order of sacrifice is reversed. The Dalit hero sacrifices for someone of a higher jati. Whereas *The Guide* presents the savarna hero's self-sacrifice as ennobling, *Seasons* suggests the horror of the Dalit hero's sacrifice of self. Rather than a liberating and ennobling acceptance of a messianic role, Shortie's jump into the well, against the exhortation of his friends that he should flee, is a more desperate reaching out across the divisions of the varna-jati complex. It is true that Murugan's language evokes an experience of freedom as Shortie swims deeper into the well, but this freedom has a touch of resignation about it rather than saintly transcendence. Commenting on his novel, Murugan observes: "My main concern is the futility, the sadness that follows the inability to escape from *soolal* (circumstances, environment), notwithstanding the many efforts to break free" (qtd. in Augustine 2005). The language in Murugan's novel (and interview) hearkens back, not to *The Guide,* but to Sivakami's observation on the sacrificial nature of the relationship of Dalits to the nation.

The concept of sacrifice resorted to in such radically different ways by Narayan, Sivakami, and Murugan testifies to the redoubtable strength of the varna-jati complex. So pervasive and powerful would the strictures of the varna-jati complex seem to be in Indian life that attempts to explore that which lies beyond it are all too often led to the brink of self-annihilation (in the case of Narayan and Murugan) or else to a consideration of the ways the self is to be made to pay in the cause of a larger redemption (Sivakami).[10] Of course, from another perspective it is Murugan and Sivakami who might be grouped together as drawing attention to the need for structural changes in society through the notion of sacrifice. *Grip* does this explicitly, while *Seasons*' subtler approach is to detail the brutality of the varna-jati complex and place it next to Shortie's horrifying sacrifice at the end. *Seasons*' structure invites the reader to transfer horror from Shortie's sacrifice to the very social system that exacts such sacrifice.

The theme of sacrifice emerging here deserves closer scrutiny for what it can teach us about the different modes in which humanism and the human may be imagined. The depictions of sacrifice examined above reveal an interest in transcending social divides. Whether it is for community (the villagers in Narayan) or for an individual of another jati (Selvan in Murugan), sacrifice negates a narrow identity based in jati as well as other forms of social division so that a larger community of human beings may be imagined and established. This negation is rather more vexed in *Grip*, since so much of the novel is focused on the utility of narrow alliances between jatis for political gain. As narrow jati identities are reinforced in political jockeying, the general social order of human beings begins to appear somewhat beside the point. Nevertheless, even here the briefly narrated inter-jati romance between the Dalit Elangovan and the "higher" jati Lalitha does offer a faith in the transcendent power of love between human beings (Sivakami

2006, 106–10). The novel does not so much refute the notion of valuing a broad human community as show only a secondary interest in it.

In the shadow of sacrifice, then, humanism emerges. The semantics of this emergence are complicated—How does one sacrifice a particular identity in the pursuit of a more universal humanism? What are the costs of this sacrifice? Are all sacrifices of particularity the same? Humanist sacrifice or human sacrifice? Such are the grim questions thrown up by the narratives of sacrifice in *The Guide, Seasons of the Palm,* and *The Grip of Change.*

Of the three novels, *Seasons* articulates the most interesting and important questions regarding humanism in the context of the varna-jati complex, and so I end this section with a few reflections on it. Limbale's materialist and humanist aesthetics gives us a critical vantage point from which to explore this theme as it emerges in the novel. Necessarily, the focus of our critical attention must be on the relationship between Shortie and Selvan and on the novel's ambiguous conclusion.

When Selvan is lost in the well, why does Shortie not run away, as in fact his friends encourage him to? Why does he jump into the well? One answer to these questions resides in the relationship between Selvan and Shortie. As we have seen, *Seasons* suggests that despite Selvan's lording over him, Shortie feels a genuine love for the son of his master. Though not untouched by resentment and an acute sense of injustice, Shortie's love for a boy he unfailingly addresses as Master has its origins in the intimacy between the boys as they spend nights together taking care of goats. In delineating the relationship between the two boys, Murugan notes not only the never-absent hierarchies and brutalities of the varna-jati complex but also the bonds of a shared boyhood. Is it this remembered intimacy that draws Shortie into the well, despite the very real prospect of a terrible punishment if Selvan has in fact drowned? An affirmative answer is suggested because it would have made much more sense for Shortie to run away.

Seasons' refusal to endorse the self-preserving option of flight could be understood as an inability on the part of the narrative to imagine Shortie breaking free of the prisonhouse of the varna-jati complex. Despite all the brutality he has faced, it might seem, Selvan cannot discern the true tyranny of the varna-jati complex; for, were he able to, would he not save himself rather than Selvan, his master? Following this vein of thought, the novel's conclusion can certainly be read as a fantasy of intercaste brotherhood that disregards the real costs exacted by the varna-jati complex.

However, another reading too is possible. The conclusion might also be read as recording not a failure of imagination (on the part of Shortie) but rather a leap of imaginative faith. By recognizing not the antagonisms of jati identity but rather a solidarity arising from a shared humanity, *Seasons* makes of Shortie the bearer of a heroic (and at the same time somber) worldview. The ending of *Seasons* becomes, then, a tortured and sorrowful (after all, it is not at all clear that Shortie himself will ever emerge from the well), but nevertheless necessary, reaching after humanism.

I am drawn to this reading because *Seasons* is quite unblinking in depicting the innumerable atrocities of the varna-jati complex. It is impossible after what has preceded to view Murugan's conclusion as a lapse into naïveté. Rather than naïveté or, worse yet, complicity, *Seasons* would seem to yearn for an inclusive humanism and at the same time to suggest in a materialist spirit of carefully attending to sociohistorical structures that until the varna-jati complex is eradicated the pursuit of such a humanism will necessarily be beset by difficulties. In this light, Shortie's leap into the well becomes a brave if tragic vault into the harsh material reality of his life. Instead of viewing the conclusion as a naive faith in human solidarity on the part of the author, in this ending we might find echoes, albeit in a more somber register, of Limbale's Dalit *satyam, shivam, sundaram*, centered as it is on *human* values.

I am reminded here too of Judith Butler's eloquent appeal in *Precarious Life* that we consider seriously the relationship between the human and the grievable—what she calls "'the human' in its grievability" (2004, 38). Butler suggests that it is necessary—I suppose it is not sufficient—that to be human an entity should be capable of being mourned.[11] It follows that someone who cannot be grieved is exiled from the community of human beings. Viewed in this light, we may read the depiction of Shortie in *Seasons* as an exploration of the grievability of the Dalit. And we can go farther and note that the novel also faithfully records Shortie's capacity to grieve. As much as grievability, the capacity to grieve is necessary—again, not therefore sufficient—for us to be human. Both by depicting Shortie's grieving commitment to Selvan in diving into the well at great risk to himself and by evoking Shortie himself as a grievable figure for us readers, Murugan establishes the humanity of his protagonist in a way that resonates with Butler's argument in the far different context of the United States in the period immediately after 9/11. In doing so, Murugan powerfully invites the reader not just to stop at horror at Shortie's sacrifice but to go beyond and recognize the horrifying nature of the varna-jati complex. Once we genuinely grieve Shortie as well as recognize his capacity for grief, can we fail to appreciate the need to expunge the social structures that oppress him?

WITNESSING DALIT LIVES

Through their narratives of sacrifice, *The Guide*, *Seasons of the Palm* and *The Grip of Change* all testify to the power of the varna-jati complex. However, a significant difference obtains between *The Guide* and the other two works in this respect. *Seasons* and *Grip* both bear witness to the atrocity of the varna-jati complex in purposeful ways, whereas *The Guide*, in keeping with what Pandian (2002, 6) calls Narayan's "masked citation" of caste in his works, obfuscates the brutality of the varna-jati complex while acknowledging its power. In *The Guide,* unlike the other two works, we cannot find a direct indictment of the varna-jati complex. Viewed in the context of Limbale's aesthetics, it might be said that *Seasons* and *Grip*, unlike *The Guide*, take seriously the duty of witnessing. Although fictional narratives, they *report* (not to be understood in a dismissive way) on the oppressiveness of the varna-jati complex.

As examples of life writing, *Karukku* and *Viramma*, the two works to which I now turn, signify witnessing even more directly. The first is an autobiography (though it bends the most conventional notions of the genre in its attempt to sometimes present the collective voice of the Paraiyars) and the second a testimonio.[12] As is often the case with the emergent literature of socially marginalized groups (consider the importance of slave narratives as well as autobiographies in the history of African American literature), nonfictional personal narratives constitute an important genre in Dalit writing. Arun Prabha Mukherjee notes in the introduction to his translation of Omprakash Valmiki's well-known Hindi Dalit autobiography *Joothan*, "Autobiography has been a favourite genre of Dalit writers. This is not surprising, in light of the emphasis placed by them on authenticity of experience" (2007, xxviii). It is, we might add, a way for Dalit writers to explore and establish their humanity. Like other socially marginalized groups, Dalits have tried through autobiographies and memoirs to bear witness to experiences of dehumanization. They have necessarily done so for Dalit as well as non-Dalit audiences.

The record produced by Dalit writers in this fashion has several aspects to it worth noting. Dalit writers describe and analyze the material conditions of their existence through the generic conventions of life-writing texts. They struggle to establish individual voices even as they articulate narratives representative of a community. Since they recount and analyze their experiences for multiple audiences—Dalit and non-Dalit, vernacular and national and even, as in the case of *Viramma*, international—their narratives have multiple foci and tensions. Alongside bearing witness against the varna-jati complex, their narratives perform personal functions. In the preface to *Joothan*, Valmiki confesses, "After a long period of procrastination, I started to write. Once again, I had to relive all those miseries, torments, neglects, admonitions. I suffered a deep mental anguish while writing this book. How terribly painful was this unraveling of my self, layer upon layer" (2007, viii). The process of writing tears the self apart; the text resulting from this writing presents a self stitched back together, albeit not seamlessly. Though Valmiki does not articulate his writing experience in this way, we can infer that the pain of remembered ignominy is succeeded in the process of writing by a renewal of the self. Life writing is a fraught as well as essential genre for Dalit writers. It forces encounters with the baleful effects of dehumanization at the same time that it offers a way to compel audiences to recognize the human self of the writer.

These aspects of Dalit autobiography are easily evident in Bama's *Karukku*, which recounts the life story of a Tamil Dalit woman. More specifically, *Karukku* presents the experiences of a politically conscious Christian Paraiyar woman. Bama's narrative begins in her childhood, but much of it is concerned with the vicious discrimination she encounters within the church hierarchy as a nun. *Karukku* is Bama's attempt to make sense of her diverse experiences in and out of the church. Eventually, Bama leaves the church and becomes a teacher. Her autobiography concludes with her exit, which forms in a sense the climactic point of her resistant narrative.

Bama describes her departure from the church through a series of comparisons—she is a strong teak tree transformed into a weak murunga by her time in the convent; she is a bird with broken wings that has been let out of a cage; she is a fish that has been returned to water (2000, 103–4). She describes her transformation in the convent as a "kind of magic" so that "eventually we become strangers even to ourselves" (103). She concludes angrily: "For the time being, I cannot see my way ahead. Yet I believe it is possible to live a meaningful life, a life that is useful to a few others. I comfort myself with the thought that rather than live with a fraudulent smile, it is better to lead a life weeping real tears" (104). *Karukku* is a powerful indictment of the manifestation of the varna-jati hierarchy within the Christian Church in India. It refutes the facile notion that the varna-jati complex is a peculiarly Hindu institution.

Like *Grip*, and unlike *The Guide*, Bama arrives at her bitter refutation of the varna-jati complex in a deliberate way. Her narrative moves from early poverty through her hopeful struggles to escape her marginalized condition by way of the church to her concluding disillusionment. The opening sections of the autobiography treat her childhood in a village divided by jati. She recounts the tensions arising from discrimination and paints in vivid colors the destitute condition of the Christian Paraiyars: "In the streets, the children used to wander, barebottomed, both boys and girls. Even if a few boys wore pants, they would usually have slipped down, hardly covering what they were supposed to cover. Their bottoms were never as big as their bellies, so their pants would not stay up. The moment it struck twelve, they'd rush off plate in hand, even the tiniest crab-like ones, for their free meal. The church bell struck the hour at twelve. That was the signal" (7). Soon, Bama gets the notion that she "could become a nun and enter a convent, and in that way work hard for other children who had struggled as I had done" (66). Her education and devotion to the church lead her to make "my first vows with many hopes and thoughts in my heart. I dream that I would share my life with the poor and the suffering, live and die for them. Instead, I was sent to a prestigious school and asked to teach there" (91). Her experiences in the school are enlightening. Gradually, she comes to realize that the church is not dedicated to the poor as she had thought, prompting her to abandon it.

The title of Bama's book is as instructive as the one Geetha comes up with for her translation of Murugan's novel. Bama informs us in her preface that *karukku* is both the palmyra leaf that scratched and tore her skin when she picked it up as a child and "the embryo and soul" of her book (xiii). Elucidating the reference further, the translator Lakshmi Holmstrom notes that *karukku* in Tamil connotes the sharp-edged palmyra leaf as well as newness (2000, vii). Valmiki's painful representation of writing in *Joothan* is echoed by Bama in *Karukku*. Bama's narrative appears both self-mutilating and self-renewing. The narrative of her childhood and subsequent life in the Catholic Church is an account of a personal trauma that is uncovered but also healed, if only partly, by the act of telling. Simultaneously, *Karukku* is an attempt to articulate the typical condition of a Dalit Christian woman. Personal as well as typical, Bama's autobiography bears witness to the material condition of Tamil Christian Dalits at the same time that it exhorts a transcendence of these very conditions: "There are other Dalit hearts like mine, with a passionate desire to create a new society made up of justice, equality and love. They, who have been the oppressed, are now themselves like the double-edged karukku, challenging their oppressors" (2000, xiii). In Bama's narrative, the karukku comes to figure several aspects of Dalit autobiography as a literature of witnessing and protest—as a literature of resistance.

Though she primarily explored literature emerging out of national struggles against colonialism in *Resistance Literature*, Barbara Harlow's assessment of the social and aesthetic location of such literature is certainly pertinent to our analysis of many Dalit works, including Bama's autobiography. "Resistance literature," notes Harlow, "calls attention to itself, and to literature in general, as a political and politicized activity. The literature of resistance sees itself furthermore as immediately and directly involved in a struggle against ascendant or dominant forms of ideological and cultural production" (1987, 28–29). As a resistant literary work, Bama's struggle against ascendant aesthetic principles is evident everywhere in her text. Resistance—witnessing and protest—is not just narrated in her text; rather, it inheres in its very language: its syntax, diction, and register.

Indeed, it is the manifestation of such linguistic resistance that poses the most fascinating questions to the translator of Bama's work. Bama's resistant language presents challenges for translation that draw attention to the politicized nature of not only literature but also translation. Of this language, Bama's translator Lakshmi Holmstrom notes: "Bama is doing something completely new in using the demotic and the colloquial regularly, as her medium for narration and even argument, not simply for reported speech. She uses a Dalit style of language which overturns the decorum and aesthetics of received upper-class, upper-caste Tamil. She breaks the rules of written grammar and spelling throughout, elides words and joins them differently, demanding a new and different pattern of reading" (2000, x–xi). Given this remarkable insight, it is surprising that Holmstrom's translation does not rise to the challenge posed by Bama's text. Her translation is content to transfer Bama into a smooth, straightforward Standard English, and so fails to capture the jaggedness of Bama's language. Instead of demanding a new pattern of reading from the reader of the translation, Holmstrom is content to domesticate Bama's language. As Anushiya Sivanarayanan perceptively observes of Holmstrom's translation, "Rather than reading *Karukku* as a Tamil novel [sic] translated into English, it would be more accurate to read it as a Tamil Dalit novel translated into literary Tamil and then into English" (2009, 148). Holmstrom writes sensitively about the demotic and vernacular power of Bama's language; nevertheless, her translation foregoes the invitation implicit in that very language to test the limits of Standard English.

It is worth underscoring here the political nature of translation decisions. Holmstrom's translation of a lively, vernacular style into a bland, standard one deflates the language, allowing some of its power of witnessing and protest to leak out. Thus it seems to me that the sentence Holmstrom translates as "They, who have been the oppressed, are now themselves like the double-edged karukku, challenging their oppressors" (quoted above) might more aptly be rendered in the following way (the passage appears on page ix in the Tamil original): "Now, these people, the crushed, becoming like the sharp double-edged karukku, slash and rip those who crush them." Holmstrom's translation dilutes and makes abstract what is a vivid metaphor of the sharp-edged palmyra leaf, sustained throughout the book—that which ripped the skin of Dalits once (in the person of the child Bama) now slashes those who oppress them. "Crushed" (rather than Holmstrom's "oppressed") echoes the original Marathi meaning of Dalit mentioned above—"broken or reduced to pieces," "the ground [down]." Surely Bama's sentence skillfully alludes to a broader, pan-Indian discourse of Dalit resistance even as it sketches out her personal experience as a Tamil Paraiyar Christian woman. In Holmstrom's translation, this allusion is lost, so Bama's ability to wed personal anguish to social commitment appears attenuated. The threatening sharpness of her language is blunted.

Nevertheless, Holmstrom's translation successfully captures many other aspects of Bama's autobiography. As in other Dalit texts, Bama's philosophical framework for understanding social commitment and liberation is humanist. In a key passage of the autobiography, she asks (the translation is Holmstrom's): "Are Dalits not human beings? Do they not have common sense? Do they not have such attributes as a sense of honor and self-respect? Are they without any wisdom, beauty, dignity?" (24; 23 in the Tamil original). Taking the cue from Bama, we might ask: If you prick a Dalit, will she not bleed? Bama's Shylockian moment is a humanist cry from the heart, quite in keeping with her bending of the generic conventions of the autobiography to articulate a collective Paraiyar voice.

In the form of rhetorical questions, Bama asserts a deeply held humanist sense of injury that is, the autobiography makes clear, personal as well as communal, psychological as well as material. An oft-cited passage from the autobiography illustrates these multiple dimensions well. In this episode, the child Bama witnesses an elder of the community carrying a morsel of food in an abject manner to a higher jati man (2000, 12–14). Watching the old man dangling the packet of food from a string so as not to "contaminate" it, Bama first laughs, "but Annan [Elder Brother] was not amused. Annan told me he wasn't being funny when he carried the package like that. He said everybody believed that Naickers were upper caste, and therefore must not touch Parayas. If they did, they would be polluted" (13). Laughter is succeeded by anger: "The thought of it infuriated me. How was it that these fellows thought so much of themselves? Because they had scraped four coins together, did that mean they must lose all human feelings? What did it mean when they called us 'Paraya'? Had the name become that obscene? But we too are human beings" (13). As Bama is shocked out of her childish innocence, she encounters both the psychological and material conditions of Dalit oppression. She encounters a poverty that is of the mind as well as of the material world; and so the naive laughter turns into humanist anger.

Unlike *Karukku*, *Viramma*, the life narrative of a twentieth-century Tamil Paraiyar woman of the same name from Pondicherry (a small Tamil-speaking state in South India), is not in a conventional sense an autobiography, though it shares many characteristics with that genre. As already noted, *Viramma*, like the more famous example of Guatemalan Rigoberta Menchú's *I, Rigoberta Menchú*, is a testimonio—a work emerging out of a collaboration between the subject of the narrative and, in this case, anthropologists. Testimonios are works in which the subjects, typically from socially marginalized groups, recount their lives to privileged interlocutors, who then compose the narrative in written form. As told to Paris-based Tamil anthropologist Josiane Racine (and composed by her and her French husband Jean-Luc Racine, also an anthropologist), *Viramma* stands out for its horrifying as well as humorous account of a Paraiyar woman from birth till the moment of recounting—the recordings in which the testimonio originates were made, we are told, between 1980 and 1990.[13] Although

Viramma does not know exactly when she was born, in the 1990s the Racines assess her age as in the sixties (Racine and Racine 1997, 309). The book not only traces Viramma's personal history (early childhood, married life, child bearing, employment) but also presents the rich cultural and social context within which this life unfolds. *Viramma* gives us lengthy accounts of rituals, festivals, typical work routines, and social and political transformations down the decades, though never at the expense of Viramma's own distinctive presence in the narrative.

Again unlike *Karukku*, *Viramma* sits uneasily under the label of resistant Dalit literature. As the life narrative of a Dalit woman born long before the rise of a radical Dalit movement in South India, *Viramma* does not offer only palatable viewpoints on the varna-jati complex. Even as she documents atrocities and contests the many humiliations of Paraiyars, Viramma, the protagonist of what might be called a collaborative text, also acquiesces to the basic ideology of the varna-jati complex, reproducing the language of purity and hierarchy by which women and men like her were and are routinely ostracized. When discussing the holy ritual of fire walking, for example, she says of Paraiyars like herself, "We know perfectly well it's impossible. We're not clean enough for that [fire-walking]!" (Viramma, Racine, and Racine 1997, 130); and of her relationship to Josiane Racine, she observes, "It doesn't matter that I'm like a mother to you or that in the bottom of my heart I think of you as my daughter, you've been born into a higher caste than me. I owe you respect" (149). Because of these and similar statements within the narrative, *Viramma* offers unique challenges as well as opportunities for criticism.

Some might regard *Viramma* as flawed because it does not offer a straightforward condemnation of the varna-jati complex. Others might argue that an authentic representation of the human emerges in its narrative precisely because of the acknowledgment that humans are shaped by, even as they shape, their cultural environment. It seems to me the Racines recognize this when they write the following words about the difficulties posed by the testimonio in whose production they have participated: "We would say to those Dalit militants who will find Viramma too submissive: please hear this voice. Doesn't it remind you of your mother, your eldest aunt, your grandmother? Does it not provide an authentic account of subjugation? Preserving this voice and memory of the past is, we believe, to contribute, however modestly, to the building of a future which will give each woman and man their share of dignity, their share of the truth" (Racine and Racine 1997,

312). Bearing witness to the humanity of the Dalit in the context of the varna-jati complex does not entail simply extolling courage and anger and resistance; it also means noting the multiple ways in which human beings accommodate themselves to oppressive realities in the interest of survival.

In *Viramma*, the act of bearing witness is intimately connected to the conventions of the genre to which the book belongs. In its very name, *testimonio* suggests witnessing. A testimonio raises interesting questions about literature. Testimonio tests the limits of what constitutes the literary by its particular form of witnessing. Citing Umberto Eco, John Beverley notes that the testimonio is "an 'open work' that implies the importance and power of literature as a form of social action, but also its radical insufficiency" (2004, 42). As an "open work," a testimonio transgresses the boundary of separation between the literary and the nonliterary. Compared to autobiographies or novels as conventionally understood, texts such as *Viramma* can more easily accommodate the kinds of insights and critiques elicited by the social sciences. Accordingly, *Viramma* is a literary form that draws its power from the domain of the aesthetic as well as beyond. Without a robust sense of this transgressiveness, *Viramma*'s representational potency is difficult to appreciate.

Commenting on the power of representation of the testimonio, Beverley notes:

> If testimonio is an art of memory, it is an art directed not only toward the memorialization of the past but also to the constitution of more heterogeneous, diverse, egalitarian, and democratic nation-states, as well as forms of community, solidarity, and affinity that extend beyond or between nation-states. To construct such forms of community, however, it is necessary to begin with the recognition of an authority that is not our own, an authority that resides in the voices of others. In this sense, testimonio, despite its ambiguities and contradictions, continues to be part of a necessary pedagogy. (2004, 24)

As an international collaboration between Viramma and the Racines, *Viramma* imagines a transnational community of solidarity. It sets out to represent to a transnational readership the vicious conundrums of the varna-jati complex as they manifest themselves in the life of a traditional Paraiyar woman. It understands this act of representation to have a pedagogical function, which is why the Racines hope in their commentary on Viramma's account that it will "contribute to that emancipation which seems impossible to her" (Racine and Racine 1997, 312).

The liberation imagined in *Viramma* cannot be understood only in the context of the varna-jati complex. Though not my focus here, it is worth noting that such emancipation also implicates a patriarchal society. *Grip*, *Karukku,* and *Viramma* all direct particular attention to Dalit women in ways that contrast to *Seasons*' story of boyhood. *Grip* does so through its female narrator and through the rape that sets the plot in motion. *Karukku* too affords its reader access to the world of Dalit women, though little direct analysis of gender is offered (in contrast to Dalit-ness, which is much reflected on in the text). *Viramma*, though the least explicitly political of the three texts, richly represents the particularities of female Dalit experience. When Viramma describes her marital relationship, or narrates how higher-jati men demand sexual favors of Dalit women, we are led to an apt if disturbing illustration of Sharmila Rege's observation that "the issue of violence against women cannot be seen as either a 'caste' issue or a 'gender' issue, but it must be located in the links between the two" (1995, 35). The works by Sivakami, Bama, and Viramma underscore the need to explore the multiple determinants of the experiences of Dalit women.[14]

As a testimonio engendered by a collaboration between Paris-based anthropologists and a Tamil Paraiyar woman, *Viramma* exports the humanist conundrums identifiable in the Dalit Panther manifesto, and in Dangle and Limbale, to the international arena. On the one hand, the Racines too take recourse to the notion of the human in their defense of what they consider to be Viramma's problematic narrative. They conclude their afterword (entitled "Routes to Emancipation: A Dalit Life Story in Context") by invoking "the simple title that Unjai Ranjan gave the Dalit journal he edits: *Manusanga*, Humans" (Racine and Racine 1997, 312). Through this reference, the Racines imagine liberation in a humanist mode, and the testimonio becomes a transnational, collaborative contribution to the emancipatory effort. Thus *Viramma* shares a humanism with Limbale. On the other hand, it seems to contravene many of the principles of Dalit humanist aesthetics elaborated by him; it memorializes an unpalatable past and often reinstates the obscene discriminations of the varna-jati complex through the words of the victim herself. What is the humanism that permits such a memorialization and reinstatement? If the contradiction in Limbale was between attending to the specific identity of the Dalit and a more general endorsement of the human, what is the contradiction at work here?

Such questions about humanism and the human are provoked not just by *Viramma* but indeed by all the Dalit (and Dalitbahujan) literary and critical texts engaged in this chapter, despite their differences in other respects. Whether by women or men, whether dealing with child or adult protagonists, whether presented in the form of literary fiction or literary criticism, all these works invest heavily in humanism and the human. At the same time, they bear the marks of their particular origin in the experiences of a particular ("untouchable") jati. Thus the vernacular confronts the universal.

HUMANISMS: COSMOPOLITAN AND VERNACULAR

In *Academic Lives: Memoir, Cultural Theory and the University Today*, Cynthia Franklin rightly notes the recent resurgence of interest in humanism and the human within the U.S. academy and characterizes it a reversal of prior tendencies. "The 1980s and 1990s," she writes, "saw a range of attacks on humanism"; the various critiques of the 1980s targeting an "exclusionary 'humanism,'" she observes, were succeeded in the 1990s by postcolonial and cultural studies disputations (2009, 19–20). The events of 9/11, however, inaugurated a significant change. Franklin cites conferences, journal special issues, and books demonstrating the return of interest in humanism and the human (20–21). Both have become significant concerns within the U.S. academy in a time of burgeoning antagonism between "America" and "the Arab world" and/or "Islam." What is our responsibility to the victim of the Taliban in Afghanistan? How may we articulate a legitimate critique without succumbing to the temptation to dehumanize an "enemy"? If not in a shared humanity, where may we locate the common aspirations of people all over the world belonging to diverse religions, cultures, and languages? These and similar questions have underpinned, Franklin makes clear, an urgent new theoretical exploration of humanism and the human by progressive-minded critics who remain skeptical of an exclusionary humanism.

Surely this American theoretical context is far different from the Dalit humanism considered in this chapter. Nevertheless, for scholars interested in the shape and form of the human and the "ism" founded on it there are lessons to be learnt in this very difference. By attending to what is shared as well as contested between the discourses of humanism emergent in the U.S. academy and articulated in the critique of caste by Dalit and allied writers, we might learn something fresh about the traditions of thought we call humanism.

A key work in the return to humanism in the United States (one with special resonance for postcolonialism) is Edward Said's final, posthumously published book. In *Humanism and Democratic Criticism*, Said argues as passionately for humanism as Limbale or Dangle. In making his argument, Said associates humanism with secularism: "The core of humanism is the secular notion that the historical world is made by men and women, and not by God, and that it can be understood rationally" (2004, 11). In offering this definition, Said insists that humanism should not be understood as a homogeneous entity, a critical stance I share. Said is keen to distinguish his notion of humanism from that of Allan Bloom, Harold Bloom, and Saul Bellow, advocates for an elitist humanism that is narrow and exclusionary. For Said, humanism in its best guise is "democratic"—open to ideas, inclusive, amenable to correction.[15] He notes: "It is possible to be critical of humanism in the name of humanism" (10). Said makes his arguments within an immediate intellectual context (the humanities sector of the North American academy) that has learnt, for the exclusionary reasons pointed out by Franklin as well as Said, to be skeptical of notions of the human.[16] Viewed within a broader context, however, Said's arguments place him within a humanistic tradition that includes writers and philosophers as diverse as Karl Marx, Frantz Fanon, and Amartya Sen.[17] This is the wide-ranging tradition that includes, I would suggest, Dalit writers such as Limbale. My claim is not that Said had read these Dalit writers or they him, but more that they are united by a global tradition of humanistic thought that owes, as Amartya Sen has insisted, much to multiple cultural traditions.[18] Said himself subscribed to a similar non-Eurocentric idea of humanism (2004, 26–27). Recognition of this global tradition of humanistic thought makes it possible to link Said's secular humanism to Limbale's forceful reappropriation of the savarna ideal of "*satyam, shivam, sundaram.*" Like Said's materialist humanism, much Dalit writing endeavors through an appeal to the human to replace God with history, narrow exclusion with democratic openness, prejudice with tolerance.

However, important distinctions also mark off Said's humanism from Dalit humanism. When Said writes, "Schooled in [the] abuses [of humanism] by the experience of Eurocentrism and empire, one could fashion a different kind of humanism that was cosmopolitan," we are in a different world from that of Dalit humanism (2004, 11). In linking humanism to cosmopolitanism, Said yokes his argument to a horse of questionable value to Dalit humanism. Chiefly, the differences between

Said's and Dalit humanism revolve around this very cosmopolitanism, a topic a wide body of critical literature has taken up in recent years. In Said, the linkage between humanism and cosmopolitanism is asserted briefly, but more extensive exemplifications can be found in the writings on cosmopolitanism by scholars like Martha Nussbaum and Kwame Anthony Appiah.[19] While cosmopolitanism is these writers' primary concern, humanism's ghost haunts their arguments.

The putative linkage in the American academy between contemporary theories of cosmopolitanism and humanism is easily perceived in *For Love of Country?*, edited by Joshua Cohen. This collection brings together a celebrated essay by Martha Nussbaum entitled "Patriotism and Cosmopolitanism," reflections on her essay by sixteen academics, and a concluding response by Nussbaum. Nussbaum's interlocutors range across the disciplines of philosophy, rhetoric, literature, political economy, and history, to mention only a few. Thus, though the essays are brief, the collection articulates the anxieties and attractions engendered by the notion of cosmopolitanism from many perspectives.

"Patriotism and Cosmopolitanism," Nussbaum's original essay, vigorously defends cosmopolitanism against the claims of patriotism—or, to pose the opposition in different words, nationalism. Nussbaum begins with a brief reading of Rabindranath Tagore's *The Home and the World*, noting how the novel opposes a dangerous if passionate nationalism to a sensible if dull cosmopolitanism. The specter of humanism appears early in the essay, for Nussbaum declares that her allegiance, like that of the character Nikhil in the novel, is to "the worldwide community of human beings" rather than to a national community (1996, 4). Nussbaum's main concern in the essay, however, is the United States and the contemporary world, rather than pre-Independence India. She argues, via reference to the ideals of Stoicism, the urgent need for a cosmopolitan education for "a citizen of the world." She declares, "Becoming a citizen of the world is often a lonely business. It is, as Diogenes said, a kind of exile—from the comfort of local truths, from the warm, nestling feeling of patriotism, from the absorbing drama of pride in oneself and one's own.... Cosmopolitanism offers no such refuge; it offers only reason and the love of humanity, which may seem at times less colorful than other sources of belonging" (15). Nussbaum, then, values cosmopolitanism for the expansive if demanding vision it offers of the world; and in so doing she presents a clear example of how cosmopolitanism articulates with humanism.

Nussbaum's respondents in "Patriotism and Cosmopolitanism" sometimes agree with her particular advocacy of cosmopolitanism, sometimes not. Most render mixed responses. One of the most insightful is offered by Immanuel Wallerstein, who suggests that the glib opposition of cosmopolitanism to patriotism might itself be the problem: "The merits of patriotism and cosmopolitanism are not abstract, and certainly not universal. We live in a deeply unequal world. As a result, our options vary according to social location, and the consequences of acting as a 'world citizen' are very different depending on time and space" (1996, 122); and

> The response to a self-interested patriotism is not a self-congratulatory cosmopolitanism. The appropriate response is to support forces that will break down existing inequalities and help create a more democratic, egalitarian world. . . . What is needed educationally is not to learn that we are citizens of the world, but that we occupy particular niches in an unequal world, and that being disinterested and global on one hand and defending one's narrow interests on the other are not opposites but positions combined in complicated ways. Some combinations are desirable, others are not. Some are desirable here but not there, now but not then. (124)

Neither patriotism, nor cosmopolitanism, then. Or: both patriotism and cosmopolitanism. The answer lies in what work one or the other does, what it enables in, as Wallerstein observes, an unequal world. In responding to Nussbaum's essay, Wallerstein's observation offers a useful perspective on the broader discourse on cosmopolitanism—rather than arguing for or against cosmopolitanism, it suggests we might want to attend to the time, place, and particular content of whatever cosmopolitanism with which we are confronted.[20]

Perusing *For Love of Country?* as well as collections such as *Cosmopolitics* (1998), edited by Pheng Cheah and Bruce Robbins, and *Cosmopolitanism* (2002), edited by Carol Breckenridge et al., makes abundantly clear that the primary point of opposition to cosmopolitanism in much critical discourse is nationalism. Although the critical discourse on cosmopolitanism is littered with contrastive references to the local, the particular, the concrete—Appiah points out that *cosmos* refers to the universe; given this etymology, how could it not be?[21]—the primary aim of most of the commentators is to adjudicate the competing claims of nationalism and cosmopolitanism. The vernacular circulates in this debate only as a necessary residual effect—an inescapable afterthought—of the more urgent concern of matching cosmopolitanism against nationalism.

Certainly, the relationship of nations and nationalism to cosmopolitanism is an urgent critical concern—but so is that of the vernacular. Thus we cross from a review of cosmopolitan humanism to one of the main concerns of this book. As we have already seen, the vernacular and the national are not the same. And because they are not, an independent and adequate accounting remains to be made between cosmopolitanism and the vernacular, despite the writings of critics such as Homi Bhabha and Sheldon Pollock. Bhabha has advanced a notion of "vernacular cosmopolitanism," relying on the oxymoronism at the heart of his formulation to uncover the supple ways in which cosmopolitanism is able to assimilate as well as be transformed by that which it seems to oppose. As I noted in chapter 1, in doing so Bhabha mainly intends to forward notions of minority discourse, not to explore the vernacular in its own right (see Bhabha 1997, 457–58). Pollock shares Bhabha's critical suppleness. He too aims to undo oppositions, but he heads in a different direction when he writes of the cosmopolitan vernacular rather than the vernacular cosmopolitan (2002, 35). In contrast to both, I explore the ways in which *vernacular* and *cosmopolitan* are opposed to each other. Rather than prematurely treating one as an adjectival modifier for the other, I want to sustain the opposition a while longer, to investigate how *vernacular* marks a point of resistance to the transnational or the cosmopolitan.

In the present context, such an investigation might take the form of considering the diverse inflections that different approaches bring to the idea of humanism. As seen in Said and Nussbaum, cosmopolitanism subsists in close association with—unavoidable dependence on—humanism. Even Kwame Anthony Appiah's advocacy of a "partial cosmopolitanism" involves balancing loyalty to "one portion of humanity—a nation, a class" with "loyalty to all of humanity" (2006, xvi–xvii). The latter, it seems, is cosmopolitanism pure and simple. Cosmopolitanism, understood as education for world citizenry (Nussbaum), as antithesis to Eurocentrism and empire (Said), as obligation to others across the world (Appiah), seems inevitably to invoke a broad human community as ethical measure. Such an appeal to a community of human beings in general is humanism at its most commonsensical. As explored in this chapter, a similar commonsensical idea of humanism is to be discerned in Dalit literature and criticism, and also in Periyar, discussed in the previous chapter, who once exhorted his "low-caste" readers: "The sense of being a low caste person seems to have mingled completely with your blood. But you must endeavor to change this. Whenever you see a person—of another caste—you must ask yourselves, if in reality there exists any difference between him and you. One cannot help a caste that is not concerned about its own self-respect to progress. Each one of you must recognize and be conscious of the fact that you are human" (qtd. in Geetha and Rajadurai 1998, 294). Surely, this is humanism. But is it cosmopolitanism?

Periyar indicates a commitment to humanism that shares ground with Said, Nussbaum, and Appiah; at the same time, in the above passage a difference emerges between the cosmopolitan humanism of these three and the humanism found in anticaste writing (Periyar's, as well as that of Dalit intellectuals like Limbale and the Dalit Panthers). As clearly evident in Periyar's words, the status of being human is something to be struggled for and won in the humanism of anticaste writing. In cosmopolitan humanism, this status is assumed. *We are all human*, the cosmopolitan humanists seem to say, *let us recognize and celebrate this*. For the cosmopolitan humanists, there is no anxiety about *their own* humanness. The anxiety rather is about reaching out and including within humanism those who might not have a similar easy and comfortable access to being human. Much is attractive about this approach to the human (and some is not), but the temper of this humanism starkly differs from the humanism of Periyar as expressed in the quoted passage, which is combative rather than inviting. *I too am human—just the way I am*, Periyar wants the low-caste person to say, not *We are all human*. A world of difference exists between *we all* and *I too*; it is the difference between a liberal humanism of tolerance and a radical humanism of assertion, between a generous humanism that speaks comfortably from within the universal and a humanism that resists exclusion and must struggle to make a place for itself within the universal.

If the humanisms of Said, Nussbaum, and Appiah are, by their own estimation, *cosmopolitan humanisms*, then the humanisms of Limbale, Murugan, and Periyar are, in all their variety, *vernacular humanisms*. Certainly, there are differences among the vernacular humanisms—Limbale is analytical and utopian, Murugan lyrical and tragic, and Periyar polemical and activist. Nevertheless, all three share the desire to lay claim to the human by redefining it from their own particular perspectives within a politics of caste. Rather than assimilative, their materialist approach is to begin with a critique that emerges out of a vernacular sensibility of their place in the world. While attracted to humanism, their vernacular experience—and we have seen in this and the previous chapter how intimately linked the vernacular and the varna-jati complex are in the Indian context—makes the easy and expansive inclusiveness of cosmopolitan humanism impossible to own. As vernacular humanists, they articulate a conflicted approach to the universal that is not yet ready to relinquish an orientation toward the rooted, the culturally autonomous, and the local.

Put in this way, the paradox of a vernacular humanism becomes immediately evident—how could that which is *particular* aspire simultaneously to the *universal* condition of the human? And yet this paradoxical aspiration is precisely what we found in Limbale's contradictory formulations, where he wished both to appeal to the human and to maintain the specificity of being Dalit. We found it too in the attempt to balance Viramma's self-staging, her accommodation of the varna-jati complex, against a broader appeal to humanism within her testimonio. In *Viramma*, a humanist recognition of her memorialization of her experiences and opinions sits uneasily next to a more programmatic humanism. Both Limbale's work and *Viramma* are fractured texts, albeit differently so. Unlike the achieved humanism of the cosmopolitans, the humanism of the vernaculars (of which Dalit humanism is but one kind) is fissured because it has yet to come to fruition. If it does not exhibit the seamlessness of cosmopolitan humanism, and has not the luxury of asserting *we are all human* in an assimilative mode, it is because it is still busy insisting *I too am human*, because it has yet to complete the transition from the margin to the center of humanism. Sometimes this insistence can surely become a form of supplication—a demeaning appeal for inclusion. However, at its best, such insistence is neither narrowly exclusionary nor a form of pleading, for in addition to *I too am human*, it adds, *just the way I am*.

For vernacular humanism, the premature assertion of *we are all human* runs the risk of aborting much too early an urgent struggle. How is the Dalit humanist to resist the blandishments of a liberal Brahminism that might invite the Dalit to become human by giving up her Dalitness, by Brahminizing herself? As the work of M. N. Srinivas has shown, such blandishments to Sanskritize oneself have had real force in the history and politics of caste.[22] Rather than succumb to the invitation to change and assimilate encoded in *We are all human*, the assertion *I too am human, just the way I am* allows the Dalit intellectual to attempt a reformation of humanism from where she is. Wallerstein's recommendation that we take note of the unequal world in assessing cosmopolitanism is worth remembering here. In an unequal world, the humanism of the wretched of the earth, of the Dalitbahujan, of the pariah, of those whose humanity is in fact routinely denied, is forced to take the form *I too am human, just the way I am,* while the humanism of the generous educators of the world, those for whom *I too am human* is already achieved, takes the form *We are all human.* The difference between the former and the latter might be regarded as the difference between a *vernacular humanism* and a *cosmopolitan humanism.* While both lay claim to the universal concept of the human, they do so from different directions, with different objectives, with different anxieties. The former is defensive and particular in its approach to humanism, whether in a combative mode like Periyar or a somber mood like Murugan in *Seasons;* the latter is tolerant and expansive. Unable to keep sight of the generous inclusiveness at the heart of humanism, the former—the humanism of the pariah—runs the risk of remaining trapped in a narrow combativeness, or in pessimism, or, if such combativeness and pessimism are to be abjured, falling into the even worse alternative of a self-insulting supplication. The latter runs the risk of imperiously—imperially—turning the pariah it ostensibly generously reaches out to into versions of itself. The tension between what I am calling vernacular humanism and cosmopolitan humanism is a tension within humanism itself, and in the figure of the Paraiyar/pariah at the center of this chapter the tension is made manifest for us.

APPROACHING THE VERNACULAR: QUESTIONS OF CRITICAL PRACTICE

In the previous chapter, the notion of the vernacular provided an opportunity to scrutinize the national. The national appeared there in the guise of the customary treatment of R. K. Narayan as an *Indian* writer in English as well as in the transformation of his novel into the Bollywood Hindi film *Guide.* In this chapter, the vernacular offered a useful vantage point from which to interrogate the tension within humanism. Pursuing the "outcaste" who goes unrepresented in novel and film led me to Dalit literature and then to humanism. In directing attention to the unrepresented Paraiyar/pariah or "outcaste," I have been interested in uncovering aspects of the human and humanism. Simultaneously, my wish has been to complement and deepen a materialist argument regarding postcolonialism begun in the first chapter. Accordingly, the first three chapters collectively explore the vernacular from a variety of directions and thus sketch out the opportunities presented to materialist criticism by recourse to the term.

The remaining two chapters take up two related topics emerging out of these explorations of the vernacular. In chapter 4 I consider translation, exploring not only how translation might be violence but also how it might *not* be, how it might also be the kind of practice that produces and makes available to readers a novel like Perumal Murugan's *Seasons of the Palm*. If the vernacular is often subjected to the violence of translation, it is also true that translation is indispensable in any extravernacular critical project of renewed attention to the vernacular. What approach to translation might we take that would allow us to recognize the enabling as well as violent possibilities of translation? This is the chief question posed in chapter 4. Following on this study of translation, the Conclusion takes up the question of comparatism. Like translation, comparatism is evoked in multiple ways by my exploration of the vernacular in a postcolonial context. Thus the next two chapters turn to questions of scholarly practice thrown up by the pursuit of a vernacular postcolonialism.

CHAPTER 4

The "Problem" of Translation

Postcolonialism, I have argued, whether understood as theory, historical condition, or literary canon, cannot be homogenized. While actually existing postcolonialism can be plotted along and between at least two axes of analysis (the transnational and the vernacular), scholarship within the North American academy has shown a strong predilection to standardize it along the first rather than the second. How can "the (post)colonial condition" be properly figured without an acknowledgment of the existence of both the vernacular and the transnational axes of orientation and, indeed, points in between? The temptation to fix and reify—to nail down one perspective on the postcolonial as "truer" than the other—is to be resisted; instead, we need an acknowledgment of existing plurality.

In practical terms, such acknowledgment would take us directly to translation, to suggest sensibly that translation has an especially important part to play in redirecting attention to that dimension I call the vernacular. It bears repeating that the vernacular is not reducible to a linguistic phenomenon; it is not exclusively a matter of a vernacular *language*. Previous chapters have been partly concerned with elucidating this assertion. I have noted that in the domain of postcolonial literature, for example, the difference between transnational and vernacular postcolonialisms cannot be sketched merely as the difference between, say, Indian literature written in English and in Tamil. Such provisos notwithstanding, the practice of translation can certainly play a role in enriching our notion of postcolonial literature by making a greater variety of colonial and postcolonial texts, sensibilities, and conundrums available for critical attention. It is worth remarking that the prevalence of an inadequate notion of the colonial and the postcolonial within the North American academy and allied academic sectors elsewhere is directly linked to the archive available for critical study. Within academic circles, it is not sufficiently acknowledged that theoretical positions emerge out of practical procedures (such as close reading in literary studies and fieldwork in anthropology); and that if the terrain available for such practical procedures is impoverished, then the effect is accordingly discernible within "theory." Because "theory" presents itself as a metadiscourse, it is easy to overlook how historically conditioned it really is.

In this context, translations present an invaluable opportunity to redress the easily observable incommensurability of theory and archive within the field of postcolonial studies. As currently constituted, the theoretical ambition of postcolonial studies bears little relationship to the reality of the impoverished archive with which the field works. It is as if a towering facade had been imposed on a shack of modest proportions, with little thought to how one fitted the other. If a suspicion of hollowness has continued to linger around postcolonial studies, it is partly because of this incommensurability between theory and archive, claim and evidence, that marks so much of the work that passes under the label of "postcolonialism." Translation has a vital role to play if this incommensurability is to be addressed. Yet translation—the actual practice, not the trope, for the recourse to trope is quite a contrast in this respect—has been generally undervalued in postcolonial theory, including within the literary and cultural studies wing of it, where the importance of translation would seem to be self-evident. Why has there been such undervaluation? Why has translation practice not appeared inviting to the postcolonial critic? Why has its absence not provoked even the kind of theoretical self-critique I am advocating here? Aside from the general disregard for translation in the North American academy, an answer to these questions may lie precisely in the tropic use to which many postcolonial critics *have* put the notion of "translation." For the point I am trying to develop here, it is worth reviewing such usage.

When discussing the variety of historical phenomena now referred to telegraphically as "colonialism" or "postcolonialism," a number of critics have exploited the undeniable tropic richness found within the notion of translation to raise it to a metaphorical level, to make it into a copious and comprehensive figure for the many different kinds of transformations worked by colonialism upon the colonized. One interesting example of such usage is Eric Cheyfitz's *The Poetics of Imperialism*, where he writes, "Translation was, and still is, the central act of European colonization and imperialism" (1991, 104), going on to add later in the book, "The imperialist believes that, literally, everything can be translated into his terms; indeed, that everything already exists in these terms and is only waiting to be liberated" (195). For Cheyfitz, it is clear, instead of translation being understood primarily as an instantiation of language, the colonial encounter is understood as an instantiation of translation. By now, this kind of tropic usage—there are, as will be evident from examples below, many others—has come to be so successful in interpreting the colonial and postcolonial situations through the prism of translation that Susan Bassnet and Harish Trivedi are able to remark in the introduction to their anthology on "post-colonial translation" that, "in current theoretical discourse . . . to speak of post-colonial translation is little short of a tautology" (1999, 13). It would seem, then, that to be postcolonial is quite simply to be translated; translation as trope has begun to eclipse translation as practice.

It is worth asking what makes such exploitation of the trope of translation for the representation of colonial and postcolonial phenomena possible. Surely such usage arises from an understanding of translation itself as a largely violent act, so that translation becomes the natural—*naturalized*—figure for the violence of imperialism. Such an estimation of translation lies behind Cheyfitz's argument; it also gives rise to the following claim by Anuradha Dingwaney, in the introduction to her coedited anthology (Dingwaney and Maier 1995): "Before translation can be defined as an enabling means (and methodology) for discussing cross-cultural 'Third World' texts, one must examine its potential pitfalls—the 'violence,' for instance, with which most self-conscious and thoughtful theorists and practitioners of translation associate it" (Dingwaney 1995, 3). Dingwaney goes on to note: "Translation is also the vehicle through which 'Third World' cultures (are made to) travel—transported or 'borne across' to and recuperated by audiences in the west" (3–4). Similarly in *Siting Translation*, another widely cited work commenting on translation from within a postcolonial theoretical context, Tejaswini Niranjana makes a close association between translation and the violence of colonialism, declaring that "translation as a practice shapes, and takes shape within, the asymmetrical relations of power that operate under colonialism" (1992, 2). Thus, in a certain species of postcolonial criticism, what is at issue is "the *problem* of translation," a resonant formulation that makes repeated appearances in Cheyfitz's work (see, for example, 1991, 7, 9, and 157; italics added). Translation is not primarily an opportunity or a tool of communication; it is rather a hindrance, an obstacle, a tool of miscommunication. I want to question this approach to translation and to point out its inadequacy.

However, I do not wish to be misunderstood as denying the potential for violence within translation. After all, it is precisely this translation as violence that I myself identify in the colonial discourse on caste. The elaboration of a discourse on the essential Indianness of caste during the colonial period can at least partly be seen as a violent act of translating a vernacular reality (of the varna-jati complex) into a highly simplified representation that could justify colonial structures and practices of governance. The example of caste under colonialism reminds us that a linguistic act of translation does not cease being violent because it is linguistic in nature. The linguistic translation of *varna/jati* into "caste" is one link in a chain of translations that ultimately encompasses the cultural, and indeed the civilizational—the chain takes in the vernacular reality of India and converts it into a civilizational representation thoroughly linked to colonialist theories and fantasies. It is a monstrous—but perfectly colonial—irony that subsequently some Indian nationalists (including Gandhi) were led to questionable defenses of (some of) the incontrovertibly abhorrent practices of the varna-jati complex, as if to defend the very India that the colonizers had constructed.

An analysis of caste discourse, then, suggests the validity of the contributions made by Cheyfitz, Niranjana, and Dingwaney on the question of translation. On the evidence of their work, and of others like them, it is not really contestable that all too often translation has been guilty of violence. Cheyfitz's brilliant study traces with subtlety and erudition the violence done to the indigenous populations of the United States through a process of translation. Niranjana's work has been valuable in initiating a settling of accounts with certain practices of translation under colonial conditions. And, in diverse ways, Dingwaney and many of the essays of her anthology offer a useful record of the asymmetry of power underlying all too many projects of translation.

Furthermore, in reviewing Cheyfitz, Niranjana, and Dingwaney, it would be remiss not to note that they do, albeit to varying degrees, counterpose to the notion of translation as violence a different kind of translation. Thus, when Dingwaney actually comes to discuss the practical work of translation, she arrives at a more refined conclusion than translation as violence—already hinted at when she grants that translation can be an "enabling means." Much more fitfully and infrequently, Cheyfitz and Niranjana too allude to a more positive notion of translation.[1] Clearly, so rich a phenomenon as translation does not lend itself to reductive theorization, and these three critical statements on translation are no exception.

Nevertheless, we are left finally in these works, as in much recent postcolonial theory, with a kind of shamefaced, apologetic attitude to translation—translation as problem. For the practice of translation, the consequences of this attitude—the result of a primary understanding of translation as a critical trope for colonial violence—are significant. If translation is virtually synonymous with (neo)colonial violence, how can the practical task of translation—an urgent need of our post-9/11 world, one might argue—not remain undervalued, unengaged, suspect, and rejected? And furthermore, if (as if to compound loss with more loss) the actual practice of translation now begins to appear altogether too daunting, how can translation practice ever become the kind of rich and pluralizing critical provocation that it could be, indeed should be? When the practical task of translation is engaged in a spirited and positive-minded if also cautious way (as opposed to shamefaced and reluctant), it makes available various materials for diverse kinds of scrutiny. When critics who do not themselves translate at least acknowledge the plurality and diversity of translation practice and retune their critical attitudes in the light of such an acknowledgment, the many instances of translation begin to emerge as opportunities for a wide variety of critical intervention rather than simply as "problems" to be bemoaned.

In the spirit of these preliminary remarks on postcolonial studies and translation, I propose that it is time to turn our collective critical attention to other dimensions of translation within a postcolonial context—that is, to dimensions other than the violence of colonialism/imperialism. I proceed now to three illustrative cases of translation, reviewing them for other issues than the violence of colonialism. Through these examples, which echo as well as further elaborate arguments about the vernacular, the national, and the transnational in previous chapters, I aim to pluralize our notions of translation, free translation from critical preconceptions, so that we come to recognize the potential it has to rouse a rich critical debate within postcolonial studies. I try to capture this potential in the titles to the three succeeding sections. I want, briefly, to open up new—and, as I hope will be clear from the way I proceed with the opening up, materialist—avenues in the study of translation and the colonial/postcolonial.[2] In practice, translation is more nuanced and interesting than can be captured by the notion of translation as violence. Today, cross-cultural communication would seem once again to be on the agenda in urgent ways, and a rehabilitated notion of translation should be central to critical concerns regarding the postcolonial: translation as opportunity rather than problem.

TRANSLATING MODERNITY

Perhaps there is no more convenient way to bridge the gap between theory and practice than by offering personal testimony, that is, by examining my own practice of translating into English Komal Swaminathan's *Thaneer, Thaneer* (*Water!*), the 1980 Tamil play discussed in some detail in the first chapter. As we saw, the central character of *Water!* is Vellaisamy (also known as Vellaidurai), a bonded laborer who escapes after murdering his tyrannical master. When Vellaisamy arrives in the drought-stricken village of Athipatti, he becomes the immediate reason for the transformation of the villagers from passive victims of postcolonial bureaucracy to men and women struggling to change their material environment and their lives. Early in the play, exhorting the villagers to take steps to better their condition, Vellaisamy declares: "Human beings have flattened mountains. They have cleared the forest and made it cultivable. With their two hands they have wrestled with nature and bent it to their convenience" (Swaminathan 2001, 10). The sentiment is repeated a number of times; but the note of confident exhortation in these words is belied by the action of the play, which ends on a tragic note. The villagers do successfully wrestle with nature and bend it to their convenience. Where they falter is in wrestling with their fellow human beings. They are defeated by a postcolonial government that will neither aid them nor stay out of their way as they aid themselves.

Translating *Water!* had its challenges. *Water!* is, I argued in chapter 1, a socialist realist play exploring notions of struggle and solidarity in the context of the radical seventies.[3] I also proposed that we think of the play's aesthetic as simultaneously shaped by a kind of vernacular realism. When it came to the task of translation, this aspect of its aesthetic raised particular concerns, for translating the play involved an encounter with a variety of Tamil dialects and idioms, some of them drawn from vernacular traditions. In the third scene of the play, for example, when one of the characters, Sevanthi, gives food to the schoolteacher Vaithilingam and to Vellaisamy, who has just arrived in the village, Vaithilingam asks her whether she has remembered to add salt, and Sevanthi replies that of course she has. Constrained by the particular nature of this reference (the way it is presented in the dialogue), I found it impossible to capture directly in an English translation the connotative significations of salt in Tamil culture, its association with concepts of community and loyalty and belonging. Instead I had recourse to a prefatory comment on these meanings.[4] Another such moment of special challenge was when *vakarisi*, rice placed in the mouth of a dead body before cremation, is referred to in an expression of courage (64). In this case, a literal fidelity to the original could be eschewed and the English bent to accommodate a meaning not natural to it. Each of these moments—and there were others like them—raised different questions of interpretation and required different strategies of translation, some more effective than others, some less violent than others.

These are familiar challenges, and no doubt familiar solutions, for practicing translators. In a memorable phrase Andre Lefevere calls translators "artisans of compromise" (1992, 6). The phrase suggests the possibilities within translation, how a combination of art, craft, and labor can often arrive at more or less adequate solutions to the challenges of translation. If the challenges of translation are many, so are the solutions. I would like to suggest that the test for the good translation cannot be whether each and every challenge has been successfully *overcome* but rather whether the challenge of the *text as a whole* has been *adequately* met.

As is often the case in such matters, the difference in attitudes toward translation I am pointing out is mainly a case of critical emphasis, which is not to say, however, that the difference is inconsequential. Significant issues lie buried within this difference: to subscribe to one view of translation (that it is mainly a matter of attacking the original word by word, sentence by sentence, rather than meeting the work as a whole in a spirit of practical accommodation) is to be left with a particular (inflated) expectation of translation. Consequently, translation cannot appear as anything other than a disappointment, a violation, a violence. I am interested in unearthing these buried issues, in bringing them forward for critical scrutiny, so that our understanding of translation is augmented and we are enabled to recognize its utility, as practice as well as provocation for critical conversation, for the study of the colonial and the postcolonial.

The examples from *Water!* provided above bring us to aspects of translation that seem to me to be of special interest in the postcolonial context. Crucial to the language in the play as a whole—this was made more and more clear as I went about translating it—is the complex interplay between different idioms of expression. The village of Athipatti is a space within which these idioms are to be found sometimes collaborating, sometimes conflicting. Accordingly the language of the play too is shot through with these collaborations and conflicts. The lives of the villagers of Athipatti are articulated not only in the vernacular idiom referred to above (salt, rice in the mouth of a dead body) but also in an idiom quite different in its associations (for example, that of liberal nationalism or radical communism). Such values as "struggle" and "courage" are presented in the play not only according to notions drawn from ritual practice and social custom peculiar to Tamils or to Hinduism but also according to those drawn from liberalism and communism—in other words, the play is, at least partly, a web of meaning composed of the interaction of such different idioms of expression.

As must be clear from the examples presented above, in translating this web of meaning the greatest challenge is posed by what one might call the vernacular idiom. Details belonging to the vernacular cultural idiom offered the greatest difficulty in translating *Water!* In other parts of the play, where a different idiom, drawn for example from liberalism or the Marxist tradition, makes its appearance, translation proved relatively easy. Equivalents in English were easier to find. It was most often the vernacular that I needed to supplement for the reader of the translation by providing the annotative machinery of a parenthetical interruption, a glossary, a footnote, or a comment in the preface, or by eschewing notions of literal fidelity as thoroughly as permissible by what I have referred to as the translation principle of *meeting* the challenge posed by the text as a whole.

This difference in translatability between the vernacular on the one hand and notions of liberalism and communism on the other is not, it seems to me, unrelated to what conventionally gets figured as the opposition between "tradition" and "modernity"—in other words, the difference between tradition and modernity can also be figured as a difference in translatability. Modernity lends itself to easy translation; tradition resists it in a variety of ways. One conclusion—about the implied "universality" of modernity—would seem to follow from this observation. Is it not because of the universalizing abstractions inherent in it that the idiom of modernity is easier to translate? On the other side from such a modernity is the vernacular particularity of tradition, which seems not so amenable to transference across linguistic boundaries. By describing modernity as a universalizing abstraction I mean only that its semantics have been injected into a variety of contexts so that, unlike tradition, it is not found constrained to one alone. It is perhaps best to think of "modernity," then, as "modular" in the sense that the conventions of thought and practice associated with it are now to be found shared in some general sense across the globe in a variety of social spaces. I identify this modularity when I refer to a *universalizing abstraction*.

Now, if modernity can be modular in this fashion it is only because of myriad particular instances of translation. If, to turn to particular examples from the play, I find it easier to translate *puratchi* as "revolution" or *therthal* as "election" than some "traditional" element, it is no doubt because my act of translating from Tamil into English has been preceded by decades of a translation practice (often gradual, collective, anonymous, oral, and anticolonial) going in the opposite direction.[5] Because many preceding acts of translation from English (as the colonial language as well as the lingua franca of the colony) into Tamil since the introduction of "modern" thought into Tamil India have made *puratchi* the Tamil cognate for "revolution" and *therthal* for "election," my own translation is made easier.

In general, the field of translation studies undervalues the significance of gradual, collective, anonymous, and oral translation (that is, the translation that happens as part of the social encounter between languages—in bus-stop conversation, over the dinner table, at a political meeting). Part of the difficulty here is precisely that such translation is gradual (its effects take years, perhaps generations, to become visible), collective (the translation practice has multiple participants), anonymous (the identity of participants is not a matter of record), and oral (the translation takes place at a distance from such putatively preservative discursive technologies as writing and film). For these reasons, such translation—let us call it social translation—is difficult to study. It is available to critical scrutiny only as the history of a language, which very fact would seem to indicate that when it comes to the general phenomenon of translation this form may well be more significant than the specifically literary, where typically an individual translator sits down to author a version of a renowned work in another language. Woven into the very fabric of a language, social translation requires the adoption of a form of critical inquiry far different from the kind found in analyses of the translation of, say, a French literary work into German (the subject of Walter Benjamin's seminal essay on translation).[6]

At the same time, it cannot be a matter for debate that literary translation—the kind, in other words, critics are prone to study—is intimately connected to social translation, for the individual translator will bring all resources, collective as well as individual, at her disposal to bear on the text being translated. No act of translation takes place in a manner hermetically sealed from the historical presence of language. Despite this elementary truth, translation is often theorized as if the social dimension were of no consequence. Because the social dimension is neglected when discussing translation, the act of translation itself begins to appear more intractable and mysterious than it truly is. It becomes hard to recognize that what might appear untranslatable at a certain time at a certain place to a particular translator might become amenable to translation over a period of time as languages share, struggle, adjust to one another, dominate one another, educate one another, through the processes of social translation. What is often a historically contingent difficulty becomes construed as an extrahistorical, natural impossibility inherent in language.[7] It should be the task of a materialist criticism to counter such obfuscation of translation.

The import of the general point about translation being developed here for my argument about postcolonialism and modernity is, I believe, self-evident. It is not because "modernity" has some *essential* abstract characteristic, I would now like to propose, that it is more easily translatable. Rather, it is because it has been translated again and again in one direction—through colonial processes, no doubt—that it now allows itself to be translated more easily than "tradition" in the opposite. In fact, it would now seem that the universally abstract appearance of modernity is really an effect of such instances of translation. The point may be captured aphoristically in the following way: if modernity enables translation now, it is because once translation enabled modernity. If modernity's aspiration to universal status enables translation, translation itself must certainly have been an enabling means for modernity—it is through myriad acts of translation that the concepts and usages of modernity must have spread around the globe.

I hope this brief discussion is enough to suggest the ways in which translation has the potential to illuminate the nature of modernity in colonial and postcolonial situations and, further, modernity in general.[8] While translation is not unique to the modern era, my examples above would seem to demonstrate that translation has enjoyed a specific relationship to modernity. Now a mutually reinforcing relationship obtains between modernity and translation. Today the untranslatable might very well be the premodern, the nonmodern, or the vernacular, though my argument also suggests that some of what appears untranslatable today could cease to be so tomorrow as acts of social translation contribute collectively to the project of intercultural communication.

Finally, these ways of thinking about "modernity" and "tradition" are available to us only when translation is understood as the multifarious and contradictory phenomenon it is.[9] If translation is always foregrounded as an act of violence, if it is always thought of as an individual rather than a social practice, the potential of translation to provoke a rich critical conversation remains unrealized.

TRANSLATING NATIONHOOD

The multifariousness and contradictoriness of translation are also illustrated by my second example, the 1992 film *Roja*, directed by Mani Ratnam and originally made in Tamil and then dubbed into Hindi—that is, not reshot for a Hindi-speaking audience. The fact that *Roja* was *not* reshot and that the dialogue of the film was merely translated from Tamil into Hindi placed the film's narrative under particular pressures, as I will explain below.

Roja, one of the biggest film hits of the nineties and often referred to as the first of Mani Ratnam's "terrorism" trilogy (the other two being *Bombay* [1995] and *Dil Se* [*From the Heart;* 1998]), concerns the turmoil in Kashmir. In the original Tamil version, the story tells of Rishi, a Tamil computer software engineer employed by the Indian government as a cryptologist, and his new wife, Roja, whom he meets on a visit to a village and then brings back to Chennai (Madras). This opening—in which a sophisticated, urban man woos and marries an innocent "girl," who is then transported to an alien, modern world—is reminiscent of other Tamil-language Mani Ratnam films such as *Mouna Raagam* (*Silent Melody;* 1986) and *Bombay*. It suggests the peculiarly gendered nature of Ratnam's imagination of the vernacular, with which the "girl" is invariably associated. In the film, soon after

Roja's marriage to Rishi, Rishi is sent to Kashmir on an assignment, and Roja, a village woman who knows only Tamil, accompanies him. The trip is to be their improbable honeymoon. In Kashmir Rishi is abducted by Kashmiri separatists and Roja is left to cajole and browbeat the Indian authorities into trying to free her husband. Her husband is indeed freed at the end, but only after many difficulties (which ultimately raise questions about the Indian state's efficacy).

Because of its provocative subject matter and its extraordinary success at the box office, *Roja* came in for sustained scholarly attention soon after its release, much of it concerning the Hindi version, though the movie was dubbed into other languages as well. In an important critique of the film in its Hindi avatar, Tejaswini Niranjana (1994) noted the disquieting nature of its depiction of Muslims and the Kashmir "problem." She located the film's success in its disavowal of the efficacy of the state and a foregrounding of the technocratic middle-class hero as personified by Rishi. Responding to Niranjana, Venkatesh Chakravarthy and M. S. S. Pandian (1994), working, it would seem, with the Tamil version (their essay is not clear on this point), claimed rather that the film affirmed a repressive state in a disguised way. In a subsequent piece, Rustom Bharucha (1994) was even more damning than either previous essay; he found in the film an ideology that bordered on fascism. Finally, in a critical intervention that took into account all three of these essays, Nicholas Dirks argued that *Roja* belonged to a type of misogynistic melodrama and revealed the limits of this genre (2001b, 182). The scholarly response, then, has been diverse, though in all this diversity there has generally been consensus about the highly problematic nature of the film. It is not difficult to accept this consensus, for *Roja* is indeed deplorable in its reductive approach to the crisis in Kashmir. However, some further nuance is introduced into the debate through attention to an aspect of the *Roja* phenomenon these essays frequently mention but leave unexplored—the differences between the various linguistic versions of the film.

Counter to the critical commentary reviewed, the "original" *Roja*—the Tamil *Roja*—is best read in the light of Mani Ratnam's ongoing preoccupation in many of his movies, often explored through displaced characters, with the place of Tamil-ness within a larger national Indian identity. In an early film such as *Mouna Raagam* (*Silent Melody*), for example, the protagonist marries and brings his new wife to Delhi, where she, like Roja in Kashmir, initially finds herself at a loss; in *Nayakan* (*Hero*; 1987), set in the Mumbai slums, a don, vividly marked as Tamil by attire and accent and behavior, must fight for his place in the underworld far from his Tamil homeland; and in *Bombay*, a Tamil couple—the husband Hindu, the wife Muslim—gets caught up in the communalist riots that erupted in Mumbai (then Bombay) in 1993, following the destruction of the Babri Mosque by Hindu fundamentalists.

In all these movies, Tamil characters are placed in non-Tamil cities, where they struggle to make a place for themselves. In these movies, non-Tamil India can be both threatening and a place of escape. At the end of *Mouna Raagam* (*Silent Melody*), the couple, finally reconciled to each other, remain in Delhi. There is no return to Tamil country. And while *Bombay* concludes with the horrifying violence of the riots in the western Indian metropolis, it includes scenes depicting the religious prejudice prevalent in the Tamil village from which the lovers are forced to flee in order to be able to marry each other. In Ratnam's films, then, there is nuance in the presentation of an opposition between Tamil-ness and a larger Indian identity. Without denying these shades of filmic meaning, I want to resort to the bare fact of the opposition itself in offering my reading of *Roja* in the context of my argument about translation. In some ways, the contrast draws on Tamil chauvinism and cultural pride; yet what keeps these filmic narratives interesting is their reluctance to rest within such chauvinism. Ratnam's purpose is more complex than can be illuminated by a simple identification of prejudice.

In different versions of *Roja*, including the Tamil, Ratnam's main concern seems to be the fraught politics of Kashmir and Hindu-Muslim relations. As the critical discourse reviewed above testifies, *Roja* is deeply problematic for its depiction of Muslims and its deliberate manipulation of nationalist ideology. Niranjana observes (she is discussing the Hindi mainly, though she refers also to the Telugu version), "This is surely a phenomenon—a box-office hit (in urban markets, at least) film that evokes from its audience not whistles and comments on the heroine but displays of 'nationalistic' fervour" (1994, 79). Niranjana goes on to argue persuasively that in *Roja* Ratnam successfully brings a populist patriotism to an urban, middle-class audience that he previously cultivated through films made according to the conventions of "middle cinema" (a cinema straddling the commercial/art divide). In a pivotal sequence of the film, Niranjana points out, one of Rishi's abductors sets fire to an Indian flag, prompting Rishi to leap forward to douse the flames with his own body.[10] The soft-spoken software engineer Rishi, the scene makes clear, is also an uncompromising nationalist. Thus the middle-class audience is led to recognize itself in him and is left in little doubt about whom to side with in the conflict between Rishi and his abductors. Niranjana's assessment of the politics of the Hindi version of *Roja* is certainly convincing; but when it comes to the Tamil version, I would like to suggest that her critique bears some reexamination. Though the Tamil version remains deeply problematic, its edifice of "'nationalistic' fervour" shows a few cracks not apparent in the Hindi version. Not surprisingly, to explore this difference requires us to turn to the question of translation.

As noted above, Ratnam did not reshoot *Roja* when preparing it for the Hindi market. Nevertheless, a number of significant—even crucial—changes were introduced into the Hindi version. The most important change is this: against all evidence of geography and common sense, the Hindi version transfers the location of Rishi's hometown—the town in which he lives and to which he brings Roja after he marries her—from Chennai (then Madras) to Meerut (that is, from a coastal city in the South to an interior town in the very heart of the Hindi belt). Against all the visual evidence on the screen (dress, houses, customs and mores, bodily morphology of the characters) the pretence is maintained that this is a movie about North Indians. Roja now is made into a woman whose first language is not Tamil but Hindi. It is worth remembering that similar changes were introduced when R. K. Narayan's novel *The Guide* was turned into the Hindi movie *Guide*. As discussed in Chapter 3, a clue to the particular conception of the national in Hindi-language Bollywood films is discernible here.

In the context of these changes, another pivotal sequence of *Roja* allows us to ask whether an alternative approach to the ideological content of the film is not possible. I would propose that this sequence is as important as the flag-burning scene, which has come in for so much critical commentary. In this sequence Roja, immediately following the frightening abduction of her husband, first runs down a road crying out and then proceeds to an Indian army camp to ask for help. The differences between the Hindi and Tamil versions of the film to which I am drawing attention are well illustrated by a comparison of the scenes in the army camp as they appear in the two versions. In the original Tamil version, Roja is unable to get immediate help because she can speak only Tamil and therefore cannot make herself understood to the Indian soldiers and officials, who speak Hindi. Officials remark in Hindi that they are unable to understand Roja because she is speaking in "Madrasi" (a common North Indian misnaming of Tamil), and they call for someone who can. Through the remainder of the Tamil version of the film, a Tamil man whom Roja encounters in Kashmir acts as her helpful interpreter. In her later encounter with a minister of the central government, Roja says in Tamil (more for the benefit of the audience than for the minister, who after all cannot understand her), "I don't understand this language," meaning Hindi.

As can be imagined, these moments of linguistic incomprehension (there are others) come under particular pressure in the Hindi version of the film. If in the Hindi version Roja's mother tongue is Hindi, the notion that she cannot make herself understood becomes absurd. Yet the unchanged—unreshot—visual material of the sequence in the army camp immediately after the abduction continues to depict a distraught Roja unable to make herself understood. What to do about this radical disjuncture between image and dialogue? How to tackle the contradiction created by this selective act of translation? The filmmakers solve the problem by implying that the first officials Roja encounters either speak in a highly marked dialect of Hindi different from her standard Hindi or are so indifferent to her pleas that even though she knows Hindi she cannot successfully communicate to them what has happened. Similar ruses become necessary in other scenes where Roja has to interact with Hindi-speaking officials. Repeatedly, through such changes, the vital difference of language (and history and culture) that separates Roja from the Hindi-speaking Indian authorities in Kashmir in the Tamil version is reduced to a far more trivial separation arising simply out of personal circumstance.[11] Dubbing in cinema—or, in other words, translation of the spoken portion of the film—is different from literary translation because of the presence of the visual image, against which the meaning of the words being spoken is continually tested. Abé Mark Nornes has provided a comprehensive introduction to the vexatious issues surrounding cinematic translation practices, noting the multiple ways in which the aesthetic vision of the source text can be marred by both dubbing and subtitling (2007). In the particular case of *Roja*, the problem of cinematic translation is compounded by the decision of the filmmakers to make as radical a change as transforming—"translating" in the tropic sense, if you will—the identities of the two central characters into North Indians and making their hometown Meerut rather than Madras (so that in one scene landlocked Meerut has an expansive seacoast!). The Tamil village of Sundara Pandiya Puram in Thirunelveli becomes the village of Sunder Bhan Pur in Chandrapore Zilla. Even the gods get translated. The deity in the temple near Sunder Bhan Pur is now Mumba Devi, not Muthalamman.

I would like to speculate that these astounding changes are made—against all on-screen visual evidence—because the filmmakers believe both that the spoken language of the film has priority over the visual medium (that, counterintuitive as it might seem, the sound of the spoken language that viewers of the film will hear has a greater claim on the characters than the visual context within which the characters are presented) and that Hindi inevitably implies a national subjectivity, which demands in its turn corresponding North Indian characters and geographical location. Given the stupendous box-office success of the Hindi version, it would appear the filmmakers were right in making this assessment of their audience.

Finally, however, the motives suggested above for these absurd-seeming changes in the Hindi version can only be speculation, for who can know the true beliefs of the filmmakers? What can be said without speculation is that the Hindi version of *Roja* is profoundly different from—even in some respects opposed to—the Tamil version. Both versions are problematic nationalist statements in the context of what the film understands as Kashmiri subnationalism. But problematic as both versions are in this respect, the Tamil version is subtler than the Hindi. In the Tamil version, Kashmiri subnationalism is contrasted to another subnational Indian identity—Tamil. It is precisely this Tamil subnational identity that becomes legible—or, more precisely, audible—to filmgoers in the sequence discussed above, in which Roja is unable to make herself understood by Hindi speakers. The very trajectory of the Tamil version of the film, which begins in the placid and highly romanticized surroundings of Roja's original Tamil village and ends in strife-torn Kashmir, serves to underscore this contrast between Kashmiri and Tamil identities and then to contrast both with a national Indian identity associated with Hindi.

These multiple contrasts among Kashmiri, Muslim, Tamil, Hindu, and Indian identities lend themselves simultaneously to two different readings of the Tamil version of *Roja*. First, it is possible to read the disjunctions as articulating a difference between a model and loyal (Hindu Tamil) minority and a violent and treacherous (Muslim Kashmiri) one. This reading is enabled most especially through the character of Rishi in such episodes as the struggle over the burning Indian flag. In these scenes, Tamil though Rishi is, he is also demonstrably patriotic—using his very body to douse the flames consuming the flag. However, an alternative reading too is possible, in which the contrasts would seem to be not so much between Muslim Kashmiri on the one hand and Hindu Tamil on the other as between these two minority identities taken together against, on the opposite side, a national Indian identity premised linguistically on Hindi and geographically and culturally on the Gangetic plain in North India (where the Meerut of the Hindi version is located). This reading would focus on the character of Roja and on such scenes as her behavior immediately after the abduction of Rishi.[12] It would note that Tamil identity, albeit Hindu, appears as foreign and incomprehensible to a national state apparatus identified linguistically with Hindi as a Kashmiri Muslim identity. It might also note that gender is crucial in this respect—it cannot be accidental that it is the female Roja (romanticized in highly stereotypical ways and made into a contrast to her two male counterparts, her husband and the male leader of the Kashmiri separatists) who becomes the bearer of this foreign and incomprehensible Tamil-ness. It is as if, in a manner much examined by historians, women were the bearers of all that is authentically traditional (in this case, Tamil).[13] Thus a reading focusing on Roja (who is after all the title character) would make of the Tamil version of the film a more intricate text than the Hindi version.

As noted above, critics do refer fleetingly to the possibility that other versions of *Roja* are more ambiguous in their articulations than the Hindi version, though this observation does not motivate them to explore the ambiguity; what enables a more thoroughgoing engagement with these differences among the various versions of the film is an appreciation of the theoretical terrain opened up by a serious consideration of translation.[14] With translation in mind, the clues to the differences I am identifying in comparing the Hindi and Tamil versions are not difficult to find—in fact, they are present even in the flag-burning scene, a scene with whose analysis by Niranjana, Bharucha, and Dirks I am largely in agreement. In both Hindi and Tamil versions of this scene, Ratnam uses as background score a song that appears in the Tamil version as "Thamizha, Thamizha" (O You Tamil!).[15] In the Hindi version, though, the opening invocation of the Tamil people is dropped and an abbreviated translation of the lyrics, presenting only a nationalist celebration of India, is used. Lines referring to Tamils appear nowhere in the Hindi version. This excision is of course the predetermined result of the identitarian difference between the two versions of *Roja* under discussion—in other words, it is the result of the difference brought into being by the translation of the location of the narrative from South India to North. Once the identities of the characters themselves have been translated from Tamil-speaking South

Indians to Hindi-speaking North Indians, the celebratory invocation of Tamil people can have no place in the film. It would surely make no sense for Tamils to be addressed in a film from which Tamils have been exiled.

As the excision of the lines referring to Tamils from the song as well as other details discussed above show, translating *Roja* produces a specific ideological effect. The song as it appears in the Tamil version of *Roja* is certainly nationalist—from the opening invocation of the Tamil people, it proceeds to a celebration of a single Indian nation to which Tamils are seen as belonging. The song makes nationalist sentiments fully available to the viewers of the Tamil version of the movie. Yet there is also in the presentation of the song a certain ambiguity—a certain contrary semantic pull that I have already identified as present in the audiovisual text of the film as a whole. Even as the viewer is invited to declare allegiance to India, a counterallegiance to Tamil-ness is exposed. In the Hindi version of the song, this ideological ambiguity is erased by the excision of the lines invoking the Tamil people. On the evidence of the Tamil version, then, it would seem that for a Tamil person, no matter how patriotic, the assertion of a nationalist sentiment is conflicted. For such a person, allegiance to India is continually in negotiation with allegiance to Tamil Nadu, which too is capable of being the vehicle for nationalist sentiment. For those identified with Hindi, on the other hand, this dual loyalty seems not to be present; in the case of *Roja* at least, their relationship to nationhood would seem to be considerably simplified.

A deep and ambiguous history, allowed only a partial though potent presence, undergirds the (vernacular) Tamil version of *Roja*, and it is this historical ambiguity that is lost in the translation to (national) Hindi. It is instructive to review this loss in some detail. The history I am referring to erupts into the narrative of the Tamil version of the film through the question of language: that is, through the circumstance of Roja's inability to speak Hindi. The importance of language politics in the formation of a modern Tamil identity is well known, as is the opposition to Hindi that was a constitutive feature of this politics through much of the twentieth century. As A. R. Venkatachalapathy observes concerning Periyar E. V. Ramasamy's attitude toward the movement to preserve Tamil against Sanskrit and Hindi during the crucial decades of the thirties and the forties, "The struggle . . . pertained not only to certain aspects of language, but was closely tied to the forging of a new identity based largely on language" (2006, 155).[16]

In *Passions of the Tongue*, her study of devotion to language in modern Tamil India, Sumathi Ramaswamy identifies four "regimes of imagination—'the religious,' the 'classicist,' the 'Indianist,' and the 'Dravidianist,'" in which "Tamil is variously conceived as a divine tongue, favored by the gods themselves; as a classical language, the harbinger of 'civilization'; as a mother tongue that enables participation in the Indian nation; and as a mother/tongue that is the essence of a nation of Tamil speakers in and of themselves" (1997, 23). Of these four regimes, the Indianist and the Dravidianist are explicitly political in that they are linked directly to a contest over territory and state formation. Each imagines the nation in its particular way, but where the Indianist is primarily anticolonial, the Dravidianist is primarily separatist (from any notion of "India") and anticaste. Dravidianism did after independence progressively moderate its antagonism to the Indian nation. Simultaneously, it remained devoted to an exceptionalist notion of Dravidian identity and of the Tamil language to which this identity was intimately connected. Indeed, devotion to the Tamil language, Ramaswamy's argument makes clear, was crucial to Dravidianism's successful conquest and retention of political power within Tamil India from the midsixties, since which time two Dravidianist parties, as I have noted in a previous chapter, have shut out the Indianist Congress Party from power and traded control over the state of Tamil Nadu. Dravidianism has achieved this conquest of power by presenting itself to varying degrees as a viable alternative to an Indianism that would ultimately dissolve Tamil identity into a national Indian identity.

The Tamil version of *Roja* presents this history of contestation between Dravidianism and Indianism within Tamil India in a coded form. The film is finally an Indianist narrative—it affirms the importance of an Indian identity. Nevertheless, it acknowledges the difficulties accompanying such an affirmation for a modern Tamil person. The incomprehensibility of Roja's Tamil pleas on behalf of her abducted husband when addressed to Hindi-speaking functionaries of the Indian state in Kashmir has a peculiar emotive power that goes beyond the merely individual and psychological when viewed from within the context of the modern devotion to the Tamil language. Roja's fruitless pleas activate a profoundly affecting history for a Tamil viewer and fracture the neat facade of national unity that the film otherwise endeavors to maintain.

All this historical complexity—present in disavowed and submerged but still potent form in the Tamil version—is lost in the translation of

Roja into its Hindi version, which attempts against all conventions of realism and common sense to erase signs of Tamil identity—with its own history of subnational separatism, we can now note—from the text of the film to leave only a stark contrast between Kashmiri separatism and Hindi-speaking Indianness. Problematic as it ultimately is in its approach to the Kashmir question, the Tamil version is more subtle in its evocation of the history of Indian nationalism. In the renarrativization of Roja's predicament as individual trauma and circumstantial failure, historical and cultural shadings are erased from the Hindi version of the film. A banal and oppressive notion of Indian identity is consolidated through the sacrifice of historical nuance. Since dominant formulations of Tamil identity during the modern period have found themselves at odds with a national Indian identity, for a Tamil viewer of the Tamil version of *Roja* (it would hardly matter whether the viewer were sympathetic to such formulations or not) the history of this tension would tend to amplify the ambiguities of the cinematic text. Alternatively, Hindi-language cinema's privileged relationship to the postcolonial project of nation building, where it has both benefited from the cultural policy of the postcolonial state and participated in the project, abets, perhaps even compels, the peculiar translation practice of the filmmakers.[17]

As I noted in chapter 2 in discussing *Guide*, film criticism has not generally pressed the distinction I have tried to keep alive between the national and the vernacular. The differences between the two versions of *Roja* (Hindi and Tamil), whether intentional or not, can be understood as corresponding to the differences between nationalist and vernacularist tendencies within postcolonial Tamil India—the differences between what Sumathi Ramaswamy calls the Indianist and Dravidianist projects of modern Tamil identity formation. Of course, my point has been to argue that the differences *between* the two versions of *Roja* are also immanent *within* each version, albeit in different ways, as a tension between Tamil-ness and Indian nationhood. In this respect *Roja* is typical of Mani Ratnam's oeuvre in general. As noted above, many Ratnam films explore the differences between Tamil India and the rest of India (especially North). Sometimes these differences are brought out narratively; at other times they remain mere suggestions, indicated through location. *Mouna Raagam* (*Silent Melody*), *Nayakan* (*Hero*), *Bombay*—all three of these key movies from the Ratnam canon cited above evidence a tension between the Tamil and the Indian, or between the vernacular and the national. With regard to *Roja*, what should be provocative to translation studies is the manner in which an act of translation (an act of translating nationhood) both exposes and glosses over these tensions.

The example of *Roja* also reinforces a point well understood in translation studies—it is not possible to translate a text without translating the cultural system of which the text is a part. Typically, translators endeavor—which is not to say that they succeed—to translate a text as wholly as possible, however the idea of the whole is understood. Their purpose is to convey the text, as well as the place the text has in the source culture, as fully as they are able. In such cases, translation is approached as an instrument of communication—as a valuable aid to intercultural contact. Yet the case of *Roja* demonstrates that translation can be used, not to communicate or make contact, but to alienate the text from its source culture and to relocate it within a new one, to pluck it from one aesthetic system (Tamil-language popular cinema) and thrust it into another (Bollywood, or Hindi-language popular cinema). In such cases translation becomes a deliberate technology of othering—of excising the foreign, the alien, the other from the text so that it can be accommodated to new social, political, and aesthetic contexts. No doubt, the two versions of *Roja* taken together provide an extreme example of such a translation practice. All the same, as postcolonial translation studies has understood all too well, the potential for such othering is always present within translation. Postcolonial translation studies has generally found this potential for othering within colonial or neocolonial situations; however, the translation practice manifested in the Hindi version of *Roja* takes place within a postcolonial one.

Translation is an unavoidable phenomenon in the cultural lives of multilingual postcolonial nations such as India. As Rukmini Bhaya Nair notes, "'India' itself is a concept that presupposes the act of translation" (2002, 7). Translation is the vehicle through which the different regions of India speak to one another. It is what makes the different parts of India intelligible to one another. It would not be an exaggeration to say that without translation there is no India (just as there is no "modernity"). In this context, it is worth considering whether intranational translation is not a more socially and politically significant phenomenon in contemporary India than international translation (that is, translation of Indian materials for an international audience). While this question (whether international or intranational translation is more important) is more easily posed rhetorically than answered in an empirically verifiable way, it does illustrate a glaring omission in postcolonial translation studies. Postcolonial theory has had something to say about the global trade in translation and how it has all too often generated a deficit for postcolonial societies. In contrast, it has said much less about intranational translation—here too we find evidence for the bias toward transnational postcolonialism in postcolonial theory. Whereas we customarily speak, as we saw at the beginning of this chapter, of the violence that is possible in the global trade in translation, the example of *Roja* would seem to suggest such violence can emerge in intranational translation as well.

Translation is a profoundly social act even as it is an individual practice. Translation studies today should recognize how the paradoxes of translation are visible within an individual translated text to the discerning eye. If the translation practice that produced the Hindi version of *Roja* works to erase ambiguities, a robust critical appreciation of translation as contradictory and various—both enabling and violent, both a technology of communication and a technology of othering, both a social and an individual phenomenon—can help reverse the erasure. It can help us figure the contradictions from which this particular translation practice emerged and that it tries violently, if only partially successfully, to eradicate. Accordingly, not only will our appreciation of translation practice be enriched, but our understanding of the social context within which a particular act of translation takes place will be augmented.

TRANSLATING THE WORLD

Multifarious as translation practice is, it possesses (most translators and translation theorists would seem to agree) a peculiar power to transform that which it touches. At the most obvious level, translation makes an idea, a sentiment, an attitude more widely available. If one believes such wider dissemination is valuable, one might conclude translation itself to be valuable. At the same time, a crucial question needs to be asked: What exactly happens during the process of translation? As the postcolonial critics reviewed at the beginning of this chapter as well as the case of *Roja* attest, the process of transferring a source from one language to another can all too easily become violation. This aspect of translation, especially evident when translation takes place under difficult social conditions, rightfully gives many commentators pause. However, even those skeptical of translation—those for whom translation is problem rather than opportunity—would seem to have a keen sense of translation's *power*. If not, what need could there be to attack translation so vehemently?

Within the domain of culture narrowly construed—the world of books and films and theater—the power of translation appears as the very power of consecration (to recall Casanova 2004, 133); for in such a domain the wide dissemination of a poem or a novel into as many languages as possible is generally regarded as a good, and translation is the indispensable vehicle for the attainment of this good. Furthermore, translation is a powerful means of canonizing a work. The moment a novel is translated, and the more it is translated, it becomes transformed within the source culture. It acquires prestige. Its accession to the canon of great literature in the source language is facilitated. At the same time, it becomes available for canonization (not the same as actually achieving such canonization) in another realm, under a rubric such as "national literature" or "world literature." It takes its place alongside other specimens of national or world literature and is now present for comparison so that it may achieve consecration. Such is the power of translation, existing in a reciprocal relationship with the fame of the original. Thus, in "The Task of the Translator," Walter Benjamin writes:

> The history of the great works of art tells us about their antecedents, their realization in the age of the artist, their potentially eternal afterlife in succeeding generations. Where this last manifests itself, it is called fame. Translations that are more than transmissions of subject matter come into being when in the course of its survival a work has reached the age of its fame. Contrary, therefore, to the claims of bad translators, such translations do not so much serve the work as owe their existence to it. The life of the originals attains in them to its ever-renewed latest and most abundant flowering. (1969, 17)

Translated texts are emanations of the original (it does not do to think of them as serving the original) that emerge out of the profound and achieved *value* of the original.

It would be a mistake to hold the prospect of accession to world literature through translation an undiluted good. What appears to be consecration can also become violation. Often enough, especially in the case of languages in a relatively weak status in the domain of world culture, only work fitting preconceived notions of what constitutes world literature or artistic merit gets translated and therefore consecrated. The translated work finds itself forced into a straitjacket of expectations. Translation becomes an unfortunate exemplification of that violence decried by Cheyfitz, Dingwaney, Niranjana, and other critics, rather than the kind of dialectical exchange between languages and works celebrated by Benjamin. Sometimes, then, it can seem better to leave a work untranslated; as Pascale Casanova notes, translation is an "ambiguous enterprise": "On the one hand, it is a means of obtaining official entry to the republic of letters; and, on the other, it is a way of systematically imposing the categories of the center upon works from the periphery, even of unilaterally deciding the meaning of such works" (2004, 154).

Casanova argues that the literary domain is in effect a global one. She traces the origin and development of a world republic of letters to late medieval Paris, when vernacular French culture wrested its autonomy from the hegemony of classical Latin influence, thereby acquiring a prestige that persists to this day. She cites the example of writers such as William Faulkner, August Strindberg, and Gao Xingjian—writers whose literary reputation was made through Paris—as evidence for the unique consecrating power of the French city. She acknowledges that the very example of Paris's revolution against Latin set the precedent for further literary secessions—this time from the influence of Paris—by other global cities. Thus London and New York have grown as rival cultural centers to Paris, though Paris continues to be the center of "the world republic of letters," with unique powers to consecrate and condemn literary productions from around the world.

Casanova rightly argues that the real life of books in the contemporary world—the elaborate processes and apparatuses of writing, influence, publishing, interpretation, careers and reputations—will remain obscured until we recognize the global arena within which books are largely conceived, produced, and consumed. Her analysis makes clear that every writer who wishes entry into the world republic of letters must now struggle against and now succumb to the structures of power—distinct from political power—peculiar to it. Casanova's argument is valuable in directing sustained attention to the notion that there is such a thing as a world republic of letters.

Yet despite her many demurrals, Casanova betrays a ferocious Eurocentrism in her argument that is most evident in the history that she traces of the emergence and consolidation of a global literary arena (Paris first, then rival European centers, then postcolonial challengers, and so on). Here is one area where a little less teleology and a lot more multipolarity would seem a good thing. Is it not possible, even likely, that a variety of centers of cultural influence emerged and competed in parallel, finding themselves dominating in some respects and dominated in others? Can it not be that the emergence of transnational cultural spheres in East Asia or North Africa or South Asia followed different trajectories before being subsumed into a world republic of letters that they also in fact helped create? Is it inconceivable that Chennai as the center of the Tamil cultural sphere, with its own resented power of consecration over adjoining areas, was and is able to use its power to sometimes resist the power of New Delhi and Paris and London, even if at other times it succumbs? And is it not possible to regard as evidence of the consecrating power that the United States exercised over Paris the way in which post-1968 French thought (deconstruction as well as other philosophical strands) was taken up and validated in the United States during the seventies and eighties?

I ask these questions to suggest all that Casanova's book leaves out. The answers to them are beyond the scope of my own argument. The world republic of letters is not in itself my concern in this book; but, as a counterpoint, Casanova's notion of a world republic of letters has relevance to my inquiry into the nature of the vernacular in a postcolonial context. As a species of thought privileging the transnational, Casanova's argument marks a point of opposition to the vernacular within a heuristic schema that includes both. What is unpersuasive about Casanova's otherwise provocative argument is the extent to which she underestimates the potency of the life-world—the sensibility, the referential frame, the practical context—that I am dubbing the vernacular. To write a credible history of the world republic of letters would require a genuine engagement with vernacular literary traditions that go beyond the largely Europhone postcolonial and Western traditions Casanova does in fact consider. It would require a more thoroughgoing comparatism than the kind exhibited by Casanova. Were such an engagement with the vernacular and such a comparatism undertaken, a more complex and fluid view of the world republic of letters might emerge. Admittedly this is speculation on my part—call it a hunch based on my own involvements with Tamil literature and culture. Such a world republic of letters would not be without hierarchies; but the unremitting teleological Eurocentrism of Casanova would have to be rethought. A less rigid world republic of letters would become visible— one whose origins and centers might be multiple and whose flows of power and literary value might tend simultaneously in diverse and contrary directions. An account of such a world republic of letters would require the review of literary traditions in many languages (including, crucially, those not in any of the European). For this reason, it would be enormously difficult for a single individual to produce credibly.

What would remain—shared with Casanova's model—in this new sketch of a world republic of letters would be a recognition of the powerful role of translation, the main subject of this chapter. Translation plays a crucial role in the delineation of a world literature and, through such delineation, of the very notion of the "world." Indeed, world literature —I content myself with this phrasing for now, though I will argue below for the alternative "literatures of the world"—has no meaningful existence separate from the phenomenon of translation, for translation is the indispensable tool through which the various texts that might make up a list of world literature are brought together. Hence the notes on translation provided in two anthologies widely used to teach world literature in U.S. universities—the *Norton Anthology of World Literature* (Lawall and Mack 2002) and the corresponding *Longman Anthology* (Damrosch and Pike 2009). Both are multivolume and purport to provide sweeping surveys of literature from around the world. Norton is the more established of the two, Longman the more attuned to recent developments in literary studies. Curiously, Norton is the one that feels compelled to include the longer essay—many pages long—on translation. By comparison, Longman's note on translation is about a page, though this brief note informs the reader that concerns about translation structure the anthology as a whole and that, beginning with the second edition, "a new Translations feature" juxtaposing alternative translations of certain selections has been added to each volume of the anthology (2009, A:xxv).[18]

Both the Norton and Longman notes acknowledge the conundrums attendant on representing diverse traditions of literature through a language (English) in which they were not originally written. If we are not reading works in their original languages, what exactly are we reading? Both anthologies recognize the difficulty of this question. Clearly the reader of the anthologies—indeed, the *consumer*, for it will not do to forget that the anthologies are also commodities—must be persuaded of the worth of the enterprise on which he is embarked. How is this to be done?

Norton assures the reader that the core elements of much literature—that which is mostly in "referential" prose—are transferred safely in translation (A4). It ends by appealing to common sense: "Literature is to be read, and the criticism that would destroy the reader's power to make some form of contact with much of the world's great writing must indeed be blown aside" (A11). In contrast, Longman's inclination is to be preemptive in its approach to the conundrum of presenting world literature in translation. "The circulation of world literature," it declares, "is always an exercise in cultural translation, and one way to define works of world literature is that they are the works that gain in translation. Some great texts remain so intimately tied to their point of origin that they never read well abroad" (A:xxv). Here, rather than considering whether translation might be a form of violation, and thus whether the enterprise of producing an anthology of "world literature" might be suspect, a circular and weakly defined notion of translatability (what could demonstrate "gain in translation" other than the fact of translation itself?) is advanced as the very foundation of world literature. Translatability, it is suggested, is ultimately an inherent feature of some texts. It is possible to hear echoes of Benjamin here, though he sought to give a greater grounding to his notion of translatability through his claims about a pure language that underlay all languages (1969, 79). Like Norton's fallback position of finally letting the reader make "some form of contact" with "the world's great writing," Longman's note on translation gives the initial impression of being commonsensical and pragmatist. It suggests a trusting reliance on a collective enterprise of translation to clear the fog around the concept of world literature. In fact, the matter is more complicated. Consider what the note really says. As texts are translated, some gain, thereby demonstrating their own world literary merit; accordingly, world literature is naturally born. The reasoning takes no account of what exactly is meant by gain and whether what is understood as gain might have something to do with history. Though the anthology acknowledges elsewhere the historical nature of translation practice (through its "Translations feature"), the note naturalizes the notion of *translatability*. It leaves unexamined the possibility that translatability itself changes (in ways suggested in my discussion of *Water!* above) from age to age and is intimately connected to questions of power, politics, and economics. While differences in translations of the same text are given historical context, translatability as a feature of the original text remains dehistoricized.

Were we discussing only literary matters, it might be possible to take a more sanguine view of the "problem" of translation as it reappears here in the Norton and Longman anthologies—or rather, to put the matter more accurately, to be more complacent about the relative lack of its appearance. As should be clear by now, my own predilection is in fact not to dwell excessively on the "problem" of translation, or at least not to the extent that the worthwhile enterprise of cross-cultural communication is itself threatened or made into a shamefaced, albeit necessary, business. I am sympathetic, then, to a commonsensical and pragmatic attitude to translation. My caution with the approach taken by these two anthologies (the problem is more pronounced in the Norton) is with the way they handle translation, tending to separate it from social and historical processes so that it acquires more of a technical gloss.

The consequences of this approach to translation are substantial, for it is possible to aver, as I have, that there is no "world" without translation. Anthologies such as Norton and Longman are not just collections of world literary texts but also representations of the world. The "world" of countless undergraduate students in a variety of U.S. universities is partly shaped by such representations. Inevitably, readers of the anthologies, or even those browsing their contents pages, are left with a highly coded representation of the world. Translation makes such representation possible; it is a key tool in the excavation of the various cultural elements that contribute to making up a "world." Accordingly, it is right to ask questions of such representation, and therefore of translation. Has translation been a tool of valid representation or a weapon of misrepresentation? Has it been plough or sword? Translation, like other uses of language, is intimately linked to processes of power. Since anthologies such as Norton and Longman delineate not only a "world literature" but also, through such delineation, a view of the world as such, it is especially pertinent to ask whether they acknowledge these elementary facts about translation.

At the same time it is worthwhile to acknowledge another aspect of translation; not only does translation facilitate the consecration of the translated text, it makes possible a certain notion of the world to be consecrated. To put it in another way: just as much as the translated text is consecrated by its importation into a canon of world literature through translation, world literature (and by extension, the world) is consecrated by the appearance of the translation within its ranks. The latter occurrence is rarely acknowledged—Is it because it seems so self-evident?—in translation studies. It is an important outcome of translation, though here too we must admit that what may be consecration in one case could be violation in another. The accommodation of a particular translation within a canon (such as that represented by an anthology) may certainly do violence to our notion of the world—it could misconstrue the world for the reader. How this violence occurs and how it might be resisted is not a matter of translation alone but also of the contexts within which translations occur and are presented. They are a matter of politics and history. Translation is of the world, and, at the same time, it produces the world. Both aspects of translation deserve scrutiny.

A. K. Ramanujan, one of the foremost twentieth-century translators of Tamil, represented in both Norton and Longman through his rendering in English of classical Tamil poetry of the Sangam period, once observed: "A major goal of comparison is contrast. Texts from different traditions, when juxtaposed, may help define each other's uniqueness. We need not add that 'comparative literature' is probably only a tactful name for 'contrastive literature'" (1999b, 331). It is this phenomenon of mutual definition that I am calling consecration of the world. Good translation elicits such definition by enabling the juxtaposition of texts from different cultures, thereby midwifing into existence a greater whole. Ramajunan makes clear elsewhere that translation's power of enabling comparison/contrasting is exerted not only across geographical space but also across historical time: "Translation . . . participates in our dream of making out of a historical past a contemporary past, creating out of the so-called linear sequential order of history a simultaneous order, an active presence" (1999a, 189). In other words, translation's power of engendering the world is exerted along the axes of both synchrony and diachrony. Ramanujan does not go so far, but it is worth extending his observation to note that diachronic translation is not the same as synchronic.

It might also be worthwhile to pause here to reconsider objections —I have already alluded to them in a previous chapter—that might be voiced against my use of *vernacular*, for just as diachronic translation is different from synchronic, the application of the term *vernacular* along the diachronic axis is different from its application along the synchronic. Many scholars of Tamil language and literature, used to applying the term along the diachronic axis, would no doubt contest my own recourse to the term. To them, the opposition would be, not between *vernacular* and *transnational,* but rather between *vernacular* and *classical.* To many admirers of Tamil language and literature, my usage would seem unfortunate, for it would seem to do disservice to a language that can rightly claim classical status, that is, ancientness or extensiveness along the axis of diachrony. Does not my reliance on Tamil examples to advance my argument about vernacular postcolonialism run counter to the demonstrable classicality of Tamil? Does it not demote Tamil from classical nobility to vernacular destitution? Such might be the counterquestions posed.

The most obvious and important observation to be made here is that *vernacular* has multiple meanings. If *vernacular* is often opposed to *classical* in usage, it is also a rough synonym for *local* or *regional*. These two usages of *vernacular* are not in reality incompatible; they simply reveal different orientations in usage, along the axis of diachrony in one case and synchrony in the other. A classical language like Tamil, when it finds itself in the position of having to resist the transnational, might become a vernacular language. In this sense, it would be possible to use the term without damaging a language's claims to classicality. Indeed, as we have seen in the discussion of Ka Na Su's poem "Situation" in the first chapter, the traditional or the classical might even in certain cases come to be harnessed in the cause of the vernacular. It can become that through which a language or a culture attempts to defend itself against the transnational (here in the guise of the neo/colonial). If the vernacular is opposed to the classical in one register, it is opposed to the transnational in another. Between these terms and registers is a complex trading of signifying power that ultimately has its origins in historical developments.

An illustration of the need to parse carefully and keep steadily in view the different meanings of *vernacular* as well as different dimensions of translation is ready to hand in the example of that very Sangam poetry (nearly two thousand years old) referred to above. Ramanujan, A. R. Venkatachalapathy, Sumathi Ramaswamy, and other scholars have discussed the intriguing story of how Sangam poetry came to attain the status of the most canonical of classical Tamil poetry. As recently as little more than a hundred years ago, before "rediscovery" by U. V. Swaminatha Aiyar and other scholars, this great body of work was relatively neglected within Tamil literary tradition. Venkatachalapathy has described in detail how the rediscovery of this body of work was closely linked to a fresh secularizing spirit in the late nineteenth century. Where, earlier, the dominant religious orientation of Tamil literary temperament through the eighteenth century had consigned these secular works to neglect, social and political upheavals in the Tamil public sphere helped create a new context for them. Subsequently, these works were taken up and assimilated into the literary canon celebrated by the emerging Dravidianist political movements discussed in this and previous chapters, for they exemplified a Tamil aesthetic as well as socius relatively free of corrupting North Indian ("Aryan") influences. Here too, as Venkatachalapathy notes, it is clear that "the uses the new literary canon was being put to in Tamil Nadu [were] to fashion a new identity for Tamils" (2006, 103).[19]

The point of this grossly truncated intellectual history is that before these poems became available for translation by Ramanujan into English they went through a complicated process of redefinition within what I am calling the Tamil vernacular sphere, a sphere comprehensible as vernacular partly in opposition to Hindi and English. Only when their status was somewhat settled within this *vernacular* sphere, when their *classicality* was demonstrably reestablished (no paradox here), were they available to be transported out of the vernacular sphere through the process of translation. Neither Norton nor Longman discusses this complex prehistory to the elevation of these poems to the canon of "world literature." Norton, which provides the longer note to these poems, focuses exclusively on the poetics of these poems (A: 1029–31). Longman's shorter note mentions their rediscovery by U.V. Swaminatha Aiyar but leaves the politics surrounding them entirely undiscussed (A: 931). The poems appear differently as they are read as part of the canon of world literature or of the canon of Tamil literature (that is, when read in Tamil within the historical context of postcolonial Tamil India). As the poems are assimilated into the canon of world literature, they are increasingly displayed as purely aesthetic objects, rather than the densely determined classical as well as vernacular, social as well as political, documents that they are.

What conclusions pertaining to translation can we draw from these observations? Some might want to regard the differences between the appearances of these poems within Tamil and world—vernacular and transnational—literary contexts as examples of translation violence, of the violence inherent to the scene of translation. It might seem that translation can only do violence along the axes of diachrony as well as synchrony—Sangam poetry as classical literature as well as vernacular literature. I am loath to come to this conclusion. A. K. Ramanujan, the translator of these poems, was certainly aware of the vernacular history briefly reviewed above. Violation, if present, is more the outcome of the presentation of these poems within these anthologies. It is important to distinguish problems of translation from those of anthologization. Anthologization is enabled by translation but is not the same as translation understood narrowly as a linguistic act. The same translation can be presented in a variety of different ways by different anthologizers. As important as it is to scrutinize individual acts of translation, it is valuable to distinguish and scrutinize separately ancillary activities such as that of anthologizing.

In *What Is World Literature?*, David Damrosch, general editor of the Longman anthology, provides an erudite discussion of various issues connected with the idea of a world literature, including translation and anthologization.[20] Throughout the book, Damrosch emphasizes what his multivolume anthology struggles to demonstrate adequately—literary works subsist in a variety of life-worlds, and the transference of a work from one life-world to another (from the vernacular to the transnational, for example) involves questions of power. Damrosch is clear that *world literature* needs to be expanded beyond its recent Eurocentrism but acknowledges at the same time the difficulty in attempting this expansion. The result is a careful argument.

If, despite the care, there is a gap between Damrosch's *argument* for world literature in his book and his *illustration* of it in his multivolume anthology, what the gap reveals is both the difficulty of putting the argument into practice within a particular pedagogical and commercial context *and* the limits of the conclusion that Damrosch (despite his argument) reaches in *What Is World Literature?*:

> The sum total of the world's literatures can be sufficiently expressed by the blanket term "literature." The idea of world literature can usefully continue to mean a subset of the plenum of literature. I take world literature to encompass all literary works that circulate beyond their culture of origin, either in translation or in their original language (Virgil was long read in Latin in Europe). In its most expansive sense, world literature could include any work that has ever reached beyond its home base, but . . . a work only has an *effective* life as world literature whenever, and wherever, it is actively present within a literary system beyond that of its original culture (2003, 4)

and "My claim is that world literature is not an infinite, ungraspable canon of works but rather a mode of circulation and of reading, a mode that is as applicable to individual works as to bodies of material, available for reading established classics and new discoveries alike" (5). As seen in these passages, Damrosch's argument is at once refined and reductive, alert to shades of meaning and eager to exclude.

Counter to Damrosch's conclusion, I want to suggest that the proper answer to the question "What is world literature?" is *nothing*. There is and can be no such thing as world literature. As the passages quoted above show, inevitably and in the final analysis *world literature* evokes a stable and comprehensively delineated field of questions, answers, and texts—whether in Damrosch or in Franco Moretti's widely read and illuminating article "Conjectures on World Literature" (2000), with its reliance on a systemic model drawn from Immanuel Wallerstein.[21] For all the reasons explored previously, such an evocation is both untenable and dangerous, especially when consumed in the undergraduate classroom in the form of anthologies. The nature of translation as well as cross-cultural exchange indicates a world beyond capture by world literature. At the same time, there is no need to flee to the extreme opposite of this position—the kind of position Damrosch reviews in order to dissociate himself from it (see 4–6 and 24–27)—and declare the impossibility of translation or of all forms of cross-cultural and comparative study. If a systematic and comprehensive notion of a world literature is not tenable, a symptomatic and partial alternative may very well be. A middle position might, then, be the most sensible—neither world literature nor its impossibility but rather *literatures of the world*. This is the true conclusion to which the details of Damrosch's own knowledgeable argument would seem to tend.

Despite occasional gestures to the contrary, neither the Longman nor the Norton volumes can be considered as constituting an anthology of (some) literatures of the world. The preface to the Norton anthology does note that there is "no one map of world literature" but adds that the anthology "takes a different point of departure [from historicizing and deconstructive alternatives], focusing first of all on literary texts—artifacts, if you will, that have a special claim on our attention because they have been read over a great period of time and are cherished by a wide variety of readers" and concludes by making *world literature* synonymous with "great literature" (xx). Though in a more nuanced way, the preface to the Longman anthology, coauthored by Damrosch, exhibits a similar stance. While referring to "the world's literatures" and acknowledging that across the world "very different ideas about what should be called 'literature' at all" exist, the preface nevertheless asserts, "Altogether, we have worked to create an exceptionally coherent and well-integrated presentation of an extraordinary variety of works from around the globe, from the dawn of writing to the present" (xxiii). How is such a coherent and well-integrated anthology to present disjuncture and incommensurability among the literary traditions of the world? Indeed, how is it to make the historically situated nature of definitions of "literature" foundational to its presentation? Apparent in the Longman volume is the difficulty of responding to these questions within the genre of an undergraduate anthology in the context of the present pedagogical arrangements in North America. Despite alternative indications and some crucial differences in organization (the Perspectives and Crosscurrents sections, for example), it is this difficulty that causes the Longman anthology's periodization and cultural selection to echo roughly the Norton anthology—that is, to aspire to a similar comprehensiveness and systematicity, to continue a reliance on the rubric of *world literature* rather than *world literatures* or, better still, *literatures of the world*.

When approached from the vantage point of the vernacular (a critical term that does the theoretical work of locating cultural specificity as well as challenging overpowering models of globality), *world literature* begs to be revised into *literatures of the world*, for the latter formulation recognizes a global context without reifying it. What one studies under the rubric *literatures of the world* are *some* questions, answers, and texts pertaining to multiple literary traditions within a comparative as well as global context. Such study is surely partial, but partiality does not foreclose a symptomatic study—a study that reads clues to globality *and* the vernacular though a contrastive and comparative juxtapositioning of literary traditions. Because of its peculiarly potent as well as conflicted relationship to translation, the vernacular vexes the seamless production of canons of world literature through anthologization, and this too can be, and should be, made the object of study without sacrificing the ability to scrutinize concomitant forces and models of global integration. For this reason, the notion of *literatures of the world* seems to me more tenable as well as productive for pedagogy and scholarship than *world literature*.

Ultimately, translation is the indispensable link between the vernacular and that which lies outside. As my discussion in this as well as previous sections of this chapter has suggested, in its guise as a link translation touches on a variety of historical and social phenomena. Translation is, I have been at pains to repeat, a multifarious and paradoxical phenomenon—multifarious and paradoxical in the way the world is. It profits us little to take too narrow a view of translation, either to celebrate it glibly or to condemn it sweepingly. To do the former is to treat a subject that is thorny and difficult as if it were facile and transparent; to do the latter is to exaggerate the difficulties of translation to the point where they begin to foreclose any possibility of cross-cultural communication. And to do either is to abstract translation from its rightful place—in the messiness of the world. It is to miss the opportunities offered by translation to engage with a variety of historical and social phenomena related to cross-cultural communication from a matchless point of vantage. It is to misconstrue the world and to leave criticism itself poorer.

A CULTURE OF TRANSLATION

I offer the discussions of translation in relationship to "modernity," "nationhood," and "the world" (altogether brief given how much there is to say) as illustrations of the complex and critically provocative character of translation. Often enough, translation is a transnational practice, and in such cases it can be guilty of the violence Cheyfitz and Dingwaney find within it. On the other hand, violence is to be found not only when translation happens transnationally. The two versions of *Roja* discussed above—translation does not take place purely in the medium of writing—serve to remind us of the kind of violation translation can become within an *intra*national context. In the pursuit of a monolithic national subjectivity, the Hindi version of *Roja* excises—or at least tries to excise, since the visual material resists the attempt—references to Tamil-ness from the cinematic text. Then there are my own experiences of translating *Water!* from Tamil, which suggest the inadequacy of approaching the question of translation exclusively through the prism of violence. They suggest that any text is composed of elements translatable to a greater or lesser degree, requiring greater or lesser compromise, and that these elements have some relationship to notions of "modernity" and "tradition." Finally, as seen in anthologies of world literature, translation bears an intimate relationship to "the world" as an aggregated representation of human communities across the globe. While problems of anthologization must be rigorously distinguished from those of translation, it is important to recognize that translation mediates the production of this world. To scrutinize this world—the point is obvious but not therefore unnecessary to make—requires scrutinizing translation, not just as trope but also as practice.

Given the plurality of issues identified here, and hardly exhausted, can violence and imperialism truly be adequate general frames for the myriad ways in which translation happens in the colonial and postcolonial contexts? My purpose has been to expand our notion of translation in diverse directions, especially by paying attention to its relationship to the vernacular within postcolonial contexts. My explorations would seem to suggest that translation bears a complicated relationship to the vernacular. On the one hand, the vernacular is that which is in need of translation. Vernacular perspectives, to become available in contexts other than those to which they are native, must be translated. At the same time, the vernacular is that which resists translation. Indeed, in a heuristic way it might be taken as a marker of that which is untranslatable—the most extreme mark of cultural difference. In practice, of course, much that partakes of the vernacular does get translated—in time, in degrees, in collective effort. In this framework, the paradox of translation—the impossibility of it, the necessity for it—can be seen to originate as well as find its practical resolution in translation's relationship to the space of the vernacular.

It is in this fecund context that I set out to draw attention to the intimate association much of postcolonial theory has established between translation and imperial violence. I want to suggest that despite the insights it has made possible, such association has now begun to foreclose other equally significant issues, increasingly urgent since 9/11, from discussion. Making translation synonymous with violence underestimates what Lawrence Venuti has called the utopian dimension in translation as a communicative act—the desire to find a community of interest between foreign and domestic audiences of a text (2000, 484–88). No doubt in typical colonial and all-too-many postcolonial translating situations the foreign text was very much deliberately subjugated to the needs of the domestic audience, thus imbuing the act of translation with violence. However, to make this claim is far different from making translation synonymous with violence.

It is apparent to me that the insistence on translation as a constitutively violent act synonymous with colonialism or imperialism is linked to what I will call the critical dead end of the notion of translational fidelity, for the violence of translation is again and again most commonly demonstrated by noting the ways in which the translation *fails* to say what the original text does. Cheyfitz's argument presents a version of this, and so does Dingwaney's. There are more and less sophisticated ways in which this argument regarding fidelity to the original text is made, but in every instance, as Kwame Anthony Appiah observes, the notion that translation "is an attempt to find ways of saying in one language something that means the same as what has been said in another" is "the simplest of beginning thoughts about translation" and should be "resisted" (2000, 418). Writing from an institutional context in India, Sujit Mukherjee concurs: "*Rupantar* (meaning 'change in form') and *anuvad* ('speaking after' or 'following') are the commonly understood senses of translation in India, and neither term demands fidelity to the original" (1981/1994, 80). Similarly, in Tamil, *mozhipeyurppu*, *mozhimaatrum*, and *mozhiyaakam*, as terms for "translation" with slightly different nuances, foreground displacement in language, transformation in language, and transcreation in language rather than fidelity.[22] Of course every translation, to a lesser or greater degree, falls short of any literal communication of the original. This does not mean, however, that the translation should be dismissed outright as violent and faithless; for the utopian horizon toward which a translation should move is not, really, a faithful *rendering* of the foreign text at the level of the literal but an informed and careful *interpretation* of it. In *After Babel*, George Steiner alerted us to this manner of approaching translation when he wrote, "The schematic model of translation is one in which a message from a source-language passes into a receptor-language via a transformational process. The barrier is the obvious fact that one language differs from the other, that an interpretive transfer, sometimes, albeit misleadingly, described as encoding and decoding, must occur so that the message 'gets through'" (1975, 29). Here translation is a species of interpretation. Citing Steiner, Damrosch observes, "A translation is always an interpretation of the source text, and as a result a translation is not a faded replica of the original but an expansive transformation of it" (2003, 167).

An act of translation, then, is an act of interpretation of meaning rather than of faithful rendering of meaning. The most obvious way a translation reveals itself to be an interpretation rather than a rendering is through such annotative contrivances as explanatory footnotes, prefaces, and glossaries. In discussing my translation of *Water!*, I have already noted the function of these devices; but there is no need to recognize the interpretive ghost only in these overt cases. The very act of transferring into one language a text that is in another is itself an act of interpretation, as every deviation from literalness shows. "A translation aims to produce," Appiah notes, "a new text that matters to one community the way another text matters to another" (2000, 425). The ways to achieve this are through myriad acts of interpretation, of which the search for literal equivalence across linguistic boundaries is just one. Of course, in the literary context translation no doubt differs from most other interpretive acts by being constituted across linguistic lines and by the nature and degree of its attention to the minutest details of the text. The conclusion to be drawn from these observations is evident: if, as I am suggesting, translation is simply a highly specialized form of interpretation, it is not clear to me why it should uniquely be saddled with the label "violent" within postcolonial studies. Translation makes interpretive choices and decisions—none of them ever exactly right—at every turn. The result of these choices is not always violent, any more than other interpretive choices that literary critics make day in and day out are, and when it *is* violent the violence is not always because of imperialism.

In the introduction to a fine collection of essays on translation coedited by him, Paul St-Pierre writes:

> Traditionally, and even within translation studies itself, the operation of translation has often been described in terms of loss, and of course betrayal, and forces have been marshaled to minimize its "negative" effects: translation is reduced to a mere reproduction (or reflection)—of an effect, of an intention, of a message. Paradoxically, however, what is being minimized in such attempts is exactly what is specific to translations, what translation brings that is new, that constitutes growth—an interaction in a new context, a new reading, a new writing. In much of what is written about translation there seems to be a desire for the certainty of what already exists, even if such certainty constitutes a form of death (the end of interpretation, even before it has begun), rather than for the indeterminacy of the future and of life. (2005, xiv)

Unfortunately, with regard to translation, much of postcolonial studies has consented to this form of death. Acknowledging that translation is interpretation, albeit a highly specialized form of it—that is, without collapsing translation into interpretation in general—has the potential to release postcolonial studies from this death embrace. It has the potential to bring new life to discussions within postcolonial studies. In the last few years—since 9/11, since globalization, in the aftermath of the various antagonisms that have erupted or worsened from Rwanda to France to India—the trafficking in meaning between cultures and communities has acquired a new urgency. Translation has a crucial role to play in this context.

Viewing translation as interpretation allows us to acknowledge the limitations of translation without experiencing critical paralysis. Translation-as-interpretation is never a finished project. Like any other kind of interpretation (what act of interpretation could ever claim to have said *everything*?), a translation is never concluded. While there will always be an incontestable place for those who know the so-called vernacular languages and read the texts of those languages in the original, translation must suffice for those who cannot. Translation can never take the place of the original text, but that does not mean that it cannot, when approached in a historically sensitive manner, effectively and ethically convey for non-native audiences aspects of the original text. Indeed translation as interpretation can go further and allow even native readers to appreciate anew aspects of the text that they thought they knew so well in the original. In this regard too translation is like any other act of interpretation.

To regard translation as interpretation is to take heed of what may be called *the culture of translation*. Now more than ever, there is need for a vigorous culture of translation—a widely disseminated and rich understanding of translation. Important as actual acts of translation are, it is also necessary to popularize a general understanding of translation that foregrounds interpretation rather than fidelity. Doing so comports well with a materialist criticism, as I hope the preceding discussion in this chapter has sufficiently illustrated. A materialist approach to translation would endeavor at one and the same time to release translation from mystification, to return translation to its place in the world, and to recognize the complexities and contradictions of translation. Making widely available a demystified, worldly, and profound understanding of translation, not only among translation practitioners and scholars but also among editors, publishers, and readers, should be considered an essential task of a materialist translation studies. The creation of such a culture of translation from a materialist perspective would ensure that translations were held accountable by standards different from that of fidelity. While it would still be possible to regard a particular translation of a particular text as inadequate or problematic, the grounds for doing so would now concern the particular interpretation the translation offered rather than whether the translation properly *captured* the *original* text. I would aver that the benefits of this shift in perspective are likely to be considerable. An urgent task for translation studies, in summary, is not just a cautious recovery of translation practice but also a dissemination of an appropriate *culture of translation* in the wider public.

It is certainly true that in our post-9/11 world translation can easily appear as an instrument of violence—as a loyal servant of imperialism gathering, for example, the myriad texts of the world and dressing them up exactly as imperialism wants them dressed. Nor, as we have seen in previous examples, would this use of translation be without historical precedent. The fate of *caste* in India is after all intimately connected to translation. Whether verbal or written, translation played an indispensable role in the dubious transformation of (often unconscionable) vernacular practice into *caste*. In spite of that, this same translation remains equally indispensable for those of us interested in advancing a different project of intercultural communication capable of acknowledging vernacular knowledges and anxieties. For those of us interested in such an alternative project of acknowledgment, translation must be opportunity for actual practice as well as for critical intervention. It cannot just, or even primarily, be violence—a problem.

Conclusion
Postcolonialism and Comparatism

In pursuit of the vernacular, I have been led to two ancillary concerns—translation and comparatism. These two topics have found iteration in my argument in multiple ways. Noting how the vernacular directed attention to the question of translation, I took up that topic in the previous chapter. I conclude by turning to comparatism and comparison, a term clearly summoned forth by the notion of comparatism. Though my focus on comparatism is narrower in scope, there are resonances between my argument about translation and my observations on comparatism and comparison in this chapter. I partly rely on these resonances to develop my remarks about comparatism and comparison.

Comparison is a commonsensical, everyday word. In contrast, the infelicitous-sounding *comparatism* is unlikely to find much purchase outside the university. Where the former is free of the taint of jargon, the latter denotes a deliberate approach to academic study. What kind of approach? And with what consequences for postcolonial studies? What kinds of intervention into postcolonial studies as an academic field does comparatism enable? What are the challenges it poses to postcolonial studies? And what challenges to comparatism does the field of postcolonial studies pose? Such are the questions I take up in this conclusion.

Given the nature of the material I have explored, my reference to comparatism might be said to invoke immediately comparative literary and cultural studies. Recently, a variety of works have taken up the task of reassessing this field of academic study. Fittingly enough, the most widely discussed are probably the two reports on the field commissioned by the American Comparative Literature Association in 1993 and 2005, presented along with responses in volumes edited by Charles Bernheimer (1995a) and Haun Saussy (2006a) respectively. Other works include those by Gayatri Spivak, Susan Bassnet, and Emily Apter. Of these, Spivak's and Bassnet's are written out of an extreme sense of crisis within comparative literature as a field of study, though both suggest possibilities for renewal. Spivak's book is entitled *Death of a Discipline* (2003), while Bassnet ends her book by noting, "Comparative literature as a discipline has had its day. Cross-cultural work in women's studies, in post-colonial theory, in cultural studies has changed the face of literary studies generally. We should look upon translation studies as the principal discipline from now on, with comparative literature as a valued but subsidiary subject area" (1993, 161). Apter, though less emphatic in her sense of crisis, too recognizes the need for a reinvention of the field as "a new comparative literature" using translation as a "fulcrum" (2006, 243). Taken together, these and other recent reflections suggest the churning within comparative literary and cultural studies; of course, it is also true that disciplinary anxiety has always seemed constitutive of the field. As Bernheimer notes in his introduction, entitled "The Anxieties of Comparison," "Comparative literature is anxiogenic" (1995b, 1).[1]

What I want to do here is not offer yet another argument about the field of comparative literary and cultural studies, or issue another call for renewal, but rather make a few observations about comparatism—a methodology of academic study that is at the heart of a variety of fields in addition to comparative literary and cultural studies: comparative sociology, comparative politics, and comparative philosophy, to name only three. Rather than entering into a discussion of the need for or problems with the field of comparative literary and cultural studies, I want to maintain my focus on postcolonialism and to reflect on the viability as well as the difficulty of comparatist critical approaches in relation to postcolonial studies. I want to assess how comparatism can intercede within postcolonial studies. It is to the credit of *Postcolonialisms: An Anthology of Cultural Theory and Criticism*, a fine recent reader on postcolonial theory edited by Gaurav Desai and Supriya Nair, that the comparative aspect of postcolonialism is sufficiently acknowledged. In their introduction, Desai and Nair write, "The large conceptual grasp of the field of postcolonial studies has meant that even scholars who define themselves as specialists in a region—say, Anglophone West Africa—have nevertheless often thought of their projects in comparative terms" (2005, 1). Desai and Nair do not note, however, that scholars in the field have not generally shown an inclination to systematically account for the place of comparison and comparatism within postcolonial studies. Instead, the predilection, as I argued in chapter 1, has been to rely on models of hybridity and similar notions to make sense of the wealth of cultural interactions that characterize the colonial and postcolonial world. The attraction to these models, I want to suggest, is precisely their apparent ability to offer cogent and powerful analyses of disparate cross-cultural processes. However, while the utility of such models in some cases cannot be denied, their ubiquity—indeed, even a dogmatic reliance on them within the field—obscures as much as it reveals about the colonial and postcolonial worlds. Many cultural phenomena, as we saw in previous chapters, simply cannot be explained by such a notion as hybridity. It is as corrective, then, that I turn to comparison and comparatism. In doing so, I suggest reasons for the reluctance to account for them within postcolonial studies even as I initiate such an accounting.

In my argument in the book thus far, I have proceeded mainly through a series of comparisons. I have relied on the juxtaposition of different linguistic and cultural traditions and forms. Tamil plays, Bollywood films in Hindi, Indian novels in English—these and other texts have been read against and alongside one another. This mode of reading has been necessitated by my desire to identify the nature of the vernacular within the contested spaces of the colonial and the postcolonial. While comparatism customarily indicates scholarly comparison across linguistic and cultural boundaries, recently arguments have advanced the notion of a comparatism broadened to include comparison across genres, media, and similar categories of critical analysis.[2] Comparison, not only linguistic and cultural, but also formal or generic, has been a valuable method for uncovering and exploring what I have referred to as the relational aspects of the notion of the vernacular—the term's existence in relationship to other terms such as *transnational, classical,* and *indigenous.* Just as much as translation, comparatism has been evoked by my pursuit of the vernacular. Since my recourse to comparatism has no doubt been shaped by my interest in the vernacular (since, that is, *vernacular* has called forth comparatism in my argument), I turn to a brief review of the idea of the vernacular as it emerges from previous chapters before considering comparatism.

THE VERNACULAR

Following the vernacular in this book has meant traveling in multiple directions. My intention has been, as Dipesh Chakrabarty puts it in *Provincializing Europe*, "to release into the space occupied by particular European histories sedimented in them [social science categories] other normative and theoretical thought enshrined in other existing life practices and their archives" (2000, 20). Through the vernacular, I have a similar interest in drawing attention to alternative life practices and archives in the context of postcolonial studies. But if the vernacular is to represent a new horizon of theoretical possibility for postcolonial criticism today, it cannot become a singular idea. Rather than offer a neatly formulated definition of the vernacular, I have tried to expose in successive readings the associations and evocations enabled by the term. Thus the vernacular was read in relationship to the transnational, the postcolonial, the colonial, the national, the classical, and the human. In each of these readings, I tried to emphasize that the vernacular represented an orientation, as well as to remain alive to nuance. The vernacular named an oppositional attitude to some of these terms (for example, the transnational or the classical), while to others it appeared as a clarifying qualification (for example, the postcolonial or the human). Contradiction too I tried to attend to—not only is the opposition of the vernacular to the transnational different from its opposition to the classical, but the two forms of opposition can themselves be at cross-purposes. Thus Tamil might in one context appear as a vernacular in relationship to Hindi, while in another it might appear as an ancient classical language in contradistinction to the relative youth of the latter, which might then be forced into the position of a vernacular. Similarly, a language such as Tamil can be at one and the same time a vernacular language (in the way Rushdie used the term) and a transnational language (in that it is to be found not only in India but also in other countries such as Malaysia). At issue in both of these examples is difference in usage. No doubt, it is because of this richness of usage that *vernacular* can appear in an oxymoronic formulation such as the "vernacular cosmopolitanism" of Homi Bhabha and the "cosmopolitan vernacular" of Sheldon Pollock.[3] While I have acknowledged the possibility of such formulations, my own intent has been to uncover and explore uses for the term within a postcolonial context that manifest themselves as resistance to cosmopolitanism and allied phenomena. It follows from the relational understanding of *vernacular* that these uses—the "content" of the vernacular in any particular situation—cannot be determined a priori. What appears as the vernacular in a situation depends on that with which it is in relation. As a term of cultural critique, *vernacular* finds its greatest resonance in a relational mode that operates along many and sometimes contradictory trajectories, and it is this relational mode that invites comparatist analysis.

In these multiple, relational, and sometimes contradictory uses of *vernacular*, much is nevertheless shared (and here we might note that, as a practice, comparatism negotiates not only difference but also commonality). As I have insisted, though vernacular might find its most common application within a linguistic sphere, it is helpful to push usage beyond this frame of reference so that we are able to speak of vernacular sensibilities. When opposing, or at least being clearly distinguished from, the terms listed above, such sensibility is oriented toward the rooted, the culturally autonomous, the local, the contingent, the practical, and the particular. It shares ground with the folk, the indigenous, and the traditional, without becoming synonymous with them. I am attracted to *vernacular* as a term of analysis precisely because it is less clearly marked in critical usage than these other terms, allowing therefore for a more liberal application. At the same time, it cannot always do the work these other terms can. In a Pacific Islands context, for example, *indigenous* represents a political claim made by some groups to historical priority in the face of past and continuing colonial encroachments. In claiming such priority, the discourse around indigeneity within a Pacific Islands context is neither reductive nor predictable. *Vernacular* does not and cannot capture the rich force of this often necessary claim to priority—a claim, in Haunani-Kay Trask's words, "defined in terms of collective aboriginal occupation prior to colonial settlement" (1993, 33). To be valuable as a critical term, the uses of *vernacular* need to be carefully delimited.

Such delimitation should be distinguished from *vernacular* as a term of denigration. We have already encountered such a deprecating application of the term in Rushdie's egregious comments on Indian literatures other than in English. Certainly, we need to be cognizant of these disparaging associations the term has acquired. However, despite such associations, it seems to me useful to retain the term. First, the use of *vernacular* as a term of disparagement is by no means universal; aside from fields such as architecture or medicine, where it is commonly used in a neutral way, *vernacular* retains an element of legitimacy even when applied to languages. To call a language a vernacular is not always to dismiss it; sometimes the intent is simply to draw attention to the locally circumscribed manifestation of a language, or to point out its lack of power relative to another language. Indeed, it is largely because of the last aspect that the term has proven useful to me.

Ultimately, questions of power—I think my arguments in previous chapters demonstrate this sufficiently—are at the heart of the constellation of issues brought to the fore by recourse to *vernacular*. The perception that *vernacular* is a term of disparagement is closely linked to the way the word more often than not indexes power or, to put the matter more accurately, subjection under power—the common perception that it is a term of denigration is intimately linked to the relative powerlessness it identifies. Often enough, to be a vernacular is to be dominated, or to be placed in a position of powerlessness in relationship to something else. My intent has been to recognize in the term a neutral—by which I mean only that no moral claim is being made on behalf of *vernacular*— index to such an economy of power, without making of it simply another term for any subjection. When *vernacular* registers power it does so in a particular way—it signals a particular kind of subjection, a particular kind of hierarchy, in which it identifies the dominated element in relation to opposing elements commonly manifested as the transnational, the national, the universal, the classical, and so on. The list of opposing terms is plural, but not without limit.

In exploring the relationship of translation to the vernacular, I found that the vernacular was that which both invited translation and resisted it; the vernacular was at one and the same time that which cried out for translation and that which could not be translated. In practice, of course, as I noted in discussing my translation of *Water!*, what appears untranslatable at a particular instant might later prove amenable to translation as languages learn to or are forced to accommodate themselves to one another; or what proves untranslatable in a particular kind of translation practice might find translation in another (for example, a notion that does not find translation in a poem might be adequately translated in a footnote to the poem). Of course, it is also true that, beyond these possibilities, some portion of the vernacular always resists translation. Contemplating the vernacular through the prism of translation only underscores the contradictoriness of the term. Because of its otherness to the transnational and the cosmopolitan, the vernacular asks—indeed demands—translation, and because of this very otherness it proves not only difficult to translate but often enough impossible.

In myriad ways, then, *vernacular* is rife with rich, if complicated and sometimes contradictory, associations. Given this richness, what other term could do the work I have asked of *vernacular* in previous chapters? With this question in mind, I turn to a more deliberate consideration of a methodological imperative prompted by the vernacular; I turn to comparatism within postcolonial contexts.

FLESH AND FISH BLOOD

I began my inquiry into the vernacular in the first chapter with a discussion of Ka Na Su's poem "Situation." "Situation," I noted, registers a complaint about what it regards as the typical condition of postcolonial intellectual production. It also raises questions about appropriate reading strategies. In a manner that might seem paradoxical, the poem appeals to readers to engage with cultural traditions on their own terms even as it invites reading by reference to multiple cultural traditions. As we saw, the poem slyly cites Ezra Pound in the final line, so that to decipher its appeal for a serious engagement with Tamil tradition is to be referred back to Pound's poem "Hugh Selwyn Mauberley." Thus the tradition of early twentieth-century Anglo-American modernism is invoked. In addition, the poem refers to the Upanishads, written in Sanskrit, and to Tagore, who wrote mostly in Bengali. It is true that the poem's reference to these two traditions is different from the reference to Pound, for it ranges them on the same side as the Tamil texts, ostensibly because of their shared Indianness; but the effect of this is to fracture the notion of a single national tradition rather than to amalgamate diverse traditions into one. The nation itself becomes multiple. My overall point is simple: Ka Na Su's poem might separate the intellectual "vociferous in thoughts not his own" from an idealized reader who has read what he discusses in the original language, but the cultural "situation" of the poem is irrevocably plural.

Ka Na Su's poem, then, might appeal for a certain kind of cultural autonomy but itself demands in rather purposeful ways a culturally diverse reading strategy. It does so by imagining its ideal reader as someone conversant with more than one language, more than one literary tradition. Given the poem's appeal for cultural autonomy, should this imagining be regarded as a contradiction? Not necessarily. After all, knowledge of a variety of literary and cultural traditions can comport with a keen sense of the specificity and autonomy of each tradition. What the poem objects to is careless vociferousness, a lazy or even appropriative mish-mash of cultural knowledge—the Upanishads known and pontificated upon through Eliot, the Tamil classics through Danielou. As the poem itself indicates, this is not the only way traditions come together. The poem's appeal for cultural autonomy is conjoined to an invocation of a reading strategy that can be described as comparatist. The intellectual at the heart of the poem is, exasperatingly for the poet, "neither flesh nor fish blood nor stone totem pole," but the poem itself is flesh *and* fish blood *and* stone totem pole. The intellectual is satirized not because he wishes to show himself familiar with different cultural traditions but rather because he does not know well enough or appropriately enough the very cultural traditions with which he claims familiarity, even identity.

In this and other ways, comparatism has slid into my arguments in previous chapters. Whether reading Ka Na Su's poem in the light of his reference to Pound or examining the Bollywood Hindi film *Guide* in relationship to R. K. Narayan's Anglophone novel *The Guide*, I have proceeded by a reading strategy that has tried to be attentive to the ways in which literary and cultural traditions sometimes share and commingle and sometimes remain, in aspiration if not always in fact, separate and autonomous. Writing about the vernacular under postcolonial conditions has required this procedure, while it has also necessitated attention to the notion of translation. Just as it is difficult to see how the argument might have proceeded without a consideration of translation, given that translation is one of the processes by which the vernacular finds (or is made to find) greater circulation, so too comparison and comparatism are evoked by the needs of the argument. The relationship of the vernacular to comparatism, I would suggest, is similar to that between the vernacular and translation. The notion of the vernacular, in the way I have had recourse to it, functions within a plural cultural situation. It both invites comparatist treatment and resists it.

Postcolonial studies has generally not responded adequately to this comparatist challenge posed by the vernacular, even though in *Comparative Literature* Bassnet describes the "cross-cultural criticism" advanced in influential anthologies of postcolonial theory such as *The Empire Writes Back* as "but comparative literature under another name" (1993, 9–10). Bassnet's point, even if valid for the anthology she cites, cannot be extended much further. It is true that aspects of

Edward Said's work can be interestingly discussed in relationship to a comparatist framework—his argument for contrapuntal readings in *Culture and Imperialism* (1993), for example, or his general admiration for Erich Auerbach's *Mimesis* as a foundational work of comparative literature, or his repeated recourse to a notion of "worldliness" that relies at least in part on a comparatist approach.[4] And it is true too that Gayatri Spivak has systematically explored translation studies and notions of comparative literature (especially in *Death of a Discipline*). However, by and large postcolonial theory has only partially followed the example of Said and Spivak, neglecting their interest in comparatism and pursuing instead their insights into *colonial discourse* as illustrated by an archive of Francophone and Anglophone material. Despite the instances of Said and Spivak, as a field postcolonial studies has generally avoided a sustained engagement with comparatist methodologies, relying instead on models of hybridity and mestizaje (as discussed in the first chapter) to account for cross-cultural communication.

The lack of engagement with comparatism within postcolonial studies is both comprehensible and a matter for wonderment. Let me begin with the comprehensible. In obvious ways, comparatism raises questions about the very grounds for comparison. As Haun Saussy notes regarding comparative literature, "The most obvious and usually untheorized, candidate for 'trunk' status [foundational category] is simply the universality of human experience" (2006b, 13). Is any comparison tenable without such a notion of the universal? Associated with this question are others: Is comparison possible without an accompanying, albeit surreptitious, element of evaluation? Does not comparison inevitably involve a kind of accusation in that if two things are compared one is found wanting in relationship to the other—as Bruce Robbins has succinctly put it, "comparison as blaming" (2007, 1648)? Within postcolonial studies, such questions have, for good reason, been linked to a critique of colonialism and imperialism.

As various commentators on the colonial scene have suggested, the idea of a universal, defined in Eurocentric ways, has been a way to coerce the colonized into aspiring to assimilate to European norms. Frantz Fanon noted long ago in *The Wretched of the Earth*: "Western bourgeois racial prejudice as regards the nigger and the Arab is a racism of contempt; it is a racism which minimizes what it hates. Bourgeois ideology, however, which is the proclamation of an essential equality between men manages to appear logical in its own eyes by inviting the sub-men to become human, and to take as their prototype Western humanity as incarnated in the Western bourgeoisie" (1963, 163). The invitation to become human is, then, a universalist subterfuge. It is an invitation to the sub-men to normalize themselves according to a *particular* idea of the human that presents itself as a universal. Were the sub-men to accept this deceptive and dangerous invitation, they would be fated to fail, for they would always be late-arriving entrants into humanity. It would be impossible for them to escape the stigma of being copies. And in being copies, they would inevitably remain inferior—never quite good enough. Thus we return to evaluation. The invitation to the sub-men to become human takes the form of a comparison, grounded on a universal notion of humanity, in the light of which the sub-men are found wanting. Given these problematic associations within colonial history how, then, could postcolonial studies not be suspicious of the universal and any comparatism founded on it? A similar question is at the heart of what I have termed above the resistance (it is, in another analytic moment, an invitation) posed to comparatism by *vernacular:* comparison can all too easily become a mode of accusation and a mode of subsumption into a "greater" whole into which the vernacular is made to disappear. The vernacular resists this act of erasure by resisting comparison. So also with postcolonialism, which too might be seen as resisting comparatism.

Nevertheless, as Desai and Nair point out, there can be no *postcolonial* without comparatism. Comparatism is indispensable for an adequate approach to "the postcolonial condition." After all, in many of the most common usages of the term the very category of the "postcolonial" is constituted comparatively. In such usages, *postcolonial literature*, for example, is used to bring together literary works from Nigeria (Achebe) and Trinidad (Naipaul) and India (Anita Desai). How many colleges around the United States, and indeed elsewhere, have courses uniting such Anglophone works under the rubric of postcolonial literature? Whether articulated or not, an implicit comparison is being made here. The suggestion is that the colonial and postindependence histories of these countries, even in all their differences, share features that allow them to be grouped together in this fashion.

The comparison implicit in the concept of postcolonialism is also evident from another direction. In this book, I have mainly deployed comparison not in a transnational direction, comparing different national contexts, but rather in an intranational one, juxtaposing different vernaculars or, indeed, the vernacular itself vis-à-vis a variety of cultural material expressive of different sensibilities. Here too different linguistic and cultural traditions are at issue. Since postcolonial countries are not homogeneous entities, the intranational mode of approaching the postcolonial too would seem naturally to invite comparatism as a methodology. In a similar vein, Mary Louise Pratt notes: "It is useful to recognize that comparativism now includes both the familiar 'horizontal' work of comparing case A with case B, and also 'vertical' work relating the global and the local. I find promising models of comparative literature degrees which require significant local expertise (and accountability) in a particular area and combine it with training in translational and global perspectives" (1995, 63–64).[5]

Yet despite the multiple ways in which its object of study is constituted comparatively, postcolonialism has had little to say about comparison and comparatism. While the notion of the postcolonial is undeniably comparative, postcolonial method has not been comparatist in any meaningful way. The reason, I would suggest, is the suspicious career of the universal within colonial history, as briefly reviewed above. This suspicion has caused postcolonial studies to ignore issues of comparison and comparatism, even as the notion of the postcolonial has relied on comparison. We cannot, in our turn, ignore this suspicion, as there is indeed much reason to be wary. At the same time, a refusal to adequately engage with comparatism is also untenable because of the fundamentally comparative nature of the "postcolonial," as observed above.

How, then, are we to begin an appropriate engagement with comparatism within postcolonial contexts? We might note that while the Eurocentric universalism (the oxymoronism is precisely the point) denounced by Fanon has played a crucially disabling role within the history of colonialism, there are alternative and more enabling versions of such universalism also at work within the postcolonial context. We encountered one such universalism in chapter 3 in the discussion of Dalit literature. In the Dalit endorsement of humanism, as well as Edward Said's similar affirmation, there is a call for a kind of universalism through the appeal to a different—more open, more oppositional, more self-reflective—humanism than the one denounced by Fanon. Fanon himself has such a humanism in mind when he ends *The Wretched of the Earth* by writing, "For Europe, for ourselves, and for humanity, comrades, we must turn over a new leaf, we must work out new concepts, and try to set afoot a new man" (1963, 316). Unfortunate as his language is in its conflation of *human* with *man*, Fanon's ending recognizes the need to continue to engage with universalism in the political struggles of decolonization.

If the very notion of the universal is to be reformulated in this way, so too in the context of my argument must be the concept of comparatism. In a passage I referred to in the previous chapter, A. K. Ramanujan noted, "Poems are unique and incomparable as poems. Only abstraction and restatement renders them comparable. A major goal of comparison is contrast. Texts from different traditions, when juxtaposed, may help define each other's uniqueness. We need not add that 'comparative literature' is probably only a tactful name for 'contrastive literature'" (1999b, 331). While contrast has always been a part of comparative work of all kinds, Ramanujan's strong iteration shifts the focus decisively from a vague notion of what is shared to what, in the midst of the shared, is not. The specification of difference also requires comparison or, rather, contrast. Difference should be as valued in comparative work as commonality. Ramanujan's brief but suggestive reference is an important warning to resist the subsumption of all manner of cultural phenomena under an overarching rubric that reduces, glosses over differences and, at its worst, colonizes. Prudent and principled attention to the incommensurable can be one bulwark against the false promises of Eurocentric universalism.

Linking the twin problems of universalism and comparatism more directly, R. Radhakrishnan notes in *Theory in an Uneven World*,

> We can either look at comparatism as a practice that is founded on the assumption that the issue of universal value that operates among and within cultures has already been normativized consensually or otherwise, or we can conceptualize comparison as but the beginning of a complex, uneven, and multilateral investigation about "the value of value" and the meaning of value. It is the latter option that I would strongly advocate. . . . To invest responsibly in the double task of believing in and acting on "universal value," while at the same time opening up axiology to critique from within and without—that would be the most exciting and transformative way to think of comparison in a multicultural world. In other words, the project of comparison has to be subsumed within the larger and more inclusive endeavor of producing a relational universality as a process without end. (2003, 78)

For Radhakrishnan, comparison is not normative; rather, it is approached "tentatively and experimentally" (78). In his careful approach, universalism remains open to refinement and redefinition. If comparison is simultaneously made to accommodate an inquiry into the value of value, as he suggests, the evaluative thrust of comparatism may be blunted. Echoing Radhakrishnan, Rey Chow contrasts a "hierarchizing frame of comparison" to one that must "be reconceptualized as an act of judging the value of different things horizontally, in sheer approximation to one another—an act that, because it is inseparable from history, would have to remain speculative rather than conclusive, and ready to subject itself to revamped semiotic relations. As much as it is inevitable (since the violent yoking together of disparate things has become inevitable in modern and postmodern times), comparison would also be an unfinalizable event because its meanings have to be repeatedly negotiated" (2006, 80–81).

In yet another recent call for a principled comparatism, Chandra Talpade Mohanty writes, "I suggest that a 'comparative feminist studies' or 'feminist solidarity' model is the most useful and productive pedagogical strategy for feminist cross-cultural work. It is this particular model that provides a way to theorize a complex relational understanding of experience, location, and history such that feminist cross-cultural work moves through the specific context to construct a real notion of the universal and of democratization rather than colonization. It is through this model that we can put into practice the idea of 'common differences' as the basis for deeper solidarity across differences and unequal power relations" (2002, 518). As is made clear elsewhere in the essay, Mohanty's comparative feminism is grounded in a materialist method.

My own critical predilections underscore Mohanty's materialism. For Mohanty, "a materialist analysis" should link "everyday lives and local gendered contexts and ideologies to the larger, transnational political and economic structures and ideologies of capitalism" (2002, 504) and should be attentive to "the material complexity, reality and agency of Third World women's bodies and lives" (510). Similarly, I have recognized the vernacular specificity of certain texts, while also acknowledging the ways in which larger national and transnational frames impinge on them. I have sought to emphasize translation's practical aspect (rather than its metaphorical usage) and to return it to its context of social and historical contestation. Like Mohanty, I aim to comprehend comparatism in materialist ways. I stress worldliness and historicity while engaging in comparatist reasoning. The ruminations on methodology offered by Radhakrishnan, Chow, and Mohanty buttress my own way of proceeding, which is to acknowledge the comparison already at work within the notion of the postcolonial and then to resuscitate comparatism as a materialist methodology in a more deliberate way.

In the pursuit of such resuscitation, there are lessons to be learnt from drawing parallels between comparatism and translation within postcolonial contexts. I suggested in the previous chapter that translation be recognized as a specialized form of interpretation. Now we might expand this formulation to note that translation is comparative cross-linguistic textual interpretation. Translation involves in the most obvious ways comparison between languages, both at the level of word and, indeed, at the level of cultural system, staged on the terrain of the text. As such, the paradox of translation provides a clue to the paradox of comparatism—enabling as well as violent, evocative of tolerant and open-minded communication as well as imperialistic appropriation. Like translation, comparatism is an interpretive act. What kind of an interpretive act depends on a variety of factors and in the manner in which the comparison is made. Paradoxically, as an interpretive act comparatism hangs suspended between generalization and particularity. Inevitably, comparatism involves generalization from particulars; such generalization may result in the careful delineation of commonalities and differences, or else it may result in the imposition of one particularity on the other, the subsumption of one under the other.

As we have seen, translation practice, which I am suggesting is a form of comparative practice, provides fascinating and concrete examples of both possibilities (careful delineation and reductive imposition). Colonialist translation of the vernacular varna-jati complex into *caste* involves an implicit, dominating comparison of India with Britain: caste-ridden India is compared to caste-less, free Britain. Such an act of comparative interpretation can be countered only by a succeeding act of interpretation, also comparative in nature, that seeks to undo what the earlier act did without thereby recuperating the multiple obscenities of the varna-jati complex. The challenge is to keep the systemic oppressions of the varna-jati complex in sight while removing the veil of colonialist discourse and making space for the kind of nuanced analysis made difficult by a term of mistranslation such as *caste*. Here one might consider an example such as V. Geetha's wonderful translation of Perumal Murugan's Tamil novel into English as *Seasons of the Palm*. This translation too is an act of comparative interpretation involving the varna-jati complex, but in this case attentive to the ethical complexities of such an act. One would have to assess these two acts of translation—the translation of the varna-jati complex as *caste* under colonial conditions and Geetha's translation—differently. So too with comparatism. Just as with translation-as-interpretation, it is prudent to keep in mind that comparatism can be a form of knowing-in-solidarity or else of knowing-as-domination. Which it is is not always easy to ascertain; nevertheless, there is no reason to be entirely pessimistic that if comparatism is approached as an open-ended and self-reflective material practice—a specific practice nested within the worldliness of human praxis—forms of knowing-in-solidarity can find expression.

The similarity between comparatism and translation I am emphasizing here might seem surprising from certain perspectives. After all, in the early years of comparative literature as a field, comparatism and translation were opposed. "From the age of philology to the age of the New Criticism, a dependence on translation was the mark of the dilettante," David Damrosch notes (1995, 130). True comparatists were scholars who worked without translation; they read in the original all the works that they wrote about. Translations were for the generalists who could not claim the specialized language skills available to the scholar working in the field of comparative literature. For the most part, the audience for whom the scholar wrote also shared the set of language skills possessed by the scholar.

It is not hard to note immediately that the notion of the dispensability of translation associated with such comparatist work depends on a narrowly demarcated cultural terrain—historically, a few parts of western and central Europe. The handful of languages employed in such comparatist work were the most dominant western and central European ones that an individual scholar might reasonably be expected to learn. As David Damrosch argues in *What Is World Literature?* (2003), such a narrow definition of the cultural terrain for comparatism is no longer possible. It is the expansion of the field of comparison to the globe as a whole that has made translation inevitable. At the same time, comparatism has risen (or fallen, depending on what aspect of it you focus on) to the condition of translation. Like translation, it is both impossible and necessary.

Comparatism, translation, the vernacular: within the postcolonial context, each marks a particular kind of critical intervention. Since 9/11 and in the midst of globalization, the tendency has been to approach the postcolonial world in overdetermined ways, whether reducing it to the menacing caricature of the Islamo-fascist or liberating it into the flat-world delirium of Thomas Friedman. Implicit in my argument is that more nuance is necessary—hardly an original and startling declaration. My sense is that renewed attention to the vernacular as a critical category, to translation as a literary and cultural practice as well as a trope, and to comparatism as a methodological imperative is a way to bring such nuance to treatments of the postcolonial world. It will not do to ignore the knowing-as-domination that each one of these terms can often enough enable and/or represent. But neither will it do to ignore the ways in which they, in a different and more scrupulous mode of materialist critical practice, can advance a form of knowing-in-solidarity.

Notes

CHAPTER I

1. Rushdie's introduction appeared originally in the 1997 *New Yorker* issue dedicated to Indian writing in English under the title "Damme, This Is the Oriental Scene for You!"

2. For some examples of such criticism, see M. Mukherjee (1999, 26), J. Rege (1999, 187–88), P. Mishra (1999, 49–51), and especially Orsini (2002), a fine essay that shares critical ground with my overall argument.

3. Perhaps it is necessary to note that *postcolonialism* is used sometimes to refer to a historical condition and sometimes more narrowly to a form of cultural and historiographical criticism and theory. This book is mainly concerned with the adequacy of certain versions of the latter to deal with the former (especially, but not exclusively, the literature that emerges out of it). It is, I think, clear from the context which meaning is meant where.

4. See also the critical anthology coedited by Bartolovich and Lazarus (2002).

5. Varadarajan's *History of Tamil Literature* (1970) is an abridged English version of an important, if dated, introduction to Tamil literature written originally in Tamil. In chapter 4 I take up the terminological relationship of "classical" to "vernacular" in some detail.

6. See Subramanyam (1994). The poem was first published in *Poetry India* 1 (April–June 1966): 9.

7. My translation. When Gnanakoothan refers to previous poets, he has in mind the great Tamil poets of antiquity he has just listed. But it is readily evident from Ka Na Su's work that he was an avid reader of English literature and was especially conversant with the modernists. In this context, Tamil readers may consult Ka Na Su's prefaces and critical essays in *Puthu Kavithaikal* (1989). K. N. Subramanyam (Ka Na Su, 1912–89), one of the most prominent figures of

modern Tamil literature, was a poet, a critic, and a novelist. "In his novels," R. Parthasarthy says, "prose fiction in Tamil reached its apotheosis" (1994, 254). While this assessment by Parthasarthy is contestable (Puthumaipithan and Mowni could easily lay rival claim), Parthasarthy's admiration for Ka Na Su on aesthetic grounds is widely shared in Tamil literary critical circles.

8. For a recent study of New Poetry, see Rama (2003).

9. As is well known, Tagore dissociated himself from overt nationalist forms of thought. However, because a song by Tagore is the national anthem of India, Tagore is also often linked to the cultural forms of the nation. Ka Na Su's poem, it seems to me, means to indicate this association. "National" is my way of identifying this association without assimilating Tagore into an ideological position that he often argued against.

10. For an overview of the concept of cultural imperialism, see Tomlinson (1991).

11. Pound's centrality for some of the most important strands of modernism is well known. Nicholls describes him as one of the "canonical modernists" (1995, vii), and one of Hugh Kenner's influential studies of the age of modernism is simply titled *The Pound Era*. The interesting echoes in Pound for postcolonial criticism are also worth noting. Pound writes in his poetic epitaph for "E. P." that "he had been born / In a half savage country, out of date" (1975, 98) and that in the modern age "Caliban casts out Ariel" (99). Such references bring to mind the postcolonial essays by Fernández Retamar (1989) on Caliban and "America."

12. The notion of a Tractor Art itself should also be scrutinized. No doubt there was much reductive literary and artistic representation under the Soviet Union. But whether all Soviet literature and art deserves this dismissive label is worth consideration.

13. For Bhabha on the "mimic man," see "Of Mimicry and Man" (1994, 87–88). Later Bhabha speaks of "colonial man" (91). Although the notion of mimicry would seem to suggest a mode of enunciation (mimicry) rather than a property of identity (hybridity), these passages illustrate the manner in which Bhabha's argument repeatedly begins with the former and ends up with the latter. For discussion of related aspects of Bhabha, see Sinfield (1996), Parry (1994), Easthope (1998), and Lazarus (1999, esp. the chapter "Disavowing Decolonization"). Alan Sinfield observes, "Bhabha's case for hybridity is related to his argument that the 'mimicry' of the colonial subject hovers, indeterminately, between respect and mockery" (1996, 282).

14. In chapter 4, I discuss in some detail my translation of *Water!* into English. The translation was published by *Asian Theatre Journal* in the United States (in a slightly abridged version) and by Seagull in India. The references here are to the Seagull version.

15. See my introduction to the Seagull version of the translation (Shankar 2001a) for a detailed discussion of the critical and popular reception of the play and for more biographical information on Swaminathan (1935–95).

16. Two ready examples of such personages are C. N. Annadurai and M. Karunanidhi. The first was chief minister of the state of Tamil Nadu when he died; the second has served in that capacity a number of times.

17. See *Oxford English Dictionary,* 2nd ed. (1989), s.v. "vernacular."

18. See Perumal (1981, esp. 4–10 and 135–51), for a discussion of the origins of Tamil drama and the persistence of traditional and folk theatrical forms in such "modern" plays meant for the auditorium as *Water! Therukoothu* is "street dance" or "street drama," and *villupaatu* literally "bow song" (a sung and spoken performance using a bow as a musical instrument). The latter has in recent decades been successfully adapted for the television in such programs as *Vayalum Vaazhvum [Field and Life]* to convey educational information to rural communities.

19. Ambai is the pseudonym of C. S. Lakshmi (b. 1944). *The Face behind the Mask* (1984) was published under the latter name.

20. There is no discussion in the cursory presentation in this chapter, for example, of Dalit writing or the literature of the Dravidian or nationalist movements. The Dravidian movements purported to advance the cause of South India (especially Tamil India) as a distinct (Dravidian) racial, political, and cultural sphere. In chapters 2 and 4 I discuss Dravidianism, and in chapter 3 I take up Dalit literature in Tamil.

21. Ambai's short story "Anil (the Squirrel)" (1993) is included in the second volume of this anthology.

22. As early as 1982, Rushdie was writing of the migrant Indian writer in England, "Our identity is at once plural and partial. Sometimes we feel that we straddle two cultures; at other times, that we fall between two stools. But however ambiguous and shifting this ground may be, it is not an infertile territory for a writer to occupy" (1991, 15). Also see, in addition to the vivid evidence of his fictional works, Rushdie's comments on the mongrel and the hybrid to Sarah Crichton on the occasion of the publication of his collection of short stories *East, West* (Crichton 1995, 59). Since 9/11, Rushdie has been very vocal about the threat posed to the West by Islam. See his op-eds in the *New York Times* (2002a, 2002c) and the *Washington Post* (2002b). The relationship between his wonted hybridity and this most recent and sweeping commentary on the Islamic world is worth considering.

23. See Wali (1963), Achebe (1975), Ngugi wa Thiong'o (1981), Chinweizu and Madubuike (1983, esp. 8–16), Bishop (1988, esp. ch. 2), and Onwuemene (1999) for a few contributions to this debate.

CHAPTER 2

1. In this respect, see also Searle-Chatterjee and Sharma (2003) and Banerjee-Dube (2008).

2. See *Oxford English Dictionary,* 2nd ed. (1989), s.v. "caste."

3. See, for example, the Buddha's long discourse "Agganna Sutta: On Knowledge of Beginnings" (1987) for a reference to the fourfold division of varna as well as a critique of it. For additional critiques see the following discourses—"Madhura Sutta" (2001d), "Kannakatthala Sutta" (2001c), "Assalayana Sutta" (2001a), and "Esukari Sutta" (2001b).

4. I am grateful to Laura Lyons for pressing the discussion in ways leading to this recognition.

5. M. S. S. Pandian points out in a personal communication (April 2008) that Periyar used the word *inam* to describe Dravidians. The primary meanings of *inam* include group, community, type or kind, and race. It is possible to argue that—contrary to some of his successors and some common notions regarding Periyar himself—the idea of Dravidians as a distinct race finds no support in Periyar's thought.

6. For other critiques of Dravidianism by Dalit intellectuals, see, for example, Thirumaavalavan (2004) and Rajkautaman (1994).

7. Aside from references elsewhere in this chapter, for a range of responses to Narayan, see Spivak (1994), Kirpal (1988), Dasenbrock (1987), Gorra (1994), and Bery (1997).

8. My discussion of Rushdie in the first chapter touches on this topic. For Rao, see R. Rao (1938/1967).

9. Thus, in studies such as Afzal-Khan (1993) and Pousse (1995), Narayan is chiefly compared to other postcolonial writers in English (such as V. S. Naipaul) or other Indian writers in English (such as Anita Desai). A similar bias is to be seen in multiauthor collections such as Kain (1993), where the essays mostly argue along one or the other of these two axes of comparison—the transnational and the national, *postcolonial* writing in English or *Indian* writing in English. See note 7, above, for other relevant references.

10. The proper title of Kamban's work is *Iramavataram*, but the work is popularly referred to as *Kamba Ramayana*, a convention observed by Narayan, and hence by me. Unlike Ramanujan in the quoted passage, I have also retained the most widely prevalent spelling for Kamban.

11. In the book, Ramasamy's name is spelt "Ramaswami." The former is the most commonly accepted rendering of his name. I have followed it everywhere except in the Works Cited section, where I have retained the spelling as it appears on the title page of the translation of his book. Regarding *Aryan,* it is perhaps necessary to note that here the word is both similar to and different from usage in the more familiar Nazi context. For a discussion of the racial politics within which the opposition between Aryan and Dravidian emerges in colonial India, see S. Ramaswamy (2004, esp. ch. 2). As noted above, Periyar's usage of these terms is not necessarily racialized.

12. Aiyar was ranged against Periyar in a controversy over separate dining for Brahmin and non-Brahmin students in a Congress Party–run school in the 1920s. This controversy was one of the catalysts for Periyar's departure from the Congress Party.

13. See Pani ([2009?], 7–8).

14. See Geetha and Rajadurai (1998, 381–85).

15. For Nehru's use of this phrase, see, for example, *Discovery of India* (1946/1981, 61–63).

16. For scholarly studies of song-and-dance sequences in Bollywood films, see Gopal and Moorti (2008). Narayan's novel thematizes *darshan*—in an Indic context, vision, spectacle, audience (as with a deity or important personage)—substantially. Providing darshan is after all what a guide does. It is interesting to note the transformation as well as reappearance of this theme within the audiovisual medium of the film *Guide* and especially within the song-and-dance sequences.

17. For other book-length studies and compilations, see Barnouw and Krishnaswamy (1980), Ganti (2004), Gokulsing and Dissanayake (1998), Pendakur (2003), and Thoraval (2000). The growing critical interest in Indian popular cinema is evident in these works, which range from histories to ethnographically oriented analyses. In all this variety, however, they for the most part continue to assume as well as explore a national and/or nationalist framework for their analyses.

CHAPTER 3

1. www.google.com, July 17, 2009.
2. See *Oxford English Dictionary*, 2nd ed. (1989), s.v. "pariah."
3. For a recent history of the Paraiyar community, see Basu (2011).
4. Italics in the original. For a more focused look at India, see Human Rights Watch and Center for Human Rights (2007).
5. Ambedkarites are often referred to as neo-Buddhists.
6. For an interesting exchange on the Indian philosophical and historical background to touch and untouchability, see Guru (2009) and Sarukkai (2009).
7. Niranjan Kumar (2005; in Hindi) discusses Hindi-language Dalit writing. For an examination of the figure of the Dalit woman in Hindi literature of the late colonial period, see Gupta (2008).
8. With respect to *Viramma*, the process by which the text came into being is not adequately described. Viramma, Jean-Luc Racine, and Josiane Racine are all identified as authors on the cover of the book. The translator's note by Will Hobson indicates that Viramma's narration in Tamil was recorded, "selected" (Hobson's word), and translated into French by Josiane Racine, herself a middle-class Tamil woman (1997, v). Hobson's translation into English is from the resulting French text. Few other details are given.
9. I am indebted to Nirmal Selvamony for help with the translation of the title of the novel, which is drawn from a dialect of the Kongu Nadu region.
10. Despite her interview observation, Sivakami's own hopeful novel of political and social change cautions against overgeneralization.
11. Necessary but not sufficient because it is after all possible to mourn the death, for example, of an animal.
12. For Bama's own views on her work, see her interview with Suchitra Behal (2003).
13. See the back of the title page.
14. On Dalit women and caste in relationship to gender, see Bhave (1988), Jogdand (1995), Liddle and Joshi (1986), and A. Rao (2003).
15. Hence the title of the book. See also p. 21.
16. On pp. 12–13, Said identifies the antihumanism emerging from opposition to such figures as Allan Bloom, Harold Bloom, and Saul Bellow in the North American academy.
17. For a broad look at humanism, see Halliwell and Mousley (2003). Though there have been numerous recent attempts to read him otherwise, Marx seems to me fundamentally a humanist. An especially powerful development of Marx as humanist thinker in a postcolonial and anticolonial context is to be

found in Rodney (1981). With regard to Fanon: it is true that he has a hard-hitting critique of humanism in *The Wretched of the Earth*. Nevertheless, he too seems to me primarily a humanist. I discuss both Fanon's humanism and his critique of it at greater length in the final chapter.

18. See Sen (2006), especially Part Two.

19. A thread in these writings concerns cosmopolitanism as a pedagogical imperative. I am unable to take up this interesting topic here.

20. Judith Butler's (1996) response to Nussbaum intersects with Wallerstein's (1996) in significant ways. Butler suggests the contingency of the universalism at the heart of cosmopolitanism. She writes of the universal as an "open-ended *ideal*" and states that "the universal begins to become articulated precisely through challenges to its existing formulations, and this challenge emerges from those not covered by it, who have no entitlement to occupy the place of the 'who,' but who nevertheless demand that the universal as such ought to be inclusive of them" (48, italics in original). The relevance of these observations to my argument below will soon be clear.

21. See p. xiv.

22. See Srinivas (1966), among other writings.

CHAPTER 4

1. See Niranjana's conclusion in *Siting Translation* (1992) and Cheyfitz (1991, xxii, xxv, and 40).

2. The three examples all concern translation within a postcolonial rather than a colonial context; despite that, they are appropriate illustrations for my broader argument about translation, since the understanding of translation as violence manifests itself in a similar way with regard to the former as well as the latter. Thus, if Cheyfitz works mainly with examples from the colonial period (though occasionally alluding to more contemporary situations), Dingawaney mainly refers to a contemporary, postcolonial context of translation. But both have similar notions of translation as violence. A further motive for my focus on postcolonial rather than colonial scenes of translation is to foreground the contemporary issues that postcolonial studies might fruitfully engage.

3. In his book on the Naxalite movement published in 1980, the same year that Swaminathan put *Water!* on stage, Sumanta Bannerjee found India to be in a state of "simmering revolution" (1980).

4. See the introduction to the translation, p. x.

5. In the Tamil of the play, *election* is sometimes simply "election" (for the word has entered the Tamil language) and sometimes "therthal." See scenes 10 and 11 for examples of the two usages. For the use of *puratchi*, see Swaminathan's preface to the play.

6. See Benjamin (1969)

7. Careful attention to this point might allow us to complicate the subtle and suggestive discussion of translation in Dipesh Chakrabarty's justly celebrated book *Provincializing Europe* (2000). Chakrabarty makes a distinction between two kinds of translation—one predicated on a mediating and universal third term, and the other dispensing with such a term (83–86). Citing examples,

Chakrabarty compares the first species of translation to a system of exchange and the second to one of barter. But it seems to me that when we begin to appreciate the *social* aspects of translation, the distinction between the two species of translation made by Chakrabarty begins to weaken. It does not seem to me obvious that a universal third term is absent in the second (barter) type of translation—only, perhaps, that it has not fully emerged through successive acts of social translation in a manner that would be visible to the observer. The difference between the two forms of translation identified by Chakrabarty, then, would seem to be not foundational but rather the result of *more* and *less* complete subjection to historical and social processes.

8. I make a distinction between the appearance of modernity in colonial and postcolonial situations and the concept of a colonial modernity. The former indicates the appearance of a set of phenomena (modes of thought, uses of technology, economic and political arrangements, etc.) commonly understood as modern within colonial and postcolonial situations; the latter, as explored in detail in my book *Textual Traffic* (Shankar 2001b), refers to the idea that the very notion of the modern is intimately linked to the history of colonialism. My discussions of modernity in this chapter concern the former rather than the latter.

9. Some studies of translation have explored the role played by foreign and ancient texts in helping to form "modern" identities without engaging the very notion of translatability as I am doing here. See Maria Tymoczko's work in the context of Ireland or David Wong's in the context of China (Tymoczko 2000; Wong 1998).

10. This sequence is made much of by Bharucha (1994) and Dirks (2001b) as well.

11. The Tamil version includes a Tamil army officer with whom Roja is able to communicate. In the Hindi version, of course, this officer's Tamil-ness is erased.

12. This would also lead me to read the character of Roja herself rather differently than Niranjana does. Niranjana (1994) argues that Roja is identified with the nation of India. I would argue that at least in the Tamil version of the film Roja is rather identified with the Tamil subnation.

13. See Sangari and Vaid (1989), Chatterjee (1993), and Mani (1998).

14. For example, see Niranjana (1994, 82).

15. My translation. The music is by well-known composer A. R. Rahman. *Roja* was the first movie for which Rahman composed the music.

16. In *Passions of the Tongue* (1997), Sumathi Ramaswamy shows how complicated was Periyar Ramasamy's attitude to language politics. While he supported efforts to preserve Tamil because he recognized the importance of linguistic independence for identity formation, his rationalism made him critical of many of the excesses of Tamil devotionalism (such as the treatment of the language as a deity, or a narrow chauvinism that regarded Tamil as the best language for everything).

17. For studies of Hindi popular cinema's institutional relationship to the postcolonial state, see Barnouw and Krishnaswamy (1980), Ganti (2004), Gokulsing and Dissanayake (1998), Pendakur (2003), Thoraval (2000), Virdi (2003), and Prasad (1998).

18. The note in Norton is by Maynard Mack, and the one in Longman is by David Damrosch and David L. Pike (in the latter it is a subsection of the preface). In my discussion below I refer to them as Norton's and Longman's notes in order to foreground what I take to be the collective, rather than individual, enterprise of anthologizing (though in my own "Works Cited" they appear under the names of the author-editors). The Longman note I refer to is from the second edition. It is a lightly revised version of the note in the first edition.

19. On this topic, see Ramaswamy (1997, 34–36, 87–88, 220–22 and elsewhere) and Ramanujan (1999a, 184–96).

20. On anthologies of world literature, see Damrosch (2003, esp. 127–31).

21. For a longer working out of his model of literary analysis, see Moretti (2007).

22. See, for example, the entries "translation," in *The Great Lifco Dictionary* (an English-English-Tamil dictionary), and "mozhipeyurppu," "mozhimaatrum," and "mozhiyaakam" in *Kriyavin Tharkala Thamizh Akrathi* (a Tamil-Tamil-English dictionary).

CONCLUSION

1. For another assessment of the field of comparative literature, especially in relationship to postcolonial studies, see Melas (2007).

2. See, for example, Pratt (1995) as well as Chow (1995).

3. See Bhabha (1997, 457) and Pollock (2002, 35).

4. Thus Said writes in *The World, the Text, and the Critic* that "criticism is worldly and in the world so long as it opposes monocentrism" (1983, 53). In addition to comments elsewhere, Said's admiration for Auerbach is fully evident in Said's last book, *Humanism and Democratic Criticism* (2004). See ch. 4, a reprint of his introduction to a reissue of *Mimesis*.

5. Margaret Higonnet notes, "The usual organization of comparative study around national Sprachliteraturen privileges the linguistic purity of a 'standard' language defined by dominant groups" and recommends that comparative study pay more attention to "gay sociolects" or "the literary specificities of a local or racial dialect" (1995, 161). The resonances with my argument about the vernacular will be immediately evident.

Works Cited

Aboul-Ela, Hosam. 2007. *Other South: Faulkner, Coloniality and the Mariategui Tradition*. Pittsburgh: University of Pittsburgh Press.
Achebe, Chinua. 1975. "The African Writer and the English Language." In *Morning Yet on Creation Day: Essays*, 91–103. Garden City, NY: Anchor/Doubleday.
Afzal-Khan, Fawzia. 1993. *Cultural Imperialism and the Indo-English Novel: Genre and Ideology in R. K. Narayan, Anita Desai, Kamala Markandaya, and Salman Rushdie*. University Park: Pennsylvania State University Press.
Ahmad, Aijaz. 1992. *In Theory: Classes, Nations, Literatures*. London: Verso.
Aiyar, V. V. S. 1965. *Kamba Ramayana: A Study*. Bombay (Mumbai): Bharatiya Vidya Bhavan.
Ambai [C. S. Lakshmi]. 1984. *The Face behind the Mask: Women in Tamil Literature*. New Delhi: Vikas.
———. 1992. "A Kitchen in the Corner of the House." In *A Purple Sea: Short Stories by Ambai*, trans. and introd. Lakshmi Holmstrom, 203–23. New Delhi: Affiliated East-West.
———. 1993. "Anil (The Squirrel)." In *Women Writing in India*, vol. 2, *The Twentieth Century*, ed. Susie Tharu and K. Lalita, 488–95. New York: Feminist Press.
Anand, S. 2003. *Touchable Tales: Publishing and Reading Dalit Literature*. Chennai: Navayana.
Anderson, Benedict. 1991. *Imagined Communities: Reflections on the Origin and Spread of Nationalism*. Rev. ed. London: Verso.
Appiah, Kwame Anthony. 2000. "Thick Translation." In *The Translation Studies Reader*, ed. Lawrence Venuti, 417–29. London: Routledge.
———. 2006. *Cosmopolitanism: Ethics in a World of Strangers*. New York: Norton.

Apter, Emily. 2006. *The Translation Zone: A New Comparative Literature.* Princeton: Princeton University Press.
Augustine, Seline. 2005. "Critical Insider." *Hindu Literary Review,* April 3, www.hindu.com/lr/2005/04/03/stories/2005040300310500.htm.
Bama. *Karukku.* 2000. Trans. Lakshmi Holmstrom. New Delhi: Macmillan. Originally published in Tamil in 1992.
———. 2003. "Labouring for the Cause of Dalits." Interview by Suchitra Behal. *Hindu* (Metro Plus sec.), March 6, 1.
Banerjee-Dube, Ishita, ed. 2008. *Caste in History.* New York: Oxford University Press.
Bannerjee, Sumanta. 1980. *India's Simmering Revolution: The Naxalite Uprising.* London: Zed.
Barnouw, Erik, and S. Krishnaswamy. 1980. *Indian Film.* 2nd ed. New York: Oxford University Press.
Bartolovich, Crystal, and Neil Lazarus, eds. 2002. *Marxism, Modernity, and Postcolonial Studies.* Cambridge: Cambridge University Press.
Bassnet, Susan. 1993. *Comparative Literature: A Critical Introduction.* Oxford: Blackwell.
Bassnet, Susan, and Harish Trivedi. 1999. Introduction to *Postcolonial Translation: Theory and Practice,* ed. Susan Bassnet and Harish Trivedi, 1–20. London: Routledge.
Basu, Raj Sekhar. 2011. *Nandanar's Children: The Paraiyans' Tryst with Destiny, Tamil Nadu, 1850–1956.* New Delhi: Sage.
Bayly, Susan. 1999. *Caste, Society and Politics in India from the Eighteenth Century to the Modern Age.* Cambridge: Cambridge University Press.
Beatina, Mary. 1993. *Narayan: A Study in Transcendence.* New York: Peter Lang.
Benjamin, Walter. 1969. "The Task of the Translator." In *Illuminations,* trans. Harry Zohn. New York: Schocken.
Bernheimer, Charles, ed. 1995a. *Comparative Literature in the Age of Multiculturalism.* Baltimore: Johns Hopkins University Press.
———. 1995b. "Introduction: The Anxieties of Comparison." In *Comparative Literature in the Age of Multiculturalism,* ed. Charles Bernheimer, 1–17. Baltimore: Johns Hopkins University Press.
Bery, Ashok. 1997. "'Changing the Script': R. K. Narayan and Hinduism." *ARIEL* 28 (2): 7–20.
Beverley, John. 2004. *Testimonio: On the Politics of Truth.* Minneapolis: University of Minnesota Press.
Bhabha, Homi. 1994. "Of Mimicry and Man: The Ambivalence of Colonial Discourse." In *The Location of Culture,* 85–92. New York: Routledge.
———. 1997. "Editor's Introduction: Minority Maneuvers and Unsettled Negotiations." *Critical Inquiry* 23 (3): 431–59.
Bharucha, Rustom. 1994. "On the Border of Fascism: Manufacture of a Consent in *Roja*." *Economic and Political Weekly,* June 4, 1389–95.
Bhave, Sumitra. 1988. *Pan on Fire: Eight Dalit Women Tell Their Story.* New Delhi: Indian Social Institute.
Bishop, Rand. 1988. *African Literature, African Critics: The Forming of Critical Standards, 1947–1966.* New York: Greenwood.

Bisztray, George. 1978. *Marxist Modes of Literary Realism.* New York: Columbia University Press.
Bombay. 1995. Dir. Mani Ratnam. Prod. Mani Ratnam and S. Sriram.
Booker, M. Keith. 1999. "Introduction: Salman Rushdie: The Development of a Literary Reputation." In *Critical Essays on Salman Rushdie,* 1–15. New York: G. K. Hall.
Breckenridge, Carol A., Sheldon Pollock, Homi K. Bhabha, and Dipesh Chakrabarty, eds. 2002. *Cosmopolitanism.* Durham, NC: Duke University Press.
Brennan, Timothy. 1997. *At Home in the World: Cosmopolitanism Now.* Cambridge, MA: Harvard University Press.
Buddha. 1987. "Agganna Sutta: On Knowledge of Beginnings." In *The Long Discourses of the Buddha,* trans. Maurice Walshe, 407–15. Boston: Wisdom Publications.
———. 2001a. "Assalayana Sutta." In *The Middle Length Discourses of the Buddha,* trans. Bhikkhu Nanamoli and Bhikkhu Bodhi, 2nd ed. Boston: Wisdom Publications.
———. 2001b. "Esukari Sutta." In *The Middle Length Discourses of the Buddha,* trans. Bhikkhu Nanamoli and Bhikkhu Bodhi, 2nd ed., 786–90. Boston: Wisdom Publications.
———. 2001c. "Kannakatthala Sutta." In *The Middle Length Discourses of the Buddha,* trans. Bhikkhu Nanamoli and Bhikkhu Bodhi, 2nd ed., 734–40. Boston: Wisdom Publications.
———. 2001d. "Madhura Sutta." In *The Middle Length Discourses of the Buddha,* trans. Bhikkhu Nanamoli and Bhikkhu Bodhi, 2nd ed., 698–703. Boston: Wisdom Publications.
Butler, Judith. 1996. "Universality in Culture." In *For Love of Country?,* by Martha Nussbaum with respondents, ed. Joshua Cohen, 45–52. Boston: Beacon.
———. 2004. *Precarious Life: The Powers of Mourning and Violence.* New York: Verso.
Casanova, Pascale. 2004. *The World Republic of Letters.* Trans. M. B. DeBevoise. Cambridge, MA: Harvard University Press.
Chakrabarty, Dipesh. 2000. *Provincializing Europe: Postcolonial Thought and Historical Difference.* Princeton: Princeton University Press.
Chakravarthy, Venkatesh, and M. S. S. Pandian. 1994. "More on *Roja.*" *Economic and Political Weekly,* March 12, 642–44.
Chakravarty, Sumita S. 1993. *National Identity in Indian Popular Cinema.* Austin: University of Texas Press.
Chatterjee, Partha. 1986. *Nationalist Thought and the Colonial World: A Derivative Discourse?* London: Zed.
———. 1993. *The Nation and Its Fragments: Colonial and Postcolonial Histories.* Princeton: Princeton University Press.
Cheah, Pheng, and Bruce Robbins, eds. 1998. *Cosmopolitics: Thinking and Feeling beyond the Nation.* Minneapolis: University of Minnesota Press.
Chellappa, Ci. Cu., ed. 1962. *Puthukurralkal* [*New Voices*]. Madras: Ezhutthu Prachuram.

Cheyfitz, Eric. 1991. *The Poetics of Imperialism: Translation and Colonization from "The Tempest" to "Tarzan."* New York: Oxford University Press.

Chinweizu, Onwuchekwa Jemie, and Ihechukwu Madubuike. 1983. *Toward the Decolonization of African Literature.* Washington, DC: Howard University Press.

Chow, Rey. 1995. "In the Name of Comparative Literature." In *Comparative Literature in the Age of Multiculturalism,* ed. Charles Bernheimer, 107–16. Baltimore: Johns Hopkins University Press.

———. 2006. *The Age of the World Target: Self-Referentiality in War, Theory, and Comparative Work.* Durham, NC: Duke University Press.

Cohen, Joshua, ed. 1996. *For Love of Country?* Boston: Beacon.

Cohn, Bernard S. 1968. "Notes on the History of the Study of Indian Society and Cultures." In *Structure and Change in Indian Society,* ed. Milton Singer and Bernard Cohn, 160–70. Chicago: Aldine.

Crichton, Sarah. 1995. "Caught between East and West, Rushdie Keeps On." *Newsweek,* February 6, 59–60.

"Dalit Panthers Manifesto." 1986. In *Untouchable! Voices of the Dalit Liberation Movement,* no trans. indicated, ed. Barbara Joshi, 141–47. London: Zed.

Damrosch, David. 1995. "Literary Study in an Elliptical Age." In *Comparative Literature in the Age of Multiculturalism,* ed. Charles Bernheimer, 122–33. Baltimore: Johns Hopkins University Press.

———. 2003. *What Is World Literature?* Princeton: Princeton University Press.

Damrosch, David, and David L. Pike, gen. eds. 2009a. *The Longman Anthology of World Literature.* Vols. A–F. 2nd ed. New York: Longman.

———. 2009b. "Translation across Cultures." In *The Longman Anthology of World Literature,* gen. ed. David Damrosch and David L. Pike, 2nd ed., [vol.] A: xxv. New York: Longman.

Dangle, Arjun. 1992a. "Dalit Literature: Past, Present and Future." Trans. Avinash S. Pandi and Daya Agrawal. In *The Poisoned Bread: Translations from Modern Marathi Dalit Literature,* ed. Arjun Dangle, 234–66. Bombay (Mumbai): Orient Longman.

———, ed. 1992b. *The Poisoned Bread: Translations from Modern Marathi Dalit Literature.* Bombay (Mumbai): Orient Longman.

Dasenbrock, Reed Way. 1987. "Intelligibility and Meaningfulness in Multicultural Literature in English." *PMLA* 102 (1): 10–19.

Desai, Gaurav, and Supriya Nair. 2005. Introduction to *Postcolonialisms: An Anthology of Cultural Theory and Criticism,* ed. Gaurav Desai and Supriya Nair, 1–12. New Brunswick: Rutgers University Press.

Devy, G. N. 1992. *After Amnesia: Tradition and Change in Indian Literary Criticism.* Hyderabad: Orient Longman.

Dharwadker, Vinay. 1994. "Indian Writing Today: A View from 1994." *World Literature Today* 68 (2): 237–41.

Dil Se. 1998. Dir. Mani Ratnam. Prod. Shekar Kapur, Mani Ratnam, and Ram Gopal Varma.

Dingwaney, Anuradha. 1995. "Introduction: Translating 'Third World' Cultures." In *Between Languages and Cultures: Translation and Cross-Cultural Texts*, ed. Anuradha Dingwaney and Carol Maier, 1–24. Pittsburgh: University of Pittsburgh Press.
Dingwaney, Anuradha, and Carol Maier, eds. 1995. *Between Languages and Cultures: Translation and Cross-Cultural Texts*. Pittsburgh: University of Pittsburgh Press.
Dirks, Nicholas. 2001a. *Castes of Mind: Colonialism and the Making of Modern India*. Princeton: Princeton University Press.
———. 2001b. "The Home and the Nation: Consuming Culture and Politics in *Roja*." In *Pleasure and the Nation: The History, Politics and Consumption of Public Culture in India*, ed. Rachel Dwyer and Christopher Pinney, 161–85. New Delhi: Oxford University Press.
Dirlik, Arif. 2003. "Globalization, Indigenism, and the Politics of Place." *ARIEL* 34 (1): 15–29.
Dumont, Louis. 1970. *Homo Hierarchicus: An Essay on the Caste System*. Trans. Mark Sainsbury. Chicago: University of Chicago Press.
Easthope, Anthony. 1998. "Bhabha, Hybridity, and Identity." *Textual Practice* 12 (2): 341–48.
Fanon, Frantz. 1963. *The Wretched of the Earth*. Trans. Constance Farrington. New York: Grove Press. Originally published as *Les damnés de la terre* in 1961.
Fernández Retamar, Roberto. 1989. *Caliban and Other Essays*. Trans. Edward Baker. Minneapolis: University of Minnesota Press.
Franklin, Cynthia. 2009. *Academic Lives: Memoir, Cultural Theory and the University Today*. Athens: University of Georgia Press.
Gandhi, Leela. 1998. *Postcolonial Theory: A Critical Introduction*. New York: Columbia University Press.
Ganti, Tejaswini. 2004. *Bollywood: A Guidebook to Popular Hindi Cinema*. New York: Routledge.
Geetha, V., and S. V. Rajadurai. 1998. *Towards a Non-Brahmin Millennium*. Calcutta (Kolkata): Samya.
Ghurye, G. S. 1961. *Caste, Class and Occupation*. 4th ed. Bombay (Mumbai): Popular Book Depot.
Gnanakoothan. 1989. Preface to *Puthu Kavithaikal* [*New Poems*], by K. N. Subramanyam, iii–vi. Madras (Chennai): Gnaanacheri.
Gokulsing, K. Moti, and Wimal Dissanayake. 1998. *Indian Popular Cinema: A Narrative of Cultural Change*. New rev. ed. Stoke on Trent: Trentham Books.
Gopal, Sangita, and Sujata Moorti. 2008. *Global Bollywood: Travels of Hindi Song and Dance*. Minneapolis: University of Minnesota Press.
Gorra, Michael. 1994. "History, Maya, Dharma: The Novels of R. K. Narayan." In *R. K. Narayan: Critical Perspectives*, ed. A. L. McLeod, 42–52. New Delhi: Sterling.
The Great Lifco Dictionary. 1993. Madras (Chennai): Little Flower.
Guide. 1965. Dir. Vijay Anand. With Dev Anand and Waheeda Rahman. Navketan.

Gupta, Charu. 2008. "(Mis)Representing the Dalit Woman: Reification of Caste and Gender in the Hindi Didactic Literature of Colonial India." *Indian Historical Review* 35 (2): 101–24.
Guru, Gopal. 2009. "Archaeology of Untouchability." *Economic and Political Weekly,* September 12, 49–56.
Halliwell, Martin, and Andy Mousley. 2003. *Critical Humanisms: Humanist/Anti-Humanist Dialogues.* Edinburgh: Edinburgh University Press.
Harlow, Barbara. 1987. *Resistance Literature.* New York: Methuen.
Higonnet, Margaret R. 1995. "Comparative Literature on the Feminist Edge." In *Comparative Literature in the Age of Multiculturalism,* ed. Charles Bernheimer, 155–64. Baltimore: Johns Hopkins University Press.
Hobson, Will. 1997. "Translator's Note." In *Viramma: Life of an Untouchable,* trans. Will Hobson, v–vi. London: Verso.
Holmstrom, Lakshmi. 2000. Introduction to *Karukku,* by Bama, vii–xii. Chennai: Macmillan.
Human Rights Watch. 2001. *Caste Discrimination: A Global Concern.* Human Rights Watch Report. September. www.hrw.org/reports/2001/globalcaste/.
Human Rights Watch and Center for Human Rights and Global Justice to the UN Committee on the Elimination of Racial Discrimination. 2007. *Hidden Apartheid: Caste Discrimination against India's "Untouchables."* Joint report. www.hrw.org/reports/2007/india0207/.
Iliah, Kancha. 1996. *Why I Am Not a Hindu: A Sudra Critique of Hindutva Philosophy, Culture and Political Economy.* Calcutta (Kolkata): Samya.
———. 2010. *The Weapon of the Other: Dalitbahujan Writings and the Remaking of Indian Nationalist Thought.* Delhi: Pearson.
Iyengar, K. R. Srinivasa. 1985. *Indian Writing in English.* Rev. and updated ed. New Delhi: Sterling.
Jogdand, P. G., ed. 1995. *Dalit Women: Issues and Perspectives.* New Delhi: Gyan.
Joshi, Barbara. 1986. "Designs for Struggle." In *Untouchable! Voices of the Dalit Liberation Movement,* ed. Barbara Joshi, 140. London: Zed.
Kain, Geoffrey. 1993. *R. K. Narayan: Contemporary Critical Essays.* East Lansing: Michigan State University Press.
Kandasamy, Meena. 2006. "And One Shall Live in Two . . . " In *The Grip of Change,* by P. Sivakami, 193–97. Hyderabad: Orient Longman.
Kenner, Hugh. 1971. *The Pound Era.* Berkeley: University of California Press.
Kersenboom, Sassia C. 1991. "The Traditional Repertoire of the Tirutanni Temple Dancers." In *Roles and Rituals for Hindu Women,* ed. Julia Leslie, 131–48. Rutherford, NJ: Fairleigh Dickinson University Press.
Kirpal, Viney. 1988. "Moksha for Raju: The Archetypal Four-Stage Journey." *World Literature Written in English* 28 (2): 356–63.
Kriyavin Tharkala Thamizh Akrathi. [In Tamil.] 1992. Chennai: Cre-A.
Kumar, Niranjan. 2005. "Dalit Sahitya ka Saundaryashastra: Kuch Vichaar." *Aalochana,* April–June, 47–54.
Lawall, Sarah, and Maynard Mack, gen. eds. 2002. *The Norton Anthology of World Literature.* 2nd ed. Vols. A–F. New York: Norton.

Lazarus, Neil. 1999. *Nationalism and Cultural Practice in the Postcolonial World*. Cambridge: Cambridge University Press.
Lefevere, Andre. 1992. *Translating Literature: Practice and Theory in a Comparative Literature Context*. New York: MLA.
Liddle, Joanna, and Rama Joshi. 1986. *Daughters of Independence: Gender, Caste and Class in India*. London: Zed.
Limbale, Sharan Kumar. 2004. *Toward an Aesthetics of Dalit Literature*. Trans. Alok Mukherjee. Hyderabad: Orient Longman.
The Longman Anthology of World Literature. See Damrosch and Pike 2009.
Loomba, Ania. 1998. *Colonialism/Postcolonialism*. New York: Routledge.
Macaulay, Thomas Babington. 2005. "Minute on Indian Education" [1835]. In *Postcolonialisms: An Anthology of Cultural Theory and Criticism*, ed. Gaurav Desai and Supriya Nair, 121–31. New Brunswick: Rutgers University Press.
Mack, Maynard. 2002. "A Note on Translation." In *The Norton Anthology of World Literature*, gen ed. Sarah Lawall and Maynard Mack, 2nd ed., [vol.] A:A1–A12. New York: Norton.
Mani, Lata. 1998. *Contentious Traditions: The Debate on Sati in Colonial India*. Berkeley: University of California Press.
McClintock, Ann. 1992. "The Angel of Progress: Pitfalls of the Term 'Postcolonialism.'" *Social Text* 31/32 (Spring): 84–98.
Melas, Natalie. 2007. *All the Difference in the World: Postcoloniality and the Ends of Comparison*. Stanford: Stanford University Press.
Menon, Dilip. 2006. *The Blindness of Insight: Essays on Caste in Modern India*. Pondicherry: Navayana.
Michael, S. M. 2007. "Dalit Vision of a Just Society." *Dalits in Modern India: Vision and Values*. 2nd ed. New Delhi: Sage.
Mishra, Pankaj. 1999. "A Spirit of Their Own." *New York Review of Books*, May 20, 47–53.
Mishra, Vijay. 1985. "Towards a Theoretical Critique of Bombay Cinema." *Screen* 26 (3–4): 116–32.
Mishra, Vijay, and Bob Hodge. 1991. "What Is Post(-)colonialism?" *Textual Practice* 5 (3): 399–414.
Mohanty, Chandra Talpade. 1988. "Under Western Eyes: Feminist Scholarship and Colonial Discourses." *Feminist Review* 30 (Autumn): 61–88.
———. 2002. "'Under Western Eyes' Revisited: Feminist Solidarity through Anticapitalist Struggles." *Signs* 28 (2): 499–535.
Mohanty, Satya. 1997. *Literary Theory and the Claims of History: Postmodernism, Objectivity, Multicultural Politics*. Ithaca: Cornell University Press.
Moretti, Franco. 2000. "Conjectures on World Literature." *New Left Review* 1 (January–February): 54–68.
———. 2007. *Graphs, Maps, Trees: Abstract Models for Literary History*. London: Verso.
Mouna Raagam. 1986. Dir. Mani Ratnam. Sujatha Film.
Mukherjee, Arun Prabha. 2007. Introduction to *Joothan: A Dalit's Life*, by Omprakash Valmiki, trans. Arun Prabha Mukherjee, xi–xlii. Kolkata: Samya.

Mukherjee, Meenakshi. 1999. Introduction to *Midnight's Children: A Book of Readings*, ed. Meenakshi Mukherjee, 9–27. Delhi: Pencraft International.

Mukherjee, Sujit. 1981/1994. *Translation as Discovery*. Hyderabad: Orient Longman.

Murugan, Perumal. 2004. *Seasons of the Palm*. Trans. V. Geetha. Chennai: Tara. Originally published in Tamil as *Koolla Madari* in 2001.

Nair, Rukmini Bhaya. 2002. Introduction to *Translation, Text and Theory: The Paradigm of India*, ed. Rukmini Bhaya Nair. New Delhi: Sage.

Narasimhaiah, C. D. 1987. "R. K. Narayan: The Comic as a Mode of Study in Maturity." In *The Swan and the Eagle: Essays on Indian English Literature*, 2nd ed. Delhi: Motilal Banarsidass.

Narayan, R. K. 1956. *Mr. Sampath*. Mysore: Indian Thought.

———. 1958. *The Guide*. New York: Penguin.

———. 1972. *The Ramayana*. New York: Penguin.

———. 1976. *The Painter of Signs*. New York: Viking.

Narayanan, Gita. n.d. "For a Potful of Water." Komal Swaminathan Archive (private collection), Chennai. N. pag.

Nayakan. 1987. Dir. Mani Ratnam. Sujatha Film.

Nehru, Jawaharlal. 1946/1981. *The Discovery of India*. New Delhi: Oxford University Press.

Ngugi wa Thiong'o. 1981. *Decolonising the Mind: The Politics of Language in African Literature*. Portsmouth, NH: Heinemann.

Nicholls, Peter. 1995. *Modernisms: A Literary Guide*. London: Macmillan.

Niranjana, Tejaswini. 1992. *Siting Translation: History, Post-Structuralism, and the Colonial Context*. Berkeley: University of California Press.

———. 1994. "Integrating Whose Nation? Tourists and Terrorists in *Roja*." *Economic and Political Weekly*, January 15, 79–82.

Nornes, Abé Mark. 2007. *Cinema Babel: Translating Global Cinema*. Minneapolis: University of Minnesota Press.

The Norton Anthology of World Literature. See Lawall and Mack 2002 and Mack 2002.

Nussbaum, Martha. 1996. "Patriotism and Cosmopolitanism." In *For Love of Country?*, by Martha Nussbaum with respondents, ed. Joshua Cohen, 2–17. Boston: Beacon.

Onwuemene, Michael C. 1999. "Limits of Transliteration: Nigerian Writers' Endeavors toward a National Literary Language." *PMLA* 114: 1055–66.

Orsini, Francesca. 2002. "India in the Mirror of World Fiction." *New Left Review* 13: 75–88.

Pandian, M. S. S. 2002. "One Step outside Modernity: Caste, Identity Politics and Public Sphere." *SEPHIS*, no. 4: 5–25.

———. 2007. *Brahmin and Non-Brahmin: Genealogies of the Tamil Political Present*. Delhi: Permanent Black.

Pani, Narendar. [2009?]. "Reservations, Exclusion and Conflict." Unpublished essay, National Institute of Advanced Studies, Bangalore, India.

Parry, Benita. 1994. "Signs of Our Times: Discussion of Homi Bhabha's *The Location of Culture*." *Third Text* 28/29 (Autumn/Winter): 5–24.

Parthasarthy, R. 1994. "Tamil Literature." *World Literature Today* 68 (2): 253–59.

Pendakur, Manjunath. 2003. *Indian Popular Cinema: Industry, Ideology and Consciousness*. Cresskill, NJ: Hampton.
Perumal, A. N. 1981. *Tamil Drama: Origin and Development*. Chennai: International Institute of Tamil Studies.
Pollock, Sheldon. 2002. "Cosmopolitan and Vernacular in History." In *Cosmopolitanism*, ed. Carol Breckenridge et al., 15–53. Durham, NC: Duke University Press.
Pound, Ezra. 1975. "Hugh Selwyn Mauberley (Contacts and Life)." In *Selected Poems, 1908–1959*, 98–112. London: Faber and Faber.
Pousse, Michel. 1995. *R. K. Narayan: A Painter of Modern India*. New York: Peter Lang.
Prasad, Madhava. 1998. *Ideology of the Hindi Film*. Delhi: Oxford University Press.
Pratt, Mary Louise. 1995. "Comparative Literature and Global Citizenship." In *Comparative Literature in the Age of Multiculturalism*, ed. Charles Bernheimer, 58–65. Baltimore: Johns Hopkins University Press.
Puthumaipithan. 1976. "Saba Vimochanam" [Deliverance from a Curse]. In *Chirukathaikal*, 1–15. New Delhi: National Book Trust.
Racine, Josiane, and Jean Luc Racine. 1997. "Routes to Emancipation: A Dalit Life Story in Context." In *Viramma: Life of an Untouchable*, by Viramma, Josiane Racine, and Jean Luc Racine, trans. Will Hobson, 306–12. London: Verso.
Radhakrishnan, R. 2003. *Theory in an Uneven World*. Oxford: Blackwell.
Rajagopalachari, C. 1957. *Ramayana*. Bombay (Mumbai): Bharatiya Vidya Bhavan.
Rajkautaman. 1994. *Talit pārvaiyil Tamilp panpāttu: Canka kālam* [Tamil Culture in Dalit Perspective: Sangam Age]. Putuccēri: Kauri Patippakam.
———. 2005. *Talittiya Vimarcanak Katturaikal* [Dalit Critical Essays]. Nakarkovil, India: Kalachuvatu Pathipakam.
Rama, N. C. 2003. "Imagery in the Poetry of Ci. Mani and Es. Vaitiswaran: A Comparative Study." PhD. diss., Madras University.
Ramanujan, A. K. 1992. "Three Hundred *Ramayanas*." In *Many Ramayanas: The Diversity of a Narrative Tradition in South Asia*, ed. Paula Richman, 22–49. New Delhi: Oxford University Press.
———. 1999a. "Classics Lost and Found." In *The Collected Essays of A. K. Ramanujan*, ed. Vinay Dharwadker, 184–96. New Delhi: Oxford University Press.
———. 1999b. "Varieties of *Bhakti*." In *The Collected Essays of A. K. Ramanujan*, ed. Vinay Dharwadker, 324–31. New Delhi: Oxford University Press.
Ramaswami [Ramasamy], Periyar E. K. 1959. *The Ramayana (A True Reading)*. Trans. not indicated. Trichy, India: Periyar Self-Respect Propaganda Institution Publications. Originally published in Tamil as *Iramayana Pathirankal* in 1930.
Ramaswamy, Sumathy. 1997. *Passions of the Tongue: Language Devotion in Tamil India, 1891–1970*. Berkeley: University of California Press.
———. 2004. *The Lost Land of Lemuria: Fabulous Geographies, Catastrophic Histories*. Berkeley: University of California Press.

Rao, Anupama, ed. 2003. *Gender and Caste*. New Delhi: Kali for Women.
Rao, Raja. 1938/1967. "Author's Foreword." In *Kanthapura*, vii–viii. New York: New Directions.
Ravikumar. 2003. "Note." In *Touchable Tales: Publishing and Reading Dalit Literature*, ed. S. Anand, 7–9. Pondicherry: Navayana.
———. 2005. "Waiting to Lose Their Patience." Trans. from the Tamil by S. Anand. In *Dalits in Dravidian Land*, by S. Viswanathan, xi–xxxviii. Pondicherry: Navayana.
Rege, Josna. 1999. "Victim into Protagonist? Midnight's Children and the Post-Rushdie National Narratives of the Eighties." In *Midnight's Children: A Book of Readings*, ed. Meenakshi Mukherjee, 182–211. Delhi: Pencraft International.
Rege, Sharmila. 1995. "Caste and Gender: The Violence against Women in India." In *Dalit Women: Issues and Perspectives*, ed. P. G. Jogdand, 18–36. New Delhi: Gyan.
Robbins, Bruce. 2007. "Afterword." *PMLA* 122 (5): 1644–51.
Rodney, Walter. 1981. *How Europe Underdeveloped Africa*. Washington, DC: Howard University Press.
Rodrigues, Valerian. 2002. Introduction to *The Essential Writings of B. R. Ambedkar*, ed. Valerian Rodrigues, 1–43. New Delhi: Oxford University Press.
Roja. 1992. Dir. Mani Ratnam. Madras Talkies.
Rushdie, Salman. 1981. *Midnight's Children*. London: Picador.
———. 1991. "Imaginary Homelands." In *Imaginary Homelands: Essays and Criticism, 1981–1991*, 9–21. London: Granta.
———. 1997a. "Damme, This Is the Oriental Scene for You!" *New Yorker*, June 23–30, 50–61.
———. 1997b. Interview with Christopher Hitchens. *Progressive*, October, 34–37.
———. 1997c. Introduction to *The Vintage Book of Indian Writing, 1947–1997*, ed. Salman Rushdie and Elizabeth West, ix–xxiii. London: Vintage.
———. 2002a. "America and Anti-Americans." *New York Times*, February 4.
———. 2002b. "A Liberal Argument for Regime Change." *Washington Post*, November 1.
———. 2002c. "No More Fanaticism as Usual." *New York Times*, November 27.
Said, Edward. 1983. *The World, the Text, and the Critic*. Cambridge, MA: Harvard University Press.
———. 1993. *Culture and Imperialism*. New York: Knopf.
———. 2004. *Humanism and Democratic Criticism*. New York: Columbia University Press.
Sangari, Kumkum, and Sudesh Vaid, eds. 1989. *Recasting Women: Essays in Indian Colonial History*. New Delhi: Kali for Women.
San Juan, E., Jr. 1998. *Beyond Postcolonial Theory*. New York: St. Martin's.
Santhanam, K. 1995. "He Made Theatre Reach Out and Communicate." *Hindu*, August 11, 14.
Sarukkai, Sundar. 2009. "Phenomenology of Untouchability." *Economic and Political Weekly*, September 12, 39–48.

Saussy, Haun, ed. 2006a. *Comparative Literature in an Age of Globalization.* Baltimore: Johns Hopkins University Press.

———. 2006b. "Exquisite Cadavers Stitched from Fresh Nightmares: Of Memes, Hives, and Selfish Genes." In *Comparative Literature in an Age of Globalization,* ed. Haun Saussy, 3–42. Baltimore: Johns Hopkins University Press.

Searle-Chatterjee, Mary, and Ursula Sharma, eds. 2003. *Contextualising Caste: Post-Dumontian Approaches.* New Delhi: Rawat.

Sen, Amartya. 2006. *The Argumentative Indian: Writings on Indian History, Culture and Identity.* New York: Picador.

Shankar, S. 2001a. "Introduction: The World and the Vision of Komal Swaminathan's *Water!*" In *Water!,* by Komal Swaminathan, trans. S. Shankar, 2–23. Calcutta (Kolkata): Seagull.

———. 2001b. *Textual Traffic: Colonialism, Modernity, and the Economy of the Text.* Albany: SUNY Press.

Sinfield, Alan. 1996. "Diaspora and Hybridity: Queer Identities and the Ethnicity Model." *Textual Practice* 10 (2): 271–93.

Sivakami, P. 2003. Interview. In *Touchable Tales: Publishing and Reading Dalit Literature,* ed. S. Anand. Pondicherry: Navayana.

———. 2006. *The Grip of Change.* Trans. P. Sivakami. Hyderabad: Orient Longman. Originally published in Tamil as *Pazhaiyana Kazhidalum* in 1989.

Sivanarayanan, Anushiya. 2004. "Translating Tamil Dalit Poetry." *World Literature Today,* May–August, 56–59.

———. 2009. "Translation and Globalization: Tamil Dalit Literature and Bama's *Karukku.*" In *Other Tongues: Rethinking the Language Debates in India,* ed. Nalini Iyer and Bonnie Zare, 135–54. Amsterdam: Rodopi.

Spivak, Gayatri Chakravorty. 1993. "In a Word." Interview by Ellen Rooney. In *Outside in the Teaching Machine,* 1–23. New York: Routledge.

———. 1994. "How to Read a 'Culturally Different' Book." In *Colonial Discourse/Post-Colonial Theory,* ed. Francis Barker et al., 126–50. Manchester: Manchester University Press.

———. 2003. *Death of a Discipline.* New York: Columbia University Press.

Srinivas, M. N. 1966. *Social Change in Modern India.* Berkeley: University of California Press.

Srinivasan, Amrit. 1985. "Reform and Revival: The Devadasi and Her Dance." *Economic and Political Weekly,* November 2, 1869–76.

Steiner, George. 1975. *After Babel: Aspects of Language and Translation.* New York: Oxford University Press.

St-Pierre, Paul. 2005. "Translation in an Era of Globalization." In *In Translation: Reflections, Refractions, Transformations,* ed. Paul St-Pierre and Prafulla C. Kar, 162–72. Delhi: Pencraft International.

Subramanyam, K. N. [Ka Na Su]. 1985. *Asura Ganam* [*Demon Breed*]. In *Moonru Navalkal* [*Three Novellas*], 208–332. Madras: Star Publications.

———. 1989. *Puthu Kavithaikal* [*New Poems*]. Madras: Gnaanacheri.

———. 1994. "Situation." In *The Oxford Anthology of Modern Indian Poetry,* ed. Vinay Dharwadker and A. K. Ramanujan, 101. Delhi: Oxford University Press.

Sunder Rajan, Rajeswari. 1993. *Real and Imagined Women: Gender, Culture, and Postcolonialism*. London: Routledge.
Swaminathan, Komal. 2001. *Water!* With Preface. Trans. S. Shankar. Calcutta (Kolkata): Seagull.
Tharu, Susie, and K. Lalita. 1991. Preface to *Women Writing in India: 600 B.C. to the Present,* ed. Susie Tharu and K. Lalita, 1:xv–xxiii. New York: Feminist Press, 1991.
Thirumaavalavan. 2004. *Uproot Hindutva: The Fiery Voice of the Liberation Panthers*. Trans. Meena Kandasamy. Kolkata: Samya.
Thomas, Rosie. 1985. "Indian Cinema: Pleasures and Popularity." *Screen* 26 (3–4): 116–32.
Thoraval, Yves. 2000. *The Cinemas of India*. New Delhi: Macmillan India.
Tomlinson, John. 1991. *Cultural Imperialism*. Baltimore: Johns Hopkins University Press.
Trask, Haunani-Kay. 1993. *From a Native Daughter: Colonialism and Sovereignty in Hawai'i*. Rev. ed. Honolulu: University of Hawai'i Press.
Tymoczko, Maria. 2000. "Translation in the Crucible of Modernity." *Eire-Ireland* 35 (1): 122–38.
Valmiki, Omprakash. 2007. *Joothan: A Dalit's Life*. Trans. Arun Prabha Mukherjee. Kolkata: Samya. Originally published in Hindi as *Joothan* in 1997.
Varadarajan, M. 1970. *A History of Tamil Literature*. New Delhi: Sahitya Akademi.
Vardapillay, T. 1837. "Seventy-Two Specimens of Castes in India." Manuscript, Yale University Beinecke Rare Book and Manuscript Library.
Venkatachalapathy, A. R. 2006. *In Those Days There Was No Coffee: Writings in Cultural History*. New Delhi: Yoda Press.
Venuti, Lawrence. 2000. "Translation, Community, Utopia." In *The Translation Studies Reader,* ed. Lawrence Venuti, 468–88. New York: Routledge.
Viramma, Josiane Racine, and Jean Luc Racine. 1997. *Viramma: Life of an Untouchable*. Trans. Will Hobson. London: Verso.
Virdi, Jyotika. 2003. *The Cinematic ImagiNation: Indian Popular Films as Social History*. New Brunswick: Rutgers University Press.
Wali, Obiajunwa. 1963. "The Dead End of African Literature?" *Transition* 10: 13–15.
Wallerstein, Immanuel. 1996. "Neither Patriotism nor Cosmopolitanism." In *For Love of Country?,* by Martha Nussbaum with respondents, ed. Joshua Cohen, 122–24. Boston: Beacon.
Webster, John C. B. 2007. "Who Is a Dalit?" In *Dalits in Modern India: Vision and Values,* 2nd ed., ed. S. M. Michael, 76–88. New Delhi: Sage.
Williams, Raymond. 1976. *Keywords: A Vocabulary of Culture and Society*. New York: Oxford University Press.
———. 1980. *Problems in Materialism and Culture: Selected Essays*. London: Verso.
Wong, David. 1998. "Translating Modernity." In *Translation and Creation: Readings of Western Literature in Early Modern China, 1840–1918,* ed. D. E. Pollard, 303–29. Amsterdam: J. Benjamins.
Zare, Bonnie, and Nalini Iyer. 2009. "Introduction: Problematizing Indian

Literary Canons." In *Other Tongues: Rethinking the Language Debates in India,* ed. Nalini Iyer and Bonnie Zare, ix–xxxvii. Amsterdam: Rodopi.

Zelliot, Eleanor. 1992. "Dalit: New Cultural Context for an Old Marathi Word." In *From Untouchable to Dalit: Essays on the Ambedkar Movement,* 267–92. New Delhi: Manohar.

Zvelebil, Kamil. 1973. *The Smile of Murugan: On Tamil Literature of South India.* Leiden: E. J. Brill.

Index

9/11, 94, 140–42, 157, 161

Aboul-Ela, Hosam, 2
Achebe, Chinua, 152, 161n23
African American literature, 25
African literature, 25
Afzal-Khan, Fawzia, 162n9
Ahmad, Aijaz, 3
Aiyar, V. V. S., 43–44, 162n12
Ambai (C. S. Lakshmi), 4, 12–16, 161n19, 161n21
Ambedkar, B. R., 67–68
Anderson, Benedict, 7, 58
Annadurai, C. N., 160n16
anthologization, 17–18, 130, 133–34
Appiah, Kwame Anthony, 96–99, 138–39
Apter, Emily, 144
area studies, 28
Aryan, 162n11
Asura Ganam (*Demon Breed*), 44

Bama, 85–90, 163n12
Bannerjee, Sumanta, 164n3
Barnouw, Erik, 163n17, 165n17
Bartolovich, Crystal, 159n4
Bassnet, Susan, 104, 144, 150
Basu, Raj Sekhar, 163n3
Bayly, Susan, 29–33, 52
Beatina, Mary, 40
Bellow, Saul, 95, 163n16
Benjamin, Walter, 125, 164n6

Bernheimer, Charles, 144
Bery, Ashok, 162n7
Beverley, John, 92
Bhabha, Homi, 7–8, 20–21, 98, 146, 160n13, 166n3
Bharatiya Janata Party, 47
Bharucha, Rustom, 114, 119, 165n10
bhasha literature, 22
Bhave, Sumitra, 163n14
Bishop, Rand, 161n23
Bisztray, George, 11
Bloom, Allan, 95, 163n16
Bloom, Harold, 95, 163n16
Bollywood, 56, 123; film criticism, 56–57, 59, 163n17; song-and-dance sequences in, 162n16
Bombay, 113–15, 122
Booker, M. Keith, 2
Brahmins, 35–36
Brennan, Timothy, 3, 23–4
Buddha, 52, 161n3
Butler, Judith, 84–85, 164n20

Casanova, Pascale, 125–28
caste, 29–34, 66, 106, 161n3; and love, 51–52, 53; and postcolonial studies, xvii, 27–29; in Tamil India, 34–36; and translation, 32–34, 106, 141–42, 156; and the vernacular, xvi, 28–29, 106, 141–42, 156. See also *varna-jati complex*

Index

Chakrabarty, Dipesh, 146, 164–65n7
Chakravarthy, Venkatesh, 114
Chakravarty, Sumita, 57, 58
Chatterjee, Partha, 27, 58, 165n13
Cheyfitz, Eric, 105–7, 126, 137, 138, 164n2
Chinweizu, Onwuchekwa Jemie, 161n23
Chow, Rey, 154–55, 166n2
classical (as term), 131–32, 146
Cohen, Joshua, 96
Cohn, Bernard, 31
colonial, the. See colonialism
colonial discourse, 7–8, 106, 151
colonialism, 31, 33, 108, 146
communism, 110
comparatism, xvi, 102, 143–45, 150–58
comparative literature, 131, 143–44, 150–51, 157, 166n1
comparison, 143, 145
Congress Party, 35, 67, 121, 162n12
cosmopolitanism, 95–99, 146, 164n19. See also humanism: cosmopolitan
Cosmopolitics, 97
cultural autonomy, 8, 21, 149–50
cultural imperialism, 6, 160n10

Dalit (term), 68–69, 73, 89
Dalitbahujan, 69–70, 73, 76, 79
Dalit lifewriting, 85–94
Dalit literature, 70–74, 153; Hindi-language, 163n7
Dalit Panthers, 68–69; Manifesto, 68–69, 71–72, 93
Dalits, 35–36, 64; and Dravidian movements, 35–36; women, 93, 163n14
Damrosch, David, 134–35, 139, 157, 166n18
Dangle, Arjun, 71–72, 93
darshan, 162n16
Dasenbrock, Reed Way, 162n7
"Deliverance from a Curse," 43
Desai, Anita, 152, 162n9
Desai, Gaurav, 144–45, 152
devadasis, 50–51, 64
Devy, G. N., 22
Dharwadker, Vinay, 17–18
Dil Se, 113
Dingwaney, Anuradha, 105–7, 126, 137, 164n2
Dirks, Nicholas, 27, 29–31, 32–33, 114, 119, 165n10
Dirlik, Arif, 24
Dissanayake, Wimal, 163n17, 165n17
Dravidianism. See Dravidian movement
Dravidian movement, 34–36, 37, 121, 132–33, 161n20, 162n5; critique of by Dalits, 35–36, 162n6
dubbing, 117–18
Dumont, Louis, 29

Easthope, Anthony, 160n13
English (as an Indian language), 37, 48, 60–61, 74

Fanon, Frantz, 95, 151–52, 153, 164n17
feminism, 14–16
Fernández Retamar, Roberto, 160n11
Franklin, Cynthia, 94, 95
Friedman, Thomas, 157

Gandhi, Leela, 3
Gandhi, M. K. (Mahatma), 35, 52, 55, 106
Ganti, Tejaswini, 163n17, 165n17
Geetha, V., 29, 30, 33, 76–77, 87, 156, 162n14
gender, 93
Ghurye, G. S., 29
globalization, 140, 157
Gnanakoothan, 5, 159n7
Gokulsing, K. Moti, 163n17, 165n17
Gopal, Sangita, 162n16
Gorra, Michael, 162n7
Grip of Change, The, 73, 78–83, 85, 87, 93, 163n10
Guide (film), 54–56, 57–64, 75, 116, 150, 162n16
Guide, The, 22–23, 40–41, 45–49, 116, 150; and Guide (film), 54–55; and the varna-jati complex, 49–54, 59–64, 74–75, 81–83, 85, 87. See also Narayan, R. K.
Gupta, Charu, 163n7
Guru, Gopal, 163n6

Halliwell, Martin, 163n17
Harlow, Barbara, 3, 88
Higonnet, Margaret, 166n5
Hindi (language and identity), 117–20, 146
Hobson, Will, 163n8
Hodge, Bob, 19
Holmstrom, Lakshmi, 87, 88–89
human. See humanism
humanism, 90, 93–94, 94–102, 146, 152, 163n17; cosmopolitan, 97–100; and sacrifice, 82–85; vernacular, 97–101
Human Rights Watch Report on Caste, 66
hybridity, 2, 7–8, 160n13, 161n22

Iliah, Kancha, 27, 69–70, 76

Indian Popular Cinema. *See* Bollywood
indigeneity, 24, 147
Iramayana Pathirankal (Characters in the Ramayana). *See Ramayana, The (A True Reading)*
Iyengar, K. R. Srinivasa, 38
Iyer, Nalini, 22

jati, 32–34
Jogdand, P. G., 163n14
Joothan, 85–86, 87
Joshi, Rama, 163n14

Kain, Geoffrey, 162n9
Kamba Ramayana: A Study, 43
Kamban, 41–42, 162n10
Ka Na Su. *See* Subramanyam, K. N.
Kandasamy, Meena, 78
Karukku, 73, 85, 86–90, 91, 93
Karunanidhi, M., 160n16
Kenner, Hugh, 160n11
Kersenboom, Sassia, 50
Kirpal, Viney, 162n7
"Kitchen in the Corner of the House," 12, 23
knowing-as-domination, 156–57, 157–58
knowing-in-solidarity, 156–57, 157–58
Koolla Madari. *See Seasons of the Palm*
Krishnaswamy, S., 163n17, 165n17
Kumar, Niranjan, 163n7

Lakshmi, C. S. *See* Ambai
Lalita, K., 17, 18
Lazarus, Neil, 3, 23, 159n4, 160n13
Lefevere, Andre, 109
Liddle, Joanna, 163n14
Limbale, Sharan Kumar, 71–73, 76, 84, 93, 95, 99–100
literatures of the world, xvii, 128, 134–36. *See also* world literature
local, 20–21
Longman Anthology of World Literature, 128–30, 131, 133, 135–36, 166n18
Loomba, Ania, 2–3, 19–20
love. *See* caste: and love
Lyons, Laura, 161n4

Macaulay, T. B., 1, 18–19, 26
Mack, Maynard, 166n18
Madubuike, Ihechukwu, 161n23
Mahabharata, the, 38
Mani, Lata, 165n13
Marx, Karl, 95, 163n17
materialism, xvii–viii, 49, 101–2, 108, 141, 155, 157

McClintock, Anne, 19
Melas, Natalie, 166n1
Menon, Dilip, 28–29, 36
Michael, S. M., 69
Midnight's Children. *See under* Rushdie, Salman
Mishra, Pankaj, 159n2
Mishra, Vijay, 19, 56–57
modernity, 110–13, 165n8
Mohanty, Chandra Talpade, 15, 155
Mohanty, Satya, 3
Moorti, Sujata, 162n16
Moretti, Franco, 135, 166n21
Mouna Ragam, 113, 114, 115, 122
Mousley, Andy, 163n17
Mowni, 160n7
Mukherjee, Arun Prabha, 85
Mukherjee, Meenakshi, 159n2
Mukherjee, Sujit, 138–39
Murugan, Perumal, 73, 75–78, 82, 87, 99–101, 156

Naipaul, V. S., 152, 162n9
Nair, Rukmini Bhaya, 123
Nair, Supriya, 144–45, 152
Narasimhaiah, C. D., 38
Narayan, R. K., 22–23, 36–41, 44–48, 49, 51, 162n7. *See also Guide, The*
nation, the, 14–15, 146, 149, 160n9, 162n9; and film criticism, 56–59, 122; and *Guide*, 54–56; and Narayan, 101; and *Roja*, 120–23. *See also* nationalism
nationalism, 61, 96–98, 110, 115–16. *See also* nation, the
Naxalite movement, 164n3
Nayakan, 114–15, 122
Nehru, Jawaharlal, 55, 57–58, 61, 162n15
neo-Buddhists, 163n5
Ngugi wa Thiong'o, 161n23
Nicholls, Peter, 160n11
Niranjana, Tejaswini: on *Roja*, 114, 115–16, 119, 165n12; on translation, 105–7, 126, 164n1
Nornes, Abé Mark, 117
Norton Anthology of World Literature, 128–30, 131, 133, 135–36, 166n18
Nussbaum, Martha, 96–97, 98, 99, 164n20

Onwuemene, Michael C., 161n23
Orsini, Francesca, 159n2

Pandian, M. S. S., 29–30, 36, 45, 85, 114, 162n5

Paraiyars, 65–66, 101, 163n3
pariah (as word in the English language), 65, 101
Parry, Benita, 3, 160n13
Parthasarthy, R., 160n7
Pazhaiyana Kazhitalum. See *Grip of Change, The*
Pendakur, Manjunath, 163n17, 165n17
Periyar (E. V. Ramasamy, E. V. Ramaswami), 30, 34–35, 37, 51–52, 98–99, 101, 162n11; attitude to Tamil, 120, 165n16; on the Ramayana, 42, 44–45, 47
Perumal, A. N., 161n18
Pike, David L., 166n18
Pollock, Sheldon, 98, 146, 166n3
Poongundranar, Kanian, xvii
postcolonialism: and caste, 27–29, and comparatism, 143, 150–58; as discipline, 2–3, 21; as object of study, 24–25, 108; as term, 159n3; and translation, 103–8; transnational, 19–26, 47; and the vernacular, xv, 19–26, 47–48, 59, 74, 146
postcolonial literary criticism, 28
postcolonial literature, 21, 25, 26, 103–4, 152, 162n9
postcolonial studies. See postcolonialism: as discipline
postcolonial theory. See postcolonialism: as discipline
Pound, Ezra, 6–7, 149, 160n11
Pousse, Michel, 162n9
Prasad, Madhava, 165n17
Pratt, Mary Louise, 153, 166n2
Puthumaipithan, 38, 43–44, 47, 160n7

Racine, Josiane and Jean-Luc, 90–91, 92, 93, 163n8
Radhakrishnan, R., 154, 155
Rahman, A. R., 165n15
Rajadurai, S. V., 29, 30, 33, 162n14
Rajagopalachari, C. (Rajaji), 42–43, 44
Rajkautaman, 74, 162n6
Ramanujan, A. K., 41–42, 131, 132, 133, 153, 166n19
Ramasamy (Ramaswami), E. V. See Periyar
Ramaswamy, Sumathi, 121, 122, 132, 165, 166n19
Ramayana, the, 36–37, 38–48
Ramayana, The (A True Reading), 42
Ranjan, Unjai, 93
Rao, Raja, 37, 162n8
Rashtriya Swayamsevak Sangh (RSS), 47
Ratnam, Mani, 113–24

Ravikumar, 35–36, 74
realism, 11–12
Rege, Josna, 159n2
Rege, Sharmila, 93
renunciation (and caste), 52–53
resistance literature, 88
Robbins, Bruce, 151
Rodney, Walter, 164n17
Rodrigues, Valerian, 67
Roja, 55, 113–24, 137, 165n12
Rushdie, Salman, 10–11, 17–19, 22, 37, 47–48, 159n1, 161n22; *Midnight's Children,* 10; on vernacular (literatures), 1–3, 4, 4–5, 15, 17–18, 146

"Saba Vimochanam." See "Deliverance from a Curse"
sacrifice, theme of (in literature about caste), 80–85
Said, Edward: comparatist, 150–51, 166n4; cosmopolitan humanist, xvi, 95–96, 98–99, 153, 163n16; materialist critic, 3, 49
Sangam poetry, 132–33
Sangari, Kumkum, 165n13
San Juan, E., 3
Sanskrit, 61
Sarukkai, Sundar, 163n6
Saussy, Haun, 144, 151
Searle-Chatterjee, Mary, 161n1
Seasons of the Palm, 73–74, 75–78, 79–83, 83–85
Self-Respect Movement, 30, 34–35, 51–52
Selvamony, Nirmal, 163n9
Sen, Amartya, xvii, 95, 164n18
"Seventy-Two Specimens of Castes in India," 33
Sharma, Ursula, 161n1
Sinfield, Alan, 160n13
"Situation," 5–8, 23, 149–50
Sivakami, P., 78–83, 103, 163n10
Sivanarayanan, Anushiya, 70
socialist realism, 11
Spivak, Gayatri, 3, 16, 144, 151, 162n7
Srinivas, M. N., 29, 100, 164n22
Srinivasan, Amrit, 50
Steiner, George, 139
St-Pierre, Paul, 140
Subramanyam, K. N. (Ka Na Su), 3, 5–8, 38, 44, 47, 149–50, 159n7
subtitling, 117
Sunder Rajan, Rajeswari, 14
Swaminathan, Komal, 3–4, 8–12, 108–10, 160n15, 164n3

Index | 185

Tagore, Rabindranath, 149, 160n9
Tamil (language), 146
Tamil cinema, 123
Tamil drama, 8, 9, 161n18
Tamil identity, 114–15, 118–22
Tamil literature, 4, 16–17, 159n7
testimonio, 90, 92
Textual Traffic, xvii, 165n8
Tharu, Susie, 17, 18
theory, 104
Thirumaavalavan, 162n6
Thomas, Rosie, 56, 57
Thoraval, Yves, 163n17, 165n17
Tomlinson, John, 160n10
Touchable Tales, 72
Tractor Art, 4–5, 10, 160n12
tradition, 21, 109–11, 113
translation, xvi, 7, 54, 66, 88–89, 102, 164n7; and anthologization, 133–34; and caste, 32–34, 106, 141–42, 156; and comparison, 155–58; culture of, 141; diachronic vs synchronic, 131; fidelity in, 138–39, 141; in film, 117–18; as interpretation, 139–41, 155–57; and nation, 123–24; as othering, 123; social, 111–112, 113; as trope, 104–5, 117; and the untranslatable, 113; and the vernacular, 108, 109, 110, 137–38; as violence, 105–7, 124, 125–26, 137–40, 148, 164n2
transnational, the, 59, 127, 131–33, 146, 162n9
Trask, Haunani-Kay, 147
Trivedi, Harish, 105
Tymoczko, Maria, 165n9

universal, the 151–55, 153–55, 164n20
untouchability, 163n6

Vaid, Sudesh, 165n13
Valmiki, Omprakash, 85, 86, 87
Varadarajan, M., 159n5
varna, 32–34, 161n3
varna-jati complex, 33–34, 49–53, 59–64, 74, 106, 156. *See also* caste
Venkatachalapathy, A. R., 120, 132
Venuti, Lawrence, 138
vernacular, xv–vi, 20–22, 24, 48, 127, 166n5; and comparatism, 150; and cosmopolitanism 97–98, 108–110; and film criticism 122; and humanism, 97–101; literature, 16, 19; and the nation, 14, 55–56; overview, 101–2, 131–33, 145–49; public sphere 37–39, 55, 62, 133; realism, 10–12, 108; and translation, 108, 109, 110, 137–38; and the varna-jati complex (caste), xvi, 28–29, 74, 106, 141–42, 156. *See also* postcolonialism: and the vernacular; Rusdhie, Salman: on vernacular (literatures)
Viramma, 73, 85, 90–94, 100, 163n8
Virdi, Jyotika, 165n17

Wali, Obiajunwa, 161n23
Wallerstien, Immanuel, 97, 135, 164n20
Water!, 8–12, 23, 108–10, 137, 148, 160n14, 164n3
Webster, John, 69
Williams, Raymond, 3, 12
Wong, David, 165n9
world literature, 125, 128–31, 133–37. *See also* literatures of the world

Zare, Bonnie, 22
Zelliot, Eleanor, 68
Zvelebil, Kamil, 5

COVER DESIGN
Sandy Drooker

TEXT
10/13 Sabon Open Type

DISPLAY
Sabon Open Type

COMPOSITOR
Modern Language Initiative

TEXT PRINTER AND BINDER
IBT Global

www.ingramcontent.com/pod-product-compliance
Lightning Source LLC
Chambersburg PA
CBHW031710230426
43668CB00006B/171